Máté Kovács

Information Flow Security in Tree-Manipulating Processes

Máté Kovács

Information Flow Security in Tree-Manipulating Processes

Verifying Safety Hyperproperties Using Abstract Interpretation and Model Checking

Südwestdeutscher Verlag für Hochschulschriften

Impressum / Imprint
Bibliografische Information der Deutschen Nationalbibliothek: Die Deutsche Nationalbibliothek verzeichnet diese Publikation in der Deutschen Nationalbibliografie; detaillierte bibliografische Daten sind im Internet über http://dnb.d-nb.de abrufbar.

Alle in diesem Buch genannten Marken und Produktnamen unterliegen warenzeichen-, marken- oder patentrechtlichem Schutz bzw. sind Warenzeichen oder eingetragene Warenzeichen der jeweiligen Inhaber. Die Wiedergabe von Marken, Produktnamen, Gebrauchsnamen, Handelsnamen, Warenbezeichnungen u.s.w. in diesem Werk berechtigt auch ohne besondere Kennzeichnung nicht zu der Annahme, dass solche Namen im Sinne der Warenzeichen- und Markenschutzgesetzgebung als frei zu betrachten wären und daher von jedermann benutzt werden dürften.

Bibliographic information published by the Deutsche Nationalbibliothek: The Deutsche Nationalbibliothek lists this publication in the Deutsche Nationalbibliografie; detailed bibliographic data are available in the Internet at http://dnb.d-nb.de.

Any brand names and product names mentioned in this book are subject to trademark, brand or patent protection and are trademarks or registered trademarks of their respective holders. The use of brand names, product names, common names, trade names, product descriptions etc. even without a particular marking in this works is in no way to be construed to mean that such names may be regarded as unrestricted in respect of trademark and brand protection legislation and could thus be used by anyone.

Coverbild / Cover image: www.ingimage.com

Verlag / Publisher:
Südwestdeutscher Verlag für Hochschulschriften
ist ein Imprint der / is a trademark of
OmniScriptum GmbH & Co. KG
Heinrich-Böcking-Str. 6-8, 66121 Saarbrücken, Deutschland / Germany
Email: info@svh-verlag.de

Herstellung: siehe letzte Seite /
Printed at: see last page
ISBN: 978-3-8381-3880-0

Zugl. / Approved by: München, TU, Diss., 2014

Copyright © 2014 OmniScriptum GmbH & Co. KG
Alle Rechte vorbehalten. / All rights reserved. Saarbrücken 2014

Contents

1 **Introduction** 1

2 **Runtime Monitor** 7
   2.1 Preliminaries 8
       2.1.1 Binary Trees 8
       2.1.2 Assembly Language for Tree Manipulation 8
       2.1.3 Information Flow Policies 13
   2.2 The Runtime Monitor through an Example 14
   2.3 Formal Treatment of the Monitor 16
   2.4 Guarantees 22
   2.5 Related Work 23

3 **Relational Abstract Interpretation** 25
   3.1 Merge over all Twin Computations 27
   3.2 Self-Compositions of Control Flow Graphs 30
   3.3 Proving Noninterference 34
       3.3.1 Case Study 40
   3.4 Practical Experiments 43
   3.5 Combining the Results of Multiple Analyses 45
   3.6 Related Work 46

4 **Model Checking** 49
   4.1 Transition Systems 50
   4.2 Temporal Information Flow Policies 52
   4.3 Model Checking Systems with Finite State Space 54
   4.4 Model Checking Systems with Infinite State Space 58
       4.4.1 Constructing the Abstract Transition System 60
       4.4.2 Constructing an Abstract State Machine Having Finite State Space 62
       4.4.3 Computing the Result 66
   4.5 Implementation 67
       4.5.1 Transforming Formulae into Büchi Automata 67
       4.5.2 The Verification Procedure 68
   4.6 Case Studies 70
   4.7 Related Work 77

5 **Conclusion** 79

6 Proofs **81**
  6.1 Proofs for Chapter 2 81
  6.2 Proofs for Chapter 3 90
  6.3 Proofs for Chapter 4 115

Chapter 1

Introduction

Today companies and organizations frequently use computer systems to store data and to execute business logic. These workflow systems bear the risk of revealing critical information through software bugs, attacks, or simple misconfiguration. Since these systems are frequently used by several principals possibly having conflicting interests, the conscious design and enforcement of information flow policies is of paramount importance.

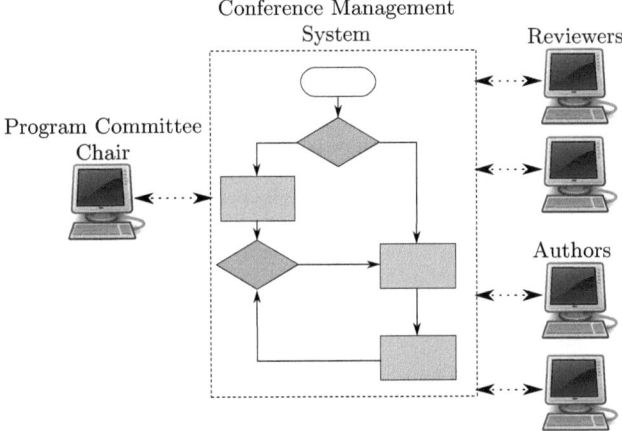

Figure 1.1: An imaginary conference management system and its cooperating partners.

As an example, Figure 1.1 illustrates the users of an imaginary conference management system like EasyChair. The users cooperate in order to successfully execute the workflow of submitting, reviewing and deciding about the acceptance of papers. The conference management system itself maintains a document base describing the state of the submission and review process. The document base stores among others the uploaded documents, the comments and scores given by the reviewers, and a value describing whether the submissions have been accepted. Some examples for conflicting interests in the context of

1

conference management systems may be the following:

- Authors might be interested in knowing the identity of their reviewers.
- Authors might wish to know about their competitors previous to the disclosure of accepted papers.

There have already been security breaches in conference management systems. For instance HotCRP [40] version 2.47 had a bug which exposed comments of reviewers to the authors, which were exclusively meant for the program committee.

There are well established programming languages and technologies for the implementation of process management systems that are responsible for the coordination of workflows of organizations. The family of standards for web services (e.g., [37, 20]) enables the platform independent communication of computer programs on a network using messages in XML [16] format. Based on this technology, high level workflows can be composed from the functionalities of individual web services using the Web Services Business Process Execution Language (BPEL) [6]. Accordingly, BPEL is designed to implement the autonomous business logic of companies and organizations that can also communicate with external, independent entities. Therefore, the information flow security of these processes may be crucial for organizations to fulfill their missions. Another central aspect of BPEL workflows is that the values of variables are document trees. Even though the goal of BPEL programs is not to carry out complex computations, still the language is Turing complete. Data manipulation can be carried out using the XML Path Language [14] (XPath), and XSL Transformations [46] (XSLT).

As motivated above, the goal of this work is to give methods for the verification and enforcement of information flow properties of programs manipulating tree-structured data. We will illustrate the developed solutions using examples that implement fragments of the imaginary conference management system sketched in Figure 1.1. We suppose that the workflow of organizing a conference consists of a series of phases. In one phase authors are allowed to upload papers, an other phase is e.g., when the submission deadline is passed, and papers are reviewed.

```
 1  <if name="If1">
 2    <condition>
 3    <![CDATA[$phase = "notify"]]>
 4    </condition>
 5    <assign> <copy> <from>$subDB </from>
 6                   <to> $toAuthors </to> </copy>
 7    </assign>
 8    <else>
 9     <sequence>
10      <if name="If2">
11       <condition> <![CDATA[$averageScore < 1.5]]>
12       </condition>
13       <assign name="EvalReject">
14        <copy> <from>"rejected"</from>
15         <to> $subDB/submission[id=$paperId]
16                /acceptance/text()
17         </to> </copy>
```

```
18      </assign>
19     <else>
20      <assign name="EvalAccept">
21       <copy> <from>"accepted"</from>
22        <to> $subDB/submission[id=$paperId]
23                  /acceptance/text()
24        </to> </copy>
25      </assign>
26     </else>
27    </if>
28    <assign> <copy> <from>$subDB </from>
29                    <to> $subDB_Output </to> </copy>
30    </assign>
31   </sequence>
32  </else>
33 </if>
```

Listing 1.1: A BPEL-like pseudo-code fragment of an imaginary conference management system.

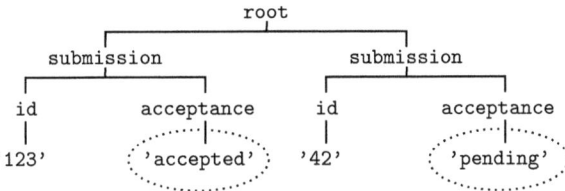

Figure 1.2: An example database mapping the identifiers of submissions to their acceptance values. The dotted rings mark the elements that can be addressed by the XPath expressions at lines 15 and 22 in Listing 1.1 depending on the value of the variable paperId.

Listing 1.1 shows a possible fragment of a document submission system like EasyChair implemented in a BPEL-like language. A tree-shaped data structure stored in variable subDB is manipulated, which contains the identifiers and acceptance states of the uploaded papers. The code covers two phases of the review process. In the phase "review" the average scores of papers are processed by the workflow engine. In this phase, the code is executed each time a review is submitted. Based on the value of variable averageScore containing the average of the scores already submitted for a paper, the program updates the acceptance status of the paper identified by the value of variable paperId. In the phase "notify" the database is sent to the authors by assigning it to the variable toAuthors.

A possible data structure representing a database is illustrated in Figure 1.2. A simple information flow policy for the document submission system could be the following:

$$\textit{"The scores of the papers may not be revealed to the authors before the notification phase."} \tag{1.1}$$

The properties this work aims to analyze belong to the class of properties called *hyperproperties* [21]. A hyperproperty is a statement about multiple runs of a system. Semantically, the requirement in (1.1) refers to at least two executions, the initial state of which may differ in the value of the variable `averageScore` and the acceptance status of documents in the database. It poses the requirement that authors should not be able to observe any difference in the outputs of any two executions until a specific point in time. The policy in (1.1) illustrates the nature of problems this work seeks to tackle.

The goal of this work is, therefore, to give methods to verify and enforce information flow security policies on programs manipulating tree-structured data, as motivated by the BPEL language. The corresponding technical challenges are the following:

1. Formalisms are needed that can express information flow policies specifying the secrecy of subtrees of document trees. Furthermore, algorithms have to be found that can either enforce the policies during runtime, or prove them in compilation time.

2. Enterprise workflows may run for an unbounded period of time, while information flow policies may change in response to events triggered by the environment. Therefore, formalisms are needed that can express the temporal nature of information flow policies, and algorithms are needed for their verification or runtime enforcement.

This work presents the following contributions:

- In Chapter 2 a runtime monitor is introduced that enforces information flow policies on tree-manipulating programs. The runtime monitor addresses challenge 1, the focus is on the properties of programs manipulating tree-structured documents. The presented solution is based on the results published in [48].

- In Chapter 3 a static analysis is developed based on relational abstract interpretation. The goal of this analysis is to prove information flow properties of programs at compilation time. Again, Chapter 3 addresses challenge 1. The presented results are based on [49].

- In Chapter 4 a model checking algorithm is described that tackles challenge 2. Policies are composed using the logic Restricted SecLTL. Restricted SecLTL extends the positive fragment of the Linear Temporal Logic with an additional modal operator, the so-called *hide* operator. The hide operator expresses that the observable behavior of the system is independent of specific pieces of secret until an event occurs. The presented algorithm extends the model checking procedure of [28] to systems with unbounded state space.

Much effort has been invested in finding adequate formalisms that describe the functionality of service orchestrations and choreography, in particular, the BPEL [6] language. The majority of the publications in this topic can be sorted into two groups. One [42, 74, 73, 61] applies formalisms based on Petri-nets [55] to model workflows, the other [39, 50, 63, 81, 18] prefers algebraic calculi like the Π-calculus [52] as the basis for investigations. The authors of [3] and [82] present security-related results using Petri-net based formalisms. A common property of these approaches is that they mostly focus on the control flow of orchestrations, sometimes with emphasis on error handling, whereas data values undergo severe abstractions: They are either considered as atomic values, or completely disregarded by handling branching decisions as nondeterminism.

The goal of this work is to provide security guarantees by taking advantage of the properties of data values. Therefore, we introduce an "assembly" language for tree manipulation that formalizes business workflows, and apply program analysis and model checking techniques in order to tackle the challenges listed above.

Chapter 2

Runtime Monitor

In this chapter we present a runtime monitor to enforce end-to-end information flow policies on programs manipulating tree-structured data. The authors of [66] note that runtime approaches [38, 77, 64] are on the rise, because they can be more permissive than static solutions, while providing the same guarantees. In our case this statement especially holds, because our monitor takes advantage of the fact that during runtime data instances are available. In principle, our monitor executes programs in parallel to the operational semantics of the language, while maintaining a state which only depends on public data. In other words, the monitor carries out a parallel computation on the public view. The computation of the public view is challenging in the case, when the result of a branching construct, whose condition depends on the secret, is about to be evaluated. In this case we apply a dataflow analysis procedure, which is a generalization of constant propagation (see e.g. [68]) for handling semi-structured data. The key difference is the hierarchic nature of lattice elements, which aligns to our purpose of preventing information leakage in tree-manipulating programs. Moreover, we gain precision by only considering a modification of a subtree inside a secret-dependent branch as potentially secret, if it does not occur in the other alternative as well, and thus must be excluded from the public view. In summary, this chapter provides the following innovations:

- A runtime monitor is introduced to support the specification of information flow policies in terms of tree-like data and their enforcement.

- The enforcement mechanism applies a generalized variant of constant propagation in order to compute the public view of the state at the end of branching instructions.

This chapter is organized as follows. In Section 2.1 we introduce the programming language, and discuss how information flow policies are composed. In Section 2.2 we illustrate the intuition behind our solution through an example, a fragment of a hypothetical paper submission system. We formalize the approach in Section 2.3, and in Section 2.4 we discuss the guarantees the monitor provides us. Finally, in Section 2.5 we relate our work to others.

2.1 Preliminaries

This section presents the necessary formalisms, languages and notations that are the basis of this work.

2.1.1 Binary Trees

In order to foster semantic clarity and simplicity, the techniques of this work are elaborated using a small but powerful "assembly" language for tree manipulation. The language is constructed to work with binary trees only. This is no restriction in general, since binary trees are in one-to-one correspondence with unranked trees. Unranked trees in turn can be considered as the natural internal representation of XML documents.

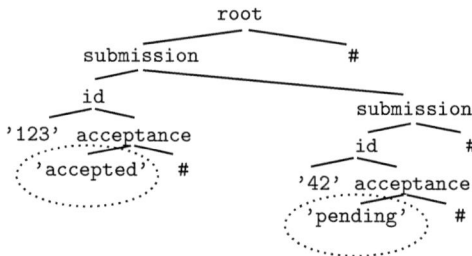

Figure 2.1: The binary representation of the database in Figure 1.2.

Definition 1 (Binary Trees). *The set of binary trees* $\mathfrak{B}_{\Sigma_2,\Sigma_0}$ *over the finite set of binary alphabet elements* Σ_2 *and the set of nullary alphabet elements* Σ_0 *is defined by the language:*

$$\tau ::= \sigma_0 \mid \sigma_2(\tau_1, \tau_2)$$

where $\sigma_0 \in \Sigma_0$, $\sigma_2 \in \Sigma_2$ *and* $\tau_1, \tau_2 \in \mathfrak{B}_{\Sigma_2,\Sigma_0}$. *The set of nullary alphabet elements* Σ_0 *does not necessarily need to be finite.*

Figure 2.1 illustrates the binary representation of the data structure of Figure 1.2 constructed using the *first-child/next-sibling* (FCNS) encoding [22]. The binary tree $\sigma_2(\tau_1, \tau_2)$ is interpreted as an unranked forest, where the root of the leftmost tree is labeled σ_2. Its content is the unranked variant of τ_1, while the forest on its right hand side is the unranked variant of τ_2. The nullary node labeled # $\in \Sigma_0$ represents the empty forest. Nullary nodes can also be labeled with *basic values* like '42', which are always between ' signs in order to emphasize that they belong to Σ_0. The FCNS encoding maps nullary nodes representing basic values to themselves.

2.1.2 Assembly Language for Tree Manipulation

The grammar of the assembly language for tree manipulation is shown in Figure 2.2. The value of a tree expression generated by the nonterminal e is either the content of a variable x, the nullary node #, or a binary tree composed of a new root labeled σ_2 having the contents of variables x_1 and x_2 as subtrees. The

2.1. PRELIMINARIES

(tree expressions) $e \;::=\; x \mid \# \mid \sigma_2(x_1,x_2) \mid x/1 \mid x/2 \mid \lambda_t(x_1,x_2,...)$
(Boolean expressions) $b \;::=\; \texttt{top}(x)\texttt{=}\sigma \mid \lambda_b(x_1,x_2,...)$
(commands) $c \;::=\; \texttt{skip} \mid x\texttt{:=}e \mid \texttt{if } b \texttt{ then } \{p_1\} \texttt{ else } \{p_2\} \mid$
                         $\texttt{while } b \texttt{ do } \{p\}$
(program) $p \;::=\; \varepsilon \mid c;p$

Figure 2.2: The grammar of the assembly language for tree manipulation, where $\sigma_2 \in \Sigma_2$ and $\sigma \in \Sigma_2 \cup \{\#\}$.

expressions $x/1$ and $x/2$ refer to the first and second subtrees of the tree stored in variable x. In case the children of leaves are addressed by $x/1$ or $x/2$ an error occurs. It is also possible to carry out an arbitrary computation based on the values of an arbitrary set of variables using interpreted functions $\lambda_t(x_1,x_2,...)$. The only constraint against these interpreted functions is that they must return a nullary node. Boolean expressions generated by the nonterminal b may test the label of the root of the tree stored in a variable, and carry out an arbitrary computation using the interpreted function $\lambda_b(x_1,x_2,...)$ returning a Boolean value. Interpreted functions $\lambda_t(x_1,x_2,...)$ and $\lambda_b(x_1,x_2,...)$ are deterministic, they do not have side effects, and the execution of λ_t can also result in the error state. In our examples we will use infix operators like less or equal to =< or equivalence = as instances for interpreted function symbols with the intuitive semantics.

$$[\![\texttt{top}(x)\texttt{=}\sigma]\!]s \;=\; s \text{ if } \sigma \in \Sigma_2 \cup \{\#\} \text{ and}$$
$$\phantom{[\![\texttt{top}(x)\texttt{=}\sigma]\!]s \;=\;} s(x) \text{ has root labeled with } \sigma$$
$$[\![\neg\texttt{top}(x)\texttt{=}\sigma]\!]s \;=\; s \text{ if } \sigma \in \Sigma_2 \cup \{\#\} \text{ and}$$
$$\phantom{[\![\neg\texttt{top}(x)\texttt{=}\sigma]\!]s \;=\;} s(x) \text{ has root labeled with some } \sigma' \neq \sigma$$
$$[\![\lambda_b(x_1,x_2,...)]\!]s \;=\; s \text{ if } [\![\lambda_b]\!](s(x_1),s(x_2),...) \text{ holds}$$

$$[\![x\texttt{:=}y]\!]s = s[x \mapsto s(y)] \qquad [\![x\texttt{:=}\#]\!]s = s[x \mapsto \#] \qquad [\![\texttt{skip}]\!]s = s$$
$$[\![x\texttt{:=}\sigma_2(x_1,x_2)]\!]s = s[x \mapsto \sigma_2(s(x_1),s(x_2))] \text{ where } \sigma_2 \in \Sigma_2$$

$$[\![x\texttt{:=}y/1]\!]s \;=\; \begin{cases} s[x \mapsto \tau_1] & \text{if } s(y) = \sigma_2(\tau_1,\tau_2) \text{ for some} \\ & \text{label } \sigma_2, \text{ and trees } \tau_1 \text{ and } \tau_2 \\ \mathbf{\mathnormal{\lightning}} & \text{otherwise} \end{cases}$$

$$[\![x\texttt{:=}y/2]\!]s \;=\; \begin{cases} s[x \mapsto \tau_2] & \text{if } s(y) = \sigma_2(\tau_1,\tau_2) \text{ for some} \\ & \text{label } \sigma_2, \text{ and trees } \tau_1 \text{ and } \tau_2 \\ \mathbf{\mathnormal{\lightning}} & \text{otherwise} \end{cases}$$

$$[\![x\texttt{:=}\lambda_t(x_1,x_2,...)]\!]s = s[x \mapsto [\![\lambda_t]\!](s(x_1),s(x_2),...)] \text{ or } \mathbf{\mathnormal{\lightning}}$$

$$[\![f]\!]\mathbf{\mathnormal{\lightning}} = \mathbf{\mathnormal{\lightning}} \text{ for assignments and expressions } f$$

Figure 2.3: State transformers of assignments and Boolean expressions. States of the form $s[x \mapsto \tau]$ stand for states, where we have $s[x \mapsto \tau](y) = s(y)$ for all $y \neq x$, and $s[x \mapsto \tau](x) = \tau$.

A structured program generated by the nonterminal p is a possibly empty sequence of commands. A command can be either the empty command skip, an assignment x:=e, which updates the value of the variable x with the value of the tree expression e, a conditional execution of alternative programs if, or an iteration while.

In this chapter the semantics of the language is defined by the transition relation $cfg \rightarrow_\rho cfg'$ between configurations of the form $\langle p, s \rangle$, where p is the program to be executed on the state s. In case of final configurations, where $p = \varepsilon$ we simply write s instead of $\langle \varepsilon, s \rangle$. The state $s : (\mathcal{X} \rightarrow \mathfrak{B}_{\Sigma_2, \Sigma_0}) \cup \{\text{\textit{\textlightning}}\}$ is a mapping from the set of variables $\mathcal{X}$ of the program to binary trees $\mathfrak{B}_{\Sigma_2, \Sigma_0}$, or the error state, denoted by \textit{\textlightning}, symbolizing that a runtime error has occurred during the execution.

The functionality of basic state transformers corresponding to assignments and Boolean expressions is defined in Figure 2.3. Note that even though the negation operator ($\neg$) is not available for programmers according to the grammar, it occurs in the semantics. The transformers in Figure 2.3 are also going to be used in later sections, where the semantics of the programming language is defined using control flow graphs. There, the application of the negation operator is necessary. On the other hand, the absence of the negation operator does not decrease the expressiveness of the programming language and simplifies the notation.

$$\text{E:} \frac{s = \text{\textlightning}}{\langle c, s \rangle \rightarrow_\rho \text{\textlightning}} \quad \text{A:} \frac{s \neq \text{\textlightning}}{\langle x{:=}e, s \rangle \rightarrow_\rho [\![x{:=}e]\!]s} \quad \text{S:} \frac{\langle c, s \rangle \rightarrow_\rho^* s'}{\langle c;p, s \rangle \rightarrow_\rho \langle p, s' \rangle}$$

$$\text{WT:} \frac{s \neq \text{\textlightning} \quad [\![b]\!]s = s \quad \langle p, s \rangle \rightarrow_\rho^* s'}{\langle \text{while } b \text{ do } \{p\}, s \rangle \rightarrow_\rho \langle \text{while } b \text{ do } \{p\}, s' \rangle}$$

$$\text{WF:} \frac{s \neq \text{\textlightning} \quad [\![\neg b]\!]s = s}{\langle \text{while } b \text{ do } \{p\}, s \rangle \rightarrow_\rho s}$$

$$\text{IT:} \frac{s \neq \text{\textlightning} \quad [\![b]\!]s = s \quad \langle p_{\text{tt}}, s \rangle \rightarrow_\rho^* s'}{\langle \text{if } b \text{ then } \{p_{\text{tt}}\} \text{ else } \{p_{\text{ff}}\}, s \rangle \rightarrow_\rho s'}$$

$$\text{IF:} \frac{s \neq \text{\textlightning} \quad [\![\neg b]\!]s = s \quad \langle p_{\text{ff}}, s \rangle \rightarrow_\rho^* s'}{\langle \text{if } b \text{ then } \{p_{\text{tt}}\} \text{ else } \{p_{\text{ff}}\}, s \rangle \rightarrow_\rho s'}$$

Figure 2.4: The semantics of the programming language.

The semantics of the programming language is shown in Figure 2.4. In the condition parts of the rules we use the relation $\rightarrow_\rho^*$, which denotes the reflexive and transitive closure of $\rightarrow_\rho$. A central rule of the semantics is S, which is responsible for executing a program, in other words a sequence of commands. The remaining rules define the effects of individual commands. Due to rule E, the error state is not modified by any command. Instead, it is passed over to the next command in the sequence, or to the final configuration. In case the state is not erroneous, the execution of an assignment is specified by rule A. The rules WT and WF execute iterations, IT and IF execute conditional selections of alternative programs as it is usual in other structured programming languages.

Because here we are concerned with end-to-end information flow policies, we assume that input values of computations are given in the initial configuration,

2.1. PRELIMINARIES

and the result is presented in the final configuration. We assume furthermore, that each variable carries a value in the initial state, therefore, no error can be triggered by a variable access.

```
1   // 1. Selecting the phase:
2     if top(phase)=notify then {
3       toAuthors := subDB;
4     }
5     else {
6
7   // 2. Initialization:
8       empty := #;
9       submissionsRev := #;
10      submissions := subDB/1;
11
12  // 3. Branching based on conditional value:
13      if averageScore < '1.5' then {
14
15  // 4/tt. Searching the elements to be modified:
16        found := false(empty,empty);
17        while top(found)=false do {
18          id := submissions/1;
19          idVal := id/1;
20          if idVal = paperId then {
21            found := true(empty,empty);
22          } else {
23            submissionsRev := submission(id,submissionsRev);
24            submissions := submissions/2;
25          };
26        };
27
28  // 5/tt. Modifying the acceptance value depending on
29  //          averageScore:
30        acceptanceVal := 'rejected';
31
32  // 6/tt. Reconstructing the data structure of the submission:
33        acceptance := acceptance(acceptanceVal,empty);
34        id := id(idVal,acceptance);
35        submissions := submissions/2;
36        submissions := submission(id,submissions);
37
38  // 7/tt. Reconstructing the data structure of the database:
39        stop := false(empty,empty);
40        while top(stop)=false do {
41          if top(submissionsRev)=submission then {
42            id := submissionsRev/1;
43            submissions := submission(id,submissions);
44            submissionsRev := submissions/2;
45          } else {
46            stop := true(empty,empty);
47          };
48        };
49
50      } else {
```

```
51
52   // 4/ff.  Searching the elements to be modified:
53        found := false(empty,empty);
54        while top(found)=false do {
55          id := submissions/1;
56          idVal := id/1;
57          if idVal = paperId then {
58            found := true(empty,empty);
59          } else {
60            submissionsRev := submission(id,submissionsRev);
61            submissions := submissions/2;
62          };
63        };
64
65   // 5/ff.  Modifying the acceptance value depending on
66   //         averageScore:
67        acceptanceVal := 'accepted';
68
69   // 6/ff.  Reconstructing the data structure of the submission:
70        acceptance := acceptance(acceptanceVal,empty);
71        id := id(idVal,acceptance);
72        submissions := submissions/2;
73        submissions := submission(id,submissions);
74
75   // 7/ff.  Reconstructing the data structure of the database:
76        stop := false(empty,empty);
77        while top(stop)=false do {
78          if top(submissionsRev)=submission then {
79            id := submissionsRev/1;
80            submissions := submission(id,submissions);
81            submissionsRev := submissions/2;
82          } else {
83            stop := true(empty,empty);
84          };
85        };
86      };
87
88   // 8.  Presenting the result.
89        subDB := root(submissions,empty);
90        subDB_Output := subDB;
91      };
```

Listing 2.1: The implementation of the functionality of the pseudo code of Listing 1.1 in the assembly language for tree manipulation.

Listing 2.1 shows the implementation of the functionality of the pseudo code of Listing 1.1 in the assembly language for tree manipulation. The program assumes that the binary representation of a database like that in Figure 2.1 is given in the variable subDB, and the modified database at the end of the computation is stored in variable subDB_Output. The identifier of the paper, the acceptance value of which is to be updated is stored in variable paperId, the average of the scores already submitted for the paper is stored in variable averageScore. Each time the program is executed, first the actual phase of the review process is determined based on the value of phase. In case we are in the "review" phase,

2.1. PRELIMINARIES

the program modifies the database based on the average score corresponding to the specified paper. In the phase "notify", the program assigns the database to the variable toAuthors, which is visible by the authors. The code itself is divided into 12 separate sections. In the first section the actual phase is determined. The second section initializes some variables that will be necessary later on during the computation. In particular, the variable submissions is initialized with the first child of the tree stored in variable subDB. The third section is a branching decision based on the value of averageScore. The corresponding Boolean expression averageScore < '1.5' at line 13 is an example of an interpreted Boolean function λ_b. The functionalities of the branches are very similar, because they implement a tree manipulation specified by identical XPath expressions at lines 15 and 22 in Listing 1.1. We tried to emphasize the correspondence of some fragments of code in the two branches. Therefore, for example, the section responsible for querying the submission identified by paperId is numbered 4/tt in the positive branch and 4/ff in the negative branch. Accordingly, the fourth section is the query in both of the branches, which selects the submission with identifier as it is stored in variable paperId. In each iteration of the loops at lines 17 and 54, the head of the list of submissions is examined, whether it corresponds to the document with the right identifier. If not, then the head is appended to the list submissionsRev. Accordingly, submissionsRev contains a prefix of the initial value of submissions in reverse order. The examination of identifiers is carried out by the branching constructs at lines 20 and 57, where the Boolean expression is idVal = paperId. This expression is an other example of an interpreted Boolean expression λ_b. The fifth section assigns a value to the variable acceptanceVal depending on the average of scores given. Next, the data structure for the actual paper is reassembled in both of the branches and appended to submissions. The seventh section reconstructs the original order of papers in the database submissions using submissionsRev. By this last iteration the database is reconstructed so that only the acceptance value of the appropriate submission is modified. Note that the list of trees as it is stored in variable submissions at the end of section 7 corresponds to a binary forest. The second child of the root of the binary representation of an unranked tree is always #. Therefore, by the first line of section 8 the binary representation of the unranked database is restored, and the second line assigns it to the output variable.

2.1.3 Information Flow Policies

In the seminal paper [26] Denning made the observation, that information flow policies must be necessarily composable in terms of lattices. Our information flow policies considering trees adhere to this observation. The simplest information flow lattice is *low* $\sqsubseteq$ *high* specifying that pieces of information classified *high* must not be observed by principals classified *low*. In this work we group the pieces of information and the principals participating in the activities of workflows into these two groups as well.

In this work we consider programs manipulating tree-shaped data, therefore, information flow policies classify nodes in trees. Our techniques can enforce information flow policies, where the secrecy level of nodes does not decrease on the paths from the root to the leaves. A policy is defined in terms of *public views* corresponding to the elements of the information flow lattice. The public view corresponding to a lattice element ξ can be obtained by replacing the greatest subtrees, the roots of which have secrecy level higher than ξ with a leaf labeled $\star$. In our case, where the information flow lattice consists of two elements, the information flow policy is defined by a single public view corresponding to the element *low*. The view corresponding to *high* is not necessary because that is identical to the entire document without nodes labeled $\star$.

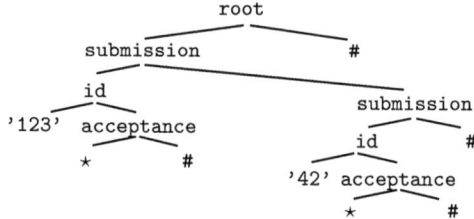

Figure 2.5: The policy specifying that the acceptance values of the submissions in the data structure of Figure 2.1 are secret.

As an example, let us compose an information flow policy specifying that the acceptance values of submissions in the database of Figure 2.1 are secret. This is done by the policy in Figure 2.5, where the leaves labeled with the acceptance values are replaced with nullary nodes labeled $\star$.

Information flow policies for programs realizing a function from the initial state to the final state are frequently defined in terms of these states. We call these policies end-to-end information flow policies, in order to emphasize their difference to temporal information flow policies characterizing the sequence of values exchanged between a system and its environment during the execution.

2.2 The Runtime Monitor through an Example

Similarly to other runtime monitors, e.g., [77, 38, 66, 64], in order to enforce information flow properties, we extend the configuration of the semantics of the language with an additional member. The new member $D : (\mathcal{X} \to \mathfrak{B}_{\Sigma_2, \Sigma_0 \cup \{\star\}}) \cup \{\bot, \top, \sharp\}$, referred to as the *monitor state*, assigns to every variable either a binary tree having the extra nullary alphabet element $\star$, or is one of the symbols $\bot$, $\top$ and $\sharp$. Intuitively, $D(x)$ stores the public view of the value of the variable x in the corresponding real state s. The monitor recalculates D in parallel to each transition of the operational semantics, and at the end the final monitor state is presented as the result of the computation for principals belonging to the security lattice element *low*.

```
1  empty:=#;
2  if top(author)=A_Mustermann then {
3    if top(topic)=Databases then {
4      rev2:=conflict(empty,rev2);
5      rev1:=listElem(doc,rev1);
6    }
7    else {
8      rev2:=conflict(empty,rev2);
```

2.2. THE RUNTIME MONITOR THROUGH AN EXAMPLE

```
9       rev3:=listElem(doc,rev3);
10    };
11  }
12  else {
13    skip;
14  };
```

Listing 2.2: Branching on a secret value.

In the next paragraphs, we informally illustrate the functionality of the runtime monitor by an example. The code fragment in Listing 2.2 could be part of a paper submission system distributing the papers to reviewers. Let us suppose that reviewer 2 declared a conflict of interest with the author A. Mustermann, and therefore the distribution system is not allowed to send information to him about the content. Therefore, from the point of view of reviewer 2, the topic of the paper of A. Mustermann is secret too. Let us suppose that the runtime monitor reaches line 3 of the code in Listing 2.2 with monitor state:

$$D_0 = \{..., \texttt{topic} \mapsto \star, \texttt{rev1} \mapsto \texttt{\#}, \texttt{rev2} \mapsto \texttt{listElem(document(...),\#)}, ...\}$$

Because the conditional expression depends on the secret, constant propagation is carried out on this branching command. We can identify the value $\star$ with the top element of constant propagation expressing that the value is not constant and therefore, may leak information about the secret. After executing the branches we get:

$$D_{\textbf{then}} = \{..., \quad \texttt{rev1} \mapsto \texttt{listElem(document(...),\#)},$$
$$\texttt{rev2} \mapsto \texttt{conflict(\#,listElem(document(...),\#))}, ...\}$$
$$D_{\textbf{else}} = \{..., \texttt{rev1} \mapsto \texttt{\#}, \texttt{rev2} \mapsto \texttt{conflict(\#,listElem(document(...),\#))}, ...\}$$

After the join computation we have:

$$D = \{..., \texttt{rev1} \mapsto \star, \texttt{rev2} \mapsto \texttt{conflict(\#,listElem(document(...),\#))}, ...\}$$

Computing the join of two states can be done by replacing the values of variables at positions where they differ, with the symbol $\star$. In this way, it is guaranteed that the monitor state is independent of the secret after the branching construct. For the join computation, therefore, it is not necessary to replace

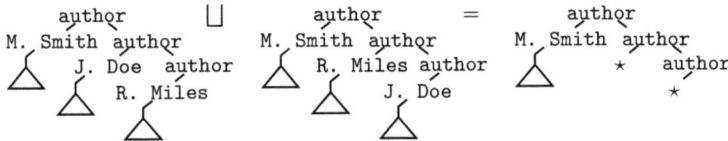

Figure 2.6: The join on document trees, where the leaves labeled # are omitted for the sake of simplicity.

the entire value of a variable with $\star$ if the two values differ only for certain subtrees. Figure 2.6 illustrates the join computation for the values of variable **authors** in monitor states $D_{\textbf{then}}$ and $D_{\textbf{else}}$ in a situation like that. The variable contains a list of authors and their documents that they submitted. Let us suppose that the order of two authors has been exchanged in one of the two secret-dependent conditional branches in order to leak information. By computing the join, we only need to replace those members of the list which were exchanged, but we can leave the others as they are. In this way, we take the semi-structured nature of data into account and gain additional precision.

Another advantage of our approach is the following. Because in the code fragment of Listing 2.2 the variable `rev2` is assigned in a secret branch, many information flow analyzers would consider its value secret. The solutions motivated by the type system of Volpano et al. [78] like Jif [56, 4], SIF [19] and Paralocks [17] do so because the variable `rev2` has been assigned in an environment, where the program counter depends on the secret and therefore is *high*. Similarly behave runtime monitors [77, 38, 66, 64] for the same reason. The program slicing [43] based solutions like Joana [41] do so, because of the control dependence edges from the conditional expressions to assignments. Our idea is based on the observation that in the final configuration the value of the variable `rev2` is independent of the value of `topic`. This could happen, perhaps, because the program noticed by the embedding branching decision, that the content of the paper is secret and behaved correctly. Accordingly, the observation of `rev2` does not give us information on the secret value. Our runtime monitor would consider the value of `rev2` as public, because it determines the confidential parts of values by means of the join computation after exiting from branching commands depending on secret values. There are approaches based on bisimulation, e.g. [51, 47], allowing public assignments in secret branches, if the equivalence of the public effects of these branches is proved. Because program equivalence is in general undecidable, these solutions rely on syntactic approximations. In our solution if programs p and q are equivalent, they do not read confidential variables, and they terminate, then the result of `if secret=0 then {p} else {q}` is recognized public regardless of the syntactic representation of p and q.

In the next section we formally elaborate the ideas introduced here.

2.3 Formal Treatment of the Monitor

In order to describe the runtime monitor formally, we need some more definitions. In the following, we regard a tree τ as a mapping from its positions $Pos(\tau)$ to the alphabet $\Sigma = \Sigma_2 \cup \Sigma_0 \cup \{\star\}$, where the domain is a prefix closed subset of $\{1, 2\}^*$. Accordingly, we use the notation $\tau(\pi)$ to refer to the alphabet element at position π of the tree τ. If a node π of τ has successors, then $\tau(\pi) \in \Sigma_2$, otherwise $\tau(\pi) \in \Sigma_0 \cup \{\star\}$. We denote the *subtrees* rooted at the first and the second child of the root of τ with $\tau/1$ and $\tau/2$ respectively.

Definition 2 (Preorder of Trees). *If $\tau_1, \tau_2 \in \mathfrak{B}_{\Sigma_2, \Sigma_0 \cup \{\star\}}$ then $\tau_1 \sqsubseteq \tau_2$ holds if one of the following is true:*

- $\tau_2(\varepsilon) = \star$.

- $\tau_2(\varepsilon) \neq \star$ and $\tau_1(\varepsilon) = \tau_2(\varepsilon)$, furthermore, if $\tau_1(\varepsilon) \in \Sigma_2$ then $\tau_1/1 \sqsubseteq \tau_2/1$ and $\tau_1/2 \sqsubseteq \tau_2/2$.

In Definition 2 the symbol $\star$ occurs as an additional nullary element, which represents a secret subtree in the public view. Similarly to the state, the monitor state can also be erroneous, denoted by $\frac{\ell}{\ell}$, meaning that the execution reached an inconsistent situation. It is also possible that the error state itself depends

2.3. FORMAL TREATMENT OF THE MONITOR

$$\mathcal{M}[\![\texttt{top}(x)\texttt{=}\sigma]\!]^\sharp D = \begin{cases} D & \text{if } D(x)(\varepsilon) = \sigma \\ D[x \mapsto \sigma(\star,\star)] & \text{if } D(x) = \star \text{ and } \sigma \in \Sigma_2 \\ D[x \mapsto \sigma] & \text{if } D(x) = \star \text{ and } \sigma \in \Sigma_0 \\ \bot & \text{otherwise} \end{cases} \quad (2.1)$$

$$\mathcal{M}[\![\neg\texttt{top}(x)\texttt{=}\sigma]\!]^\sharp D = \begin{cases} D & \text{if } D(x)(\varepsilon) \neq \sigma \\ \bot & \text{if } D(x)(\varepsilon) = \sigma \end{cases} \quad (2.2)$$

$$\mathcal{M}[\![x\texttt{:=}y]\!]^\sharp D = D[x \mapsto D(y)] \qquad \mathcal{M}[\![x\texttt{:=\#}]\!]^\sharp D = D[x \mapsto \#]$$
$$\mathcal{M}[\![x\texttt{:=}\sigma_2(x_1,x_2)]\!]^\sharp D = D[x \mapsto \sigma_2(D(x_1),D(x_2))] \text{ where } \sigma_2 \in \Sigma_2 \quad (2.3)$$
$$\mathcal{M}[\![\texttt{skip}]\!]^\sharp D = D$$

$$\mathcal{M}[\![x\texttt{:=}y/1]\!]^\sharp D = \begin{cases} D[x \mapsto \tau_1] & \text{if } D(y) = \sigma_2(\tau_1,\tau_2) \text{ for some } \sigma_2 \\ \top & \text{if } D(y) = \star \\ \lightning & \text{otherwise} \end{cases}$$
$$\mathcal{M}[\![x\texttt{:=}y/2]\!]^\sharp D = \begin{cases} D[x \mapsto \tau_2] & \text{if } D(y) = \sigma_2(\tau_1,\tau_2) \text{ for some } \sigma_2 \\ \top & \text{if } D(y) = \star \\ \lightning & \text{otherwise} \end{cases} \quad (2.4)$$

$$\mathcal{M}[\![\lambda_b(x_1,x_2,\ldots)]\!]^\sharp D = D'$$
$$\text{where } D' = \bigsqcap\{D^* \mid \forall s \sqsubseteq D : [\![\lambda_b(x_1,x_2,\ldots)]\!]s \sqsubseteq D^*\} \quad (2.5)$$

$$\mathcal{M}[\![x\texttt{:=}\lambda_t(x_1,x_2,\ldots)]\!]^\sharp D = D'$$
$$\text{where } D' = \bigsqcap\{D^* \mid \forall s \sqsubseteq D : [\![x\texttt{:=}\lambda_t(x_1,x_2,\ldots)]\!]s \sqsubseteq D^*\} \quad (2.6)$$

$$\mathcal{M}[\![f]\!]^\sharp D = D \text{ if } D \in \{\lightning, \top, \bot\}$$
$$\text{for all assignments and Boolean expressions } f \quad (2.7)$$

Figure 2.7: Monitor state transformers of assignments and Boolean expressions.

on the secret. This happens for instance, if one conditional branch of a decision depending on the secret exhibits an error, while the other does not. We have introduced the top element $\top$ to represent this case. For the monitor state, a data flow analysis will be performed to approximate the public view after a secret-dependent branching construct. For this analysis, a bottom element (denoting unreachability) comes in handy to obtain a complete lattice (see Definition 3).

Definition 3 (Complete Lattice of Monitor States). *The complete lattice of monitor states is* $\mathbb{D} = (\mathcal{X} \to \mathfrak{B}_{\Sigma_2, \Sigma_0 \cup \{\star\}}) \cup \{\mathbf{\xi}, \top, \bot\}$. *For any* $D_1, D_2 \in \mathbb{D}$ *the relation* $D_1 \sqsubseteq D_2$ *holds if one of the following is true:*

- $D_1 = \bot$
- $D_2 = \top$
- $D_1 = \mathbf{\xi}$ *and* $D_2 = \mathbf{\xi}$
- *If* $D_1, D_2 \notin \{\mathbf{\xi}, \top, \bot\}$ *then for all variables x it holds that* $D_1(x) \sqsubseteq D_2(x)$ *according to Definition 2.*

The idea of the monitored execution is to carry out the state transformations on the real state and on the monitor state in parallel. For each assignment or Boolean expression f the function $[\![f]\!]$ is carried out on the real state s, and the function $\mathcal{M}[\![f]\!]^\sharp$ is carried out on the monitor state D. The function $\mathcal{M}[\![f]\!]^\sharp$ is defined so that whenever $s \sqsubseteq D$ then $[\![f]\!]s \sqsubseteq \mathcal{M}[\![f]\!]^\sharp D$ holds too. The intuitive meaning of the relation $\sqsubseteq$ between the real state and the monitor state is that they agree on public values, and this is the property our monitor guarantees along the run.

The state transformers for monitor states are shown in Figure 2.7, where the effects of Boolean expressions are displayed by formulae (2.1) and (2.2). Boolean expressions are transformations on the monitor state just as tree expressions are. Basically, a Boolean expression b holds on the monitor state D (i.e., $\mathcal{M}[\![b]\!]^\sharp D = D$) if there is potentially a state s where $s \sqsubseteq D$ and $[\![b]\!]s = s$. In the other case the result is $\bot$, which represents unreachability. In (2.1) however, additional modifications are carried out on the monitor state. The content of the variable x is transformed to the greatest tree that does not equal to $\star$, for which the Boolean expression holds. The purpose of the transformation is to enhance precision while preserving soundness.

```
1  if top(x)=σ₂ then {
2      y:=x/2;
3      ...
4  } else { ... };
```

Consider the listing above having an assignment y:=x/2 in the positive branch of a branching construct. Since the condition tests the label of the root of the tree in x for the symbol $\sigma_2 \in \Sigma_2$, it is impossible that the root of the value in x at line 2 is labeled with an element of Σ_0. Therefore, the monitor state after the assignment does not need to represent the error state, which cannot happen for any real state anyway. On the other hand, soundness is preserved by the fact that the monitor state of the negative branch is not modified by the Boolean expression (2.2). Therefore, the final monitor states of both branches are in the desirable relation with all possible real states, given that the relation was also present initially.

2.3. FORMAL TREATMENT OF THE MONITOR

The monitor state transformers corresponding to assignments as shown by (2.3) and (2.4) are almost identical to the real state transformers in Figure 2.3. The only difference is in (2.4), where there is an additional case for the situation, when the children of a leaf with label $\star$ are addressed. Depending on the secret, the result of the expression on the corresponding real state may possibly be $\frac{1}{2}$ but it is not necessary. Therefore, the monitor state must be switched to $\top$, in order to indicate that the occurrence of the error state may depend on confidential information.

$$\text{CA:} \quad \frac{D \notin \{\frac{1}{2}, \top\}}{\langle x := e, n, (s, D) \rangle \to_\gamma (\llbracket x := e \rrbracket s, \mathcal{M}\llbracket x := e \rrbracket^\sharp D)}$$

$$\text{CCE:} \quad \frac{D \in \{\frac{1}{2}, \top\} \quad \langle c, s \rangle \to_\rho^* s'}{\langle c, n, (s, D) \rangle \to_\gamma (s', D)} \qquad \text{CS:} \quad \frac{\langle c, n, (s, D) \rangle \to_\gamma^* (s', D')}{\langle c; p, n, (s, D) \rangle \to_\gamma \langle p, n, (s', D') \rangle}$$

$$\text{CIT:} \quad \frac{D \notin \{\frac{1}{2}, \top\} \quad \mathcal{M}\llbracket \neg b \rrbracket^\sharp D = \bot \quad \langle p_{\mathtt{tt}}, n, (s, D) \rangle \to_\gamma^* (s', D')}{\langle \mathtt{if}\ b\ \mathtt{then}\ \{p_{\mathtt{tt}}\}\ \mathtt{else}\ \{p_{\mathtt{ff}}\}, n, (s, D) \rangle \to_\gamma (s', D')}$$

$$\text{CIF:} \quad \frac{D \notin \{\frac{1}{2}, \top\} \quad \mathcal{M}\llbracket b \rrbracket^\sharp D = \bot \quad \langle p_{\mathtt{ff}}, n, (s, D) \rangle \to_\gamma^* (s', D')}{\langle \mathtt{if}\ b\ \mathtt{then}\ \{p_{\mathtt{tt}}\}\ \mathtt{else}\ \{p_{\mathtt{ff}}\}, n, (s, D) \rangle \to_\gamma (s', D')}$$

$$\text{CIH:} \quad \frac{\begin{array}{c} D \notin \{\frac{1}{2}, \top\} \quad \mathcal{M}\llbracket b \rrbracket^\sharp D \neq \bot \quad \mathcal{M}\llbracket \neg b \rrbracket^\sharp D \neq \bot \\ \langle \mathtt{if}\ b\ \mathtt{then}\ \{p_{\mathtt{tt}}\}\ \mathtt{else}\ \{p_{\mathtt{ff}}\}, s \rangle \to_\rho^* s' \\ \langle\langle \mathtt{if}\ b\ \mathtt{then}\ \{p_{\mathtt{tt}}\}\ \mathtt{else}\ \{p_{\mathtt{ff}}\}\rangle, s, D \rangle \to_\mu^* D' \end{array}}{\langle \mathtt{if}\ b\ \mathtt{then}\ \{p_{\mathtt{tt}}\}\ \mathtt{else}\ \{p_{\mathtt{ff}}\}, n, (s, D) \rangle \to_\gamma (s', D')}$$

$$\text{CWT:} \quad \frac{D \notin \{\frac{1}{2}, \top\} \quad \mathcal{M}\llbracket \neg b \rrbracket^\sharp D = \bot \quad \langle p, n, (s, D) \rangle \to_\gamma^* (s', D')}{\langle \mathtt{while}\ b\ \mathtt{do}\ \{p\}, n, (s, D) \rangle \to_\gamma \langle \mathtt{while}\ b\ \mathtt{do}\ \{p\}, n, (s', D') \rangle}$$

$$\text{CWF:} \quad \frac{D \notin \{\frac{1}{2}, \top\} \quad \mathcal{M}\llbracket b \rrbracket^\sharp D = \bot}{\langle \mathtt{while}\ b\ \mathtt{do}\ \{p\}, n, (s, D) \rangle \to_\gamma (s, D)}$$

$$\text{CWH:} \quad \frac{\begin{array}{c} D \notin \{\frac{1}{2}, \top\} \quad \mathcal{M}\llbracket b \rrbracket^\sharp D \neq \bot \quad \mathcal{M}\llbracket \neg b \rrbracket^\sharp D \neq \bot \\ \langle \mathtt{while}\ b\ \mathtt{do}\ \{p\}, s \rangle \to_\rho^* s' \quad \langle(\mathtt{while}\ b\ \mathtt{do}\ \{p\})(n), D \rangle \to_\mu^* D' \end{array}}{\langle \mathtt{while}\ b\ \mathtt{do}\ \{p\}, n, (s, D) \rangle \to_\gamma (s', D')}$$

Figure 2.8: The monitored semantics.

The transformers corresponding to interpreted functions λ_b and λ_t are specified by (2.5) and (2.6). Since the real semantics of these functions are unknown, the equations only specify the conditions that need to be fulfilled by all possible sound runtime monitors. Accordingly, the resulting monitor state D' needs to be greater or equal to all possible resulting real states. An additional requirement against D' is that it needs to be the least among those that fulfill the previous requirement. This way, the resulting monitor state is the smallest among those that are sound with respect to the concrete state transformer.

The semantics of the monitored execution is defined in the form of relations $cfg \to_\gamma cfg'$ between configurations of the form $\langle p, n, (s, D) \rangle$, where p is a pro-

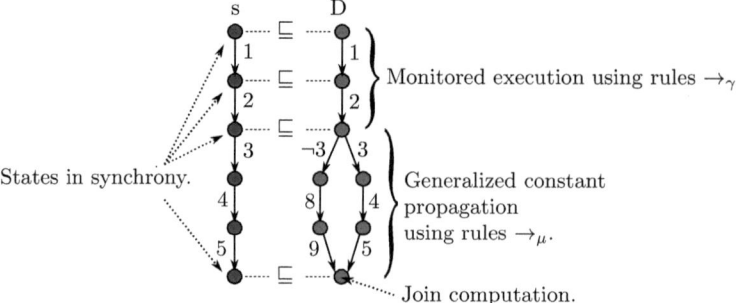

Figure 2.9: A monitored execution of the example program at Listing 2.2, where the numbers of edges identify the line in the code they stand for. In particular, the meaning of ¬3 is that the negated version of the Boolean expression of line 3 is executed.

gram to be executed and s is the state of the execution. The member D is the public view of the state s, which we call the monitor state, s is called the real state. The member n is a natural number influencing the precision of the monitor when computing the public effect of branching constructs. Larger values correspond to enhanced precision and longer computation time. In the initial configuration $\langle p_0, n, (s_0, D_0)\rangle$ it holds that $s_0 \sqsubseteq D_0$. Furthermore, there are no trees with nodes labeled $\star$ in the contents of s_0.

The transition rules of the monitored semantics are shown in Figure 2.8, and a monitored execution of the program in Listing 2.2 is illustrated in Figure 2.9. As long as the monitored semantics does not execute a branching construct, the condition of which depends on the secret, the monitored execution carries out the transformations on s and D simultaneously. Accordingly, assignments are executed in parallel on s and on D as it is defined by rule CA. If the monitor state $D \in \{\top, \bot, \notin\}$, then it is simply propagated to the next command in the sequence using rule CCE. The truth values of Boolean expressions are determined based on the monitor state. If $\mathcal{M}[\![b]\!]^\sharp D = \bot$, then we assume $\neg b$ to be true. Accordingly, since the content of the variable author does not depend on the secret, line 2 of Listing 2.2 is executed on the monitor and the real state using rule CIT in Figure 2.8. In case $\mathcal{M}[\![b]\!]^\sharp D \neq \bot$ and $\mathcal{M}[\![\neg b]\!]^\sharp D \neq \bot$ simultaneously, we execute a branching construct, the condition of which may depend on the secret. In this case, according to rules CIH and CWH, the result of the branching command on the real state is computed using the original semantics of Figure 2.4, the resulting monitor state is computed using a generalized constant propagation algorithm. This is visualized in Figure 2.9, where multiple branches of a branching construct are executed on the monitor state using rules $\rightarrow_\mu$. At the common final node of the branches the results of the branches are joined in order to compute the result of the whole branching construct.

The parameter n in the configuration of the monitored execution is used by the generalized constant propagation algorithm. Assume that the command c in the configuration $\langle c; p, n, (s, D)\rangle$ is a branching construct, the condition of which depends on the secret. In this case we apply the generalized constant

2.3. FORMAL TREATMENT OF THE MONITOR

propagation on the command $c(n)$, which we construct based on c by replacing all occurrences of the command while b do $\{p\}$ in the program text of c by while(n) b do $\{p\}$.

$$\text{MCE:} \frac{D \in \{\top, \bot, \text{\textsc{\textonehalf}}\}}{\langle c, D \rangle \to_\mu D} \quad \text{MA:} \frac{D \notin \{\top, \bot, \text{\textsc{\textonehalf}}\}}{\langle \texttt{x:=}e, D \rangle \to_\mu \mathcal{M}[\![\texttt{x:=}e]\!]^\sharp D}$$

$$\text{MS:} \frac{\langle c, D \rangle \to_\mu^* D'}{\langle c;p, D \rangle \to_\mu \langle p, D' \rangle}$$

$$\text{MI:} \frac{\langle p_{\texttt{tt}}, \mathcal{M}[\![b]\!]^\sharp D \rangle \to_\mu^* D_{\texttt{tt}} \quad \langle p_{\texttt{ff}}, \mathcal{M}[\![\neg b]\!]^\sharp D \rangle \to_\mu^* D_{\texttt{ff}}}{\langle \texttt{if } b \texttt{ then } \{p_{\texttt{tt}}\} \texttt{ else } \{p_{\texttt{ff}}\}, D \rangle \to_\mu D'}$$

$$\text{MWT:} \frac{D \notin \{\top, \bot, \text{\textsc{\textonehalf}}\} \quad \mathcal{M}[\![\neg b]\!]^\sharp D = \bot \quad n > 0 \quad \langle p, \mathcal{M}[\![b]\!]^\sharp D \rangle \to_\mu^* D'}{\langle \texttt{while}(n) \ b \texttt{ do } \{p\}, D \rangle \to_\mu \langle \texttt{while}(n-1) \ b \texttt{ do } \{p\}, D' \rangle}$$

$$\text{MWF:} \frac{D \notin \{\top, \bot, \text{\textsc{\textonehalf}}\} \quad \mathcal{M}[\![b]\!]^\sharp D = \bot}{\langle \texttt{while}(n) \ b \texttt{ do } \{p\}, D \rangle \to_\mu D}$$

$$\text{MWH:} \frac{(\mathcal{M}[\![\neg b]\!]^\sharp D \neq \bot \wedge \mathcal{M}[\![b]\!]^\sharp D \neq \bot) \vee n \leq 0}{D \notin \{\top, \bot, \text{\textsc{\textonehalf}}\} \quad \langle p, \mathcal{M}[\![b]\!]^\sharp D \rangle \to_\mu^* D_1 \quad D' = D_1 \sqcup D \quad D' \not\sqsubseteq D}{\langle \texttt{while}(n) \ b \texttt{ do } \{p\}, D \rangle \to_\mu \langle \texttt{while}(n-1) \ b \texttt{ do } \{p\}, D' \rangle}$$

$$\text{MWX:} \frac{(\mathcal{M}[\![\neg b]\!]^\sharp D \neq \bot \wedge \mathcal{M}[\![b]\!]^\sharp D \neq \bot) \vee n \leq 0}{D \notin \{\top, \bot, \text{\textsc{\textonehalf}}\} \quad \langle p, \mathcal{M}[\![b]\!]^\sharp D \rangle \to_\mu^* D_1 \quad D' = D_1 \sqcup D \quad D' \sqsubseteq D}{\langle \texttt{while}(n) \ b \texttt{ do } \{p\}, D \rangle \to_\mu D}$$

Figure 2.10: Generalized constant propagation.

The *generalized constant propagation* algorithm is defined in Figure 2.10, which is basically the rule-based formalization of a syntax-directed fixed-point computation algorithm on the program text as it is presented in [15]. The lattice is the set of possible monitor states according to Definition 3.

The rules defining the functionality of assignment (MA), sequential execution of commands (MS), and the propagation of the states $\top$, $\bot$ and $\text{\textsc{\textonehalf}}$ (MCE) are very similar to rules A, S and E of the original semantics. The only difference is at rule MCE, which propagates the states $\bot$ and $\top$ unmodified as well.

The rule MI is responsible for computing the monitor state transformation corresponding to an if command. It evaluates both branches with initial states $\mathcal{M}[\![b]\!]^\sharp D$ and $\mathcal{M}[\![\neg b]\!]^\sharp D$ and then joins the results.

The rules MWT, MWF, MWH and MWX are used to compute the public effect of iterations. If the parameter n is less or equal to zero, or the condition b is secret-dependent, then a fixed point is computed by rules MWH and MWX. If, however, the condition is independent of the secret, and n is greater than zero, the monitor executes the body of the loop iteratively by applying rules MWT and MWF. At the same time this might not terminate. So the purpose of n is to allow the user to specify how many times the monitor should apply the rule MWT before switching to the fixed point computation. In particular, setting the parameter n to zero in the initial configuration of the monitored execution $\langle p, n, (s, D) \rangle$ amounts to choosing to omit the application of rules MWT and MWF, and use only the fixed point computation offered by rules MWH and MWX. At the same time this might result in an unnecessarily inaccurate monitor state.

Because the complete lattice of Definition 3 has the ascending chain condition, as Theorem 1 states below, the fixed point computation always terminates.

Theorem 1. *If there is an s' so that $s \sqsubseteq D$ and $\langle p, s \rangle \rightarrow_\rho^* s'$, then there is a D' so that $\langle p, n, (s, D) \rangle \rightarrow_\gamma^* (s', D')$.*

Proof. The idea behind the proof is the following: If there is no branching construct executed having a secret-dependent condition along the monitored execution, then the state transitions are carried out simultaneously on the real state and on the monitor state.

In the case of a branching construct having a secret-dependent condition, the public effect is computed by the algorithm in Figure 2.10. The only rule, which could be applied an unbounded number of times is MWH, but because the lattice of Definition 3 has the ascending chain condition, the fixed point computation terminates. For the detailed proof of this case please refer to Lemma 3 in Section 6.1. □

2.4 Guarantees

In this section we formally discuss the guarantees provided by the runtime monitor.

Similarly to other language-based information flow controlling solutions [27, 56, 4, 65, 64, 41, 38, 77], our approach enforces a variant of *termination-insensitive noninterference* [7] tailored for our computational model. Accordingly, we do not consider covert channels like the timing channel, the heat channel, or the memory consumption channel, or any other channel that could result from the properties of a specific implementation or runtime environment.

Definition 4 (Termination-Insensitive Noninterference[1])**.** *Program p satisfies termination-insensitive noninterference relative to the initial and final public views D and D' if and only if for all $s_1, s_2 \sqsubseteq D$ it is true that if*

- $\langle p, s_1 \rangle \rightarrow_\rho^* s_1'$ *and*
- $\langle p, s_2 \rangle \rightarrow_\rho^* s_2'$

then $s_1' \sqsubseteq D'$ and $s_2' \sqsubseteq D'$ hold too. In this case we say that D' is an appropriate final public view corresponding to the program p and the initial public view D.

The monitored execution $\langle p, n, (s, D) \rangle \rightarrow_\gamma^* (s', D')$ computes a pair (s', D') based on (s, D), where D' is an appropriate final public view corresponding to p and D. We may consider the public view D as an indistinguishability relation between

---
[1]There is an algebraically equivalent and simpler formulation to this definition: Program p satisfies termination-insensitive noninterference relative to D and D', if for all $s \sqsubseteq D$ from $\langle p, s \rangle \rightarrow_\rho^* s'$ it follows that $s' \sqsubseteq D'$.

any initial states s^*, for which it holds that $s^* \sqsubseteq D$. The meaning of the resulting monitor state D' is that by observing it, we do not gain information on which s^* was the initial state. Accordingly, we can communicate parts or the entire final public view D' to principals having security clearance *low*, and we can consider nodes labeled $\star$ as a default value that secret pieces of information have been replaced with. If $D' = \top$, then the observers of the public do not gain more information than the fact that the execution of the program terminated. Still, principals with security clearance *high* may observe the resulting real state s', and use the computed values.

The following theorem assures us that our monitor computes indeed an appropriate final public view corresponding to the program and the initial public view:

Theorem 2. *If there are two initial states s_1 and s_2 so that $s_1, s_2 \sqsubseteq D$, then if*

- $\langle p, n, (s_1, D) \rangle \to_\gamma^* (s'_1, D'_1)$ *and*
- $\langle p, n, (s_2, D) \rangle \to_\gamma^* (s'_2, D'_2)$

then $D'_1 = D'_2 = D'$ and $s'_1 \sqsubseteq D'$ and $s'_2 \sqsubseteq D'$.

Proof. The result follows from Lemma 9 and Lemma 8 in Section 6.1. □

2.5 Related Work

We have presented an approach to enforce information flow security in tree manipulating processes during runtime. Since practical information flow policies refer to the structure of data, approaches where security specifications are bound to variables such as [4, 56, 41, 17, 19, 38, 77] may not suffice. In their paper [64], Russo et al. aim at a similar goal like us. In their formal model of JavaScript, they consider one DOM tree representing the data in a Web browser. However, their formalism is still quite different to ours. Their computational model operates on a single unranked tree using a pointer on one specific working node, and supports operations like insertion, modification and removal. Since their monitor maintains the security levels of the positions of the DOM tree during the run, it can be considered as a generalization of the idea of binding secrecy levels to variables. Our monitor, on the other hand, maintains the concrete values of public nodes making it possible to take the semantics of branches into account where the conditional depends on the secret, and compute the public effect by means of a value-based comparison of the resulting states.

An approach based on abstract interpretation has been presented in [34], where the security of programs is investigated depending on the observational capabilities of attackers. If the public input values are handled as constants in the initial state, then no information leaks to public variables in the final state, if the property that the attackers can observe can be proved to be constant. Our generalized constant propagation used to compute the public effect of secret-dependent branching constructs is based on a similar observation.

Chapter 3

Relational Abstract Interpretation

In this chapter we introduce a framework for proving 2-hypersafety properties of programs by means of abstract interpretation. The main idea is to apply abstract interpretation on the self-compositions of the control flow graphs (CFG) of programs. As a result, our method is inherently capable of analyzing relational properties of even dissimilar programs.

Constructing self-compositions of control flow graphs is nontrivial. Therefore, we present an algorithm for constructing quality self-compositions driven by a tree distance measure between the abstract syntax trees of subprograms. Finally, we demonstrate the applicability of the approach by proving intricate information flow properties of programs written in the assembly language for tree manipulation motivated by the Web Services Business Process Execution Language (BPEL) [6].

Abstract interpretation [23] is a well established approach for proving safety properties of programs. However, an interesting class of properties, namely information flow properties, are best formalized not as safety properties, but as *safety hyperproperties* [21]. Safety hyperproperties are not invariants maintained by individual runs of systems but are properties of multiple runs.

The authors of [21] have observed that the verification of k-hypersafety properties can be reduced to the verification of ordinary safety properties of the k-fold self-composition of programs. In this chapter we apply this idea to control-flow graphs, and present a method for proving 2-hypersafety properties. We apply the general approach for proving the noninterference of programs written in the assembly language for tree manipulation as presented in Figure 2.2.

Noninterference means that two executions are indistinguishable based on public observations if their initial states differ in secret data only [36]. Consider, e.g., the code fragment in Listing 1.1 written in a pseudo language similar to BPEL. Our goal is to prove that the value of variable `averageScore` only interferes with the acceptance status in the description of the corresponding submission, but neither with its identifier nor with the size of the database etc. It is challenging, because data manipulation is carried out in different branches depending on the secret. By comparing two executions corresponding to the two branches of the `if` construct at line 10 in Listing 1.1, we notice, however, that only the acceptance status of the paper with the given id can be different in the results, while all public data remains equal. In this chapter we show a method to prove properties like this automatically using static analysis.

We regard the execution of a program as the sequence of assignments and condition evaluations that take place during the computation. We take advantage of the fact that inserting skip instructions into arbitrary places of an execution does not change the result. Therefore, different *alignments* of a pair of executions can be achieved by the insertion of skip instructions. Knowing an initial abstract value describing the potential set of pairs of initial states, we are interested in computing the final abstract value describing the possible set of pairs of states that can result from any pairs of executions. For that we require a relational abstract domain describing *pairs* of concrete states, together with abstract transformers for *pairs* of instructions set in alignment within the two executions. The abstract effect of a given pair of executions w.r.t. a fixed alignment of instructions is obtained by applying the composition of the occurring transformers to the initial abstract value. Since the abstract effect of any alignment results in a safe overapproximation of the desired outcome, we can approximate it by the greatest lower bound over all alignments. In order to obtain a safe approximation for all pairs of executions reaching a given pair of program points, we then take the least upper bound of the values provided for each pair of executions individually. We refer to this value as the *merge over all twin computations* (MTC) solution, and consider it as the ideal solution of the analysis problem.

In general, it might be difficult to compute the MTC solution directly. Instead, we propose to select one promising static alignment of instructions for each pair of executions resulting in a *self-composition* of the CFG of the program. Here, the key problem is to find decent self-compositions of CFGs, which is nontrivial. Therefore, we present an algorithm to construct them recursively based on the abstract syntax trees of programs. In order to achieve good precision, the structural similarities of two subprograms are taken into account using a tree distance measure during the construction. Once a particular self-composition of the CFG is ready, an over-approximation of the MTC solution is obtained as a solution to a constraint system formulated based on the self-composition.

Our goal is to apply the general approach described above to verify the security of web service orchestrations implemented, e.g., in BPEL. Accordingly, information flow policies are composed in terms of public views of document trees specifying the potential positions of secrets. We introduce an abstract domain based on regular sets of public views of documents together with abstract transformers modeling operations on document trees using Horn clauses. During the analysis implications are generated to specify the relations of abstract values corresponding to the nodes of the self-composition of the CFG. These implications fall into a special class, which can be solved e.g., using $\mathcal{H}_1$-normalization [60, 79].

In order to simplify the presentation and concentrate on the key issues of information flow, we restricted ourselves to the assembly language for tree manipulation as it is presented in Figure 2.2.

To summarize, this chapter presents the following contributions:

- We define the ideal solution of the analysis problem of pairs of executions of a program, and propose to overapproximate it by applying abstract interpretation on a particular self-composition of the corresponding CFG.

- A concrete algorithm for the construction of self-compositions of CFGs is proposed, which is driven by a tree distance measure in order to take into account the similarities of subprograms.

- The applicability of the general framework is demonstrated using a complex abstract domain for semi-structured data. Based on the self-composition of the CFG of a tree-manipulating program, a translation is proposed into Horn clauses, which can be solved, e.g., by means of $\mathcal{H}_1$-normalization [60, 79].

- The approach is evaluated on case studies found in the literature [29, 11, 2].

The rest of this chapter is structured as follows. In Section 3.1 the theoretical framework is elaborated. In Section 3.2 we present a method to construct the necessary self-compositions of CFGs based on structured programs, while in Section 3.3 we instantiate our approach for the case of the assembly language for tree-manipulation and information flow policies composed as regular sets of public views of document trees. In Section 3.4 we validate the presented analysis using practical experiments on case studies found in the literature. In Section 3.5 we describe a technique to enhance the precision of the analysis using multiple self-compositions of a CFG. Finally, in Section 3.6 we relate our work to others.

3.1 Merge over all Twin Computations

In this section we establish the formal foundations for proving 2-hypersafety properties using relational abstract interpretation.

We define the semantics of programs by means of control flow graphs (CFG). A CFG is a tuple $G = (N, E, n_{in}, n_{fi})$ consisting of a set of nodes N including the unique initial and final nodes n_{in} and n_{fi}, and a set of directed and labeled edges E. Members of the set E are of the form (n_1, f, n_2), where the nodes $n_1 \in N$ and $n_2 \in N$ are the initial and final nodes of the edge and the label is f. Labels f of edges represent state transformers $[\![f]\!] : S \nrightarrow S$, which are partial mappings on the set of states S. We presume the existence of a special label skip with $[\![\text{skip}]\!]s = s$ for all $s \in S$. A run or execution of a program is defined by a path from the initial node to the final node. The effect of the sequence of labels $\pi = f_1...f_n$ of edges in a run is given by the composition of the effects of the individual labels: $[\![\pi]\!]s_0 = [\![f_1...f_n]\!]s_0 = ([\![f_n]\!] \circ ... \circ [\![f_1]\!])s_0$. In the remainder, we denote the set of sequences of labels of paths from node n_1 to node n_2 by $n_1 \leadsto n_2$.

Properties we aim to verify in this chapter are defined below:

Definition 5 (2-Hypersafety Properties). *We define a 2-hypersafety property by an initial and a final relation of program states $\rho_{in}, \rho_{fi} \subseteq S \times S$. A program given by CFG $G = (N, E, n_{in}, n_{fi})$ satisfies the 2-hypersafety property specified by ρ_{in} and ρ_{fi}, if for all pairs of initial states $(s_0, t_0) \in \rho_{in}$ and all pairs of final states $s = [\![\pi_1]\!]s_0$ and $t = [\![\pi_2]\!]t_0$ reachable by arbitrary computations $\pi_1, \pi_2 \in n_{in} \leadsto n_{fi}$, it holds that $(s, t) \in \rho_{fi}$.*

When applying abstract interpretation to this problem, we may choose a *Cartesian* abstraction of pairs of states. This means that each program state in the pairs is abstracted separately. Let us briefly argue why this approach may often return unsatisfactory results. Consider, e.g., the program if h>'5' then {l:=1+'2';} else {l:=1+'2';};, with integer variables h and l. Assume that ρ_1 and ρ_2 consist of all pairs of states where the values of variable l are equal. Since the precise initial values for l are unknown, the final values for l will also be unknown, implying that their equality cannot be inferred. Therefore, better results can be obtained by using a *relational* abstraction of pairs of program states. A relational abstraction of pairs of program states may record the fact that the variables l in the two program states tracked in parallel, are equal, and that this equality is preserved by all possible pairs of program executions.

The following definition is necessary in order to formalize the relation between concrete states and abstract values.

Definition 6 (Galois Connections). *A Galois connection* $(\mathbb{A}, \alpha, \gamma, \mathbb{B})$ *between lattices* $(\mathbb{A}, \sqsubseteq_\mathbb{A})$ *and* $(\mathbb{B}, \sqsubseteq_\mathbb{B})$ *is a pair of functions* $\alpha : \mathbb{A} \to \mathbb{B}$ *and* $\gamma : \mathbb{B} \to \mathbb{A}$ *so that the following holds:*

$$\alpha(a) \sqsubseteq_\mathbb{B} b \Leftrightarrow a \sqsubseteq_\mathbb{A} \gamma(b)$$

In general, let $(\mathbb{D}_{rel}, \sqsubseteq)$ be a complete lattice forming a Galois connection $(\mathcal{P}(S \times S), \alpha, \gamma, \mathbb{D}_{rel})$ with the powerset of pairs of states $\mathcal{P}(S \times S)$, where $\alpha : \mathcal{P}(S \times S) \to \mathbb{D}_{rel}$ is an abstraction function and $\gamma : \mathbb{D}_{rel} \to \mathcal{P}(S \times S)$ is a concretization function. The only requirement against abstract transformers $\mathcal{S}\left[\begin{smallmatrix}f\\g\end{smallmatrix}\right]^\sharp$ of pairs of labels $\left[\begin{smallmatrix}f\\g\end{smallmatrix}\right]$ (otherwise called *twin steps*) is that they must satisfy the following property:

$$\gamma(\mathcal{S}\left[\begin{matrix}f\\g\end{matrix}\right]^\sharp d) \supseteq \{\left[\begin{matrix}s'\\t'\end{matrix}\right] \mid \exists \left[\begin{matrix}s\\t\end{matrix}\right] \in \gamma(d) : [\![f]\!]s = s' \wedge [\![g]\!]t = t'\} \qquad (3.1)$$

Given two sequences, π_1 and π_2, the set of all possible *alignments* is defined by the nonterminal $A\left[\begin{smallmatrix}\pi_1\\\pi_2\end{smallmatrix}\right]$ according to the following grammar:

$$\begin{array}{llll}
A\left[\begin{matrix}\varepsilon\\\varepsilon\end{matrix}\right] \xrightarrow{1} \varepsilon & & A\left[\begin{matrix}f\pi\\\varepsilon\end{matrix}\right] \xrightarrow{6} \left[\begin{matrix}\text{skip}\\\text{skip}\end{matrix}\right] A\left[\begin{matrix}f\pi\\\varepsilon\end{matrix}\right] & \\
A\left[\begin{matrix}\varepsilon\\\varepsilon\end{matrix}\right] \xrightarrow{2} \left[\begin{matrix}\text{skip}\\\text{skip}\end{matrix}\right] A\left[\begin{matrix}\varepsilon\\\varepsilon\end{matrix}\right] & & A\left[\begin{matrix}f\pi_1\\g\pi_2\end{matrix}\right] \xrightarrow{7} \left[\begin{matrix}\text{skip}\\g\end{matrix}\right] A\left[\begin{matrix}f\pi_1\\\pi_2\end{matrix}\right] & \\
A\left[\begin{matrix}\varepsilon\\g\pi\end{matrix}\right] \xrightarrow{3} \left[\begin{matrix}\text{skip}\\g\end{matrix}\right] A\left[\begin{matrix}\varepsilon\\\pi\end{matrix}\right] & & A\left[\begin{matrix}f\pi_1\\g\pi_2\end{matrix}\right] \xrightarrow{8} \left[\begin{matrix}f\\\text{skip}\end{matrix}\right] A\left[\begin{matrix}\pi_1\\g\pi_2\end{matrix}\right] & (3.2)\\
A\left[\begin{matrix}\varepsilon\\g\pi\end{matrix}\right] \xrightarrow{4} \left[\begin{matrix}\text{skip}\\\text{skip}\end{matrix}\right] A\left[\begin{matrix}\varepsilon\\g\pi\end{matrix}\right] & & A\left[\begin{matrix}f\pi_1\\g\pi_2\end{matrix}\right] \xrightarrow{9} \left[\begin{matrix}f\\g\end{matrix}\right] A\left[\begin{matrix}\pi_1\\\pi_2\end{matrix}\right] & \\
A\left[\begin{matrix}f\pi\\\varepsilon\end{matrix}\right] \xrightarrow{5} \left[\begin{matrix}f\\\text{skip}\end{matrix}\right] A\left[\begin{matrix}\pi\\\varepsilon\end{matrix}\right] & & A\left[\begin{matrix}f\pi_1\\g\pi_2\end{matrix}\right] \xrightarrow{10} \left[\begin{matrix}\text{skip}\\\text{skip}\end{matrix}\right] A\left[\begin{matrix}f\pi_1\\g\pi_2\end{matrix}\right] & \\
\end{array}$$

We denote the language generated by the nonterminal $A\left[\begin{smallmatrix}\pi_1\\\pi_2\end{smallmatrix}\right]$ by $L\left(A\left[\begin{smallmatrix}\pi_1\\\pi_2\end{smallmatrix}\right]\right)$. According to (3.2), an alignment of two sequences of labels of a CFG, π_1 and π_2, is a sequence of twin steps ω representing both of the original runs. Note, that the insertion of skip labels does not change the result of a run. Therefore, if $[\![\pi_1]\!]s_0 = s$, $[\![\pi_2]\!]t_0 = t$, $\omega \in L\left(A\left[\begin{smallmatrix}\pi_1\\\pi_2\end{smallmatrix}\right]\right)$ and $\omega = \left[\begin{smallmatrix}f_1\\g_1\end{smallmatrix}\right]\ldots\left[\begin{smallmatrix}f_n\\g_n\end{smallmatrix}\right]$, then we can write that $\left[\begin{smallmatrix}s\\t\end{smallmatrix}\right] = [\![\omega]\!]\left[\begin{smallmatrix}s_0\\t_0\end{smallmatrix}\right] = \left[\![\begin{smallmatrix}f_1\\g_1\end{smallmatrix}\right]\ldots\left[\begin{smallmatrix}f_n\\g_n\end{smallmatrix}\right]\!]\left[\begin{smallmatrix}s_0\\t_0\end{smallmatrix}\right] = \left[\![\begin{smallmatrix}f_n\\g_n\end{smallmatrix}\right]\!] \circ \ldots \circ \left[\![\begin{smallmatrix}f_1\\g_1\end{smallmatrix}\right]\!]\left[\begin{smallmatrix}s_0\\t_0\end{smallmatrix}\right]$, where $\left[\begin{smallmatrix}s_i\\t_i\end{smallmatrix}\right] = \left[\![\begin{smallmatrix}f_i\\g_i\end{smallmatrix}\right]\!]\left[\begin{smallmatrix}s_{i-1}\\t_{i-1}\end{smallmatrix}\right]$ if $s_i = [\![f_i]\!]s_{i-1}$ and $t_i = [\![g_i]\!]t_{i-1}$ so that $s = s_n$ and $t = t_n$.

3.1. MERGE OVER ALL TWIN COMPUTATIONS

In later sections we are going to apply the alignment construction of (3.2) to programs, i.e., sequences of commands. For the sake of clarity, in this case, the alignment is denoted by Ω, where the members are pairs of commands.

Given two runs π_1, π_2 and an abstract value d_0, we are interested in the most precise abstract value d that can be computed using the abstract semantics of twin steps:

$$d = \bigsqcap_{\omega \in L\left(A\left[\begin{smallmatrix}\pi_1\\\pi_2\end{smallmatrix}\right]\right)} \mathcal{S}[\![\omega]\!]^\sharp d_0$$

Since there can be multiple pairs of paths executed on the members of the concretization of an initial abstract value, we obtain a sound overapproximation for the abstract value at any pair of nodes by computing the least upper bound of the abstract effects for all possible pairs of paths of the CFG reaching these nodes.

Definition 7 (The MTC Solution). *Given a CFG $G = (N, E, n_{in}, n_{fi})$ and the initial abstract value d_0, the merge over all twin computations solution is defined by:*

$$MTC(G, d_0) = \bigsqcup_{\substack{\pi_1 \in n_{in} \leadsto n_{fi}\\\pi_2 \in n_{in} \leadsto n_{fi}}} \bigsqcap_{\omega \in L\left(A\left[\begin{smallmatrix}\pi_1\\\pi_2\end{smallmatrix}\right]\right)} \mathcal{S}[\![\omega]\!]^\sharp d_0$$

The MTC solution can be considered as the extension of the *meet over all paths* (MOP) solution of Kam and Ullman [45] to pairs of paths on the CFG. We have:

Theorem 3. *Consider a pair of sequences of labels $\pi_1, \pi_2 \in n_{in} \leadsto n_{fi}$ on the CFG $G = (N, E, n_{in}, n_{fi})$, and states $s_0, s, t_0, t \in S$, where $s = [\![\pi_1]\!]s_0$, $t = [\![\pi_2]\!]t_0$ and $\left[\begin{smallmatrix}s_0\\t_0\end{smallmatrix}\right] \in \gamma(d_0)$. In this case $d \sqsupseteq MTC(G, d_0)$ implies $\left[\begin{smallmatrix}s\\t\end{smallmatrix}\right] \in \gamma(d)$.*

The proof of Theorem 3 can be found in Section 6.2.

According to Theorem 3, the MTC solution is an abstraction of all possible pairs of states resulting from any pair of executions of the program. In general it might be difficult, though, to compute the MTC solution directly. A perhaps less precise, but still sound solution is obtained by restricting the set of alignments $L(A\left[\begin{smallmatrix}\pi_1\\\pi_2\end{smallmatrix}\right])$ for which the greatest lower bound is computed in the MTC solution. In particular, we may even fix a single alignment for each pair of paths. A fixed alignment like that can be obtained by constructing a self-composition GG of the CFG G. Here, we define more generally, when a graph is a composition of two CFGs.

Definition 8 (Composition of CFGs). *Given the CFGs $G = (N^G, E^G, n_{in}^G, n_{fi}^G)$ and $H = (N^H, E^H, n_{in}^H, n_{fi}^H)$, $GH = (N', E', n'_{in}, n'_{fi})$ is a composition of G and H, if each edge in E' has a label $\left[\begin{smallmatrix}f\\g\end{smallmatrix}\right]$ where f and g are labels of G and H respectively, or **skip**, and furthermore for all $\pi_G \in n_{in}^G \leadsto n_{fi}^G$ and $\pi_H \in n_{in}^H \leadsto n_{fi}^H$ there is an $\omega \in n'_{in} \leadsto n'_{fi}$ so that $\omega \in L\left(A\left[\begin{smallmatrix}\pi_G\\\pi_H\end{smallmatrix}\right]\right)$.*

According to Definition 8, a CFG GG is considered to be a self-composition of G, if for all pairs of paths on G there is a path on GG so that the latter is an alignment of the former two paths. Note that due to the insertion of skip operations, a self-composition may be quite different from the Cartesian product of the two graphs, where every two aligned paths have exactly the same length.

Theorem 4. *Given the CFG $G = (N, E, n_{in}, n_{fi})$ and one of its self-compositions $GG = (N', E', n'_{in}, n'_{fi})$, the following holds for all d_0:*

$$\bigsqcup_{\omega \in n'_{in} \rightsquigarrow n'_{fi}} \mathcal{S}[\![\omega]\!]^\sharp d_0 \sqsupseteq MTC(G, d_0)$$

Again, the proof of Theorem 4 can be found in Section 6.2. By Theorem 4, any overapproximation of the analysis problem [45] corresponding to the self composition GG of G is a safe overapproximation of $MTC(G, d_0)$.

Proving a 2-hypersafety property by means of our methods proceeds in two steps. First, a self-composition GG of the CFG is constructed. The graph GG gives rise to a constraint system over a suitable relational abstract domain, which describes how relations of states are transformed by pairs of edges. A solution to this constraint system then provides the analysis result. Accordingly, the two key practical problems consist in finding a *decent* self-composition and a *decent* abstract domain that achieve reasonable precision at an acceptable price. Note that different analysis results can be obtained if different self-compositions are chosen. Theorem 4 guarantees that all results are sound, and therefore, their greatest lower bound can be considered as the final result of the analysis.

3.2 Self-Compositions of Control Flow Graphs

When an appropriate alignment of computations is chosen, we assume that abstract transformers $\mathcal{S}\left[\!\!\left[\begin{smallmatrix} f \\ f' \end{smallmatrix} \right]\!\!\right]^\sharp$ for pairs of identical or similar actions f, f' are more precise than abstract transformers for arbitrary pairs. Therefore, the goal is to maximize the number of edges labeled $\left[\begin{smallmatrix} f \\ f' \end{smallmatrix} \right]$ in a self-composition of a CFG. If the program in question has been specified by means of a structured programming language, a quality self-composition can be obtained by means of syntactically matching abstract syntax trees (ASTs) of program fragments. In order to illustrate the approach, assume that programs are generated by the nonterminal p of the grammar in Figure 2.2.

CFGs of programs are constructed by two mutually recursive functions "program to CFG" (p2cfg) and "command to CFG" (c2cfg). The CFG corresponding to a program p can be obtained by means of the function p2cfg(p, n_{in}, n_{fi}), where the initial and final nodes of the resulting graph n_{in} and n_{fi} need to be given as parameters. In case $p = c_1; ...; c_m;$, then $m - 1$ fresh nodes are instantiated, and c2cfg(c_i, n_{i-1}, n_i) is called for each i to construct the CFG fragment corresponding to the command c_i so that $n_0 = n_{in}$ and $n_m = n_{fi}$. c2cfg(skip, n_i, n_{i+1}) = (n_i, skip, n_{i+1}) and c2cfg(x:=e, n_i, n_{i+1}) = (n_i, x:=e, n_{i+1}), furthermore, the CFG fragments corresponding to branching constructs are shown in Figure 3.1.

A self-composition of the CFG corresponding to a program can be constructed by two mutually recursive functions "pair of programs to CFG" (pp2cfg) and "pair of commands to CFG" (pc2cfg). The function pp2cfg can also be

3.2. SELF-COMPOSITIONS OF CONTROL FLOW GRAPHS

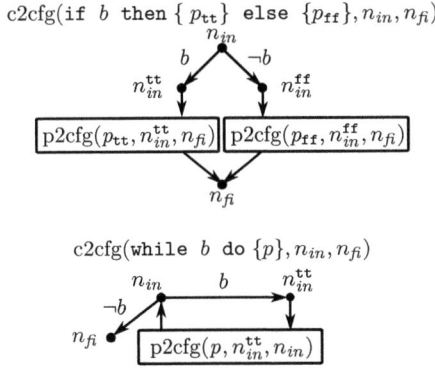

Figure 3.1: CFGs corresponding to branching constructs

called for two different programs in order to align the two alternatives in a conditional. The function makes use of a distance measure for trees as introduced, e.g., in [69]. The evaluation of pp2cfg(p_1, p_2, n_{in}, n_{fi}) proceeds in two steps:

Step 1: Computing a Best Alignment of Two Programs. Here, we adapt the definition of alignments (3.2) to two sequences of commands. An optimal alignment of two sequences of commands, $c_1;...;c_k$; and $d_1;...;d_l$;, with respect to a tree distance measure td is the sequence of pairs of commands Ω_{opt}, where the sum of the distances $td(c_i^{\Omega_{\text{opt}}}, d_i^{\Omega_{\text{opt}}})$ of the ASTs of the aligned pairs of commands $\begin{bmatrix} c_i^{\Omega_{\text{opt}}} \\ d_i^{\Omega_{\text{opt}}} \end{bmatrix}$ is minimal. Formally, an optimal alignment Ω_{opt} of $p_1 = c_1;...;c_k$; and $p_2 = d_1;...;d_l$; is defined as:

$$\Omega_{\text{opt}} = \arg\min_{\Omega \in L\left(A\begin{bmatrix} p_1 \\ p_2 \end{bmatrix}\right)} \sum_{1 \leq i \leq |\Omega|} td(\Omega[i].1, \Omega[i].2) \quad (3.3)$$

In (3.3), $\Omega[i]$ stands for the ith pair of commands in the sequence Ω, and $\Omega[i].1$ and $\Omega[i].2$ denote the first and second components of the pair respectively. In our implementation we use the *Robust Tree Edit Distance* described in [62] as tree distance measure.

Step 2: Computing the Compositions of CFGs of Pairs of Commands. If the alignment is ready, the function pc2cfg(c_i, d_i, n_{i-1}, n_i) is called for each aligned pair of commands c_i and d_i to construct the corresponding subgraph in the self-composition between the nodes n_{i-1} and n_i. Assume that the chosen alignment of the two programs is $\Omega = \begin{bmatrix} c_1 \\ d_1 \end{bmatrix}, ..., \begin{bmatrix} c_k \\ d_k \end{bmatrix}$. In this case for each $1 \leq i \leq k-1$ we instantiate a fresh node, and call pc2cfg(c_i, d_i, n_{i-1}, n_i) so that $n_0 = n_{in}$ and $n_k = n_{fi}$.

Now we discuss how the subgraphs corresponding to pairs of commands are constructed. First, the roots of the abstract syntax trees corresponding to the commands are examined. The roots of the ASTs corresponding to c and d are considered *composable* in the following cases:

The resulting CFG of pc2cfg(c_1, c_2, n_{in}, n_{fi}), where
$c_1 =$ if b_1 then $\{p^1_{tt}\}$ else $\{p^1_{ff}\}$, and
$c_2 =$ if b_2 then $\{p^2_{tt}\}$ else $\{p^2_{ff}\}$:

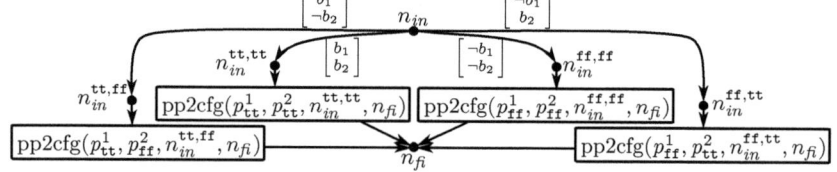

The resulting CFG of pc2cfg(while b_1 do $\{p_1\}$, while b_2 do $\{p_2\}, n_{in}, n_{fi}$):

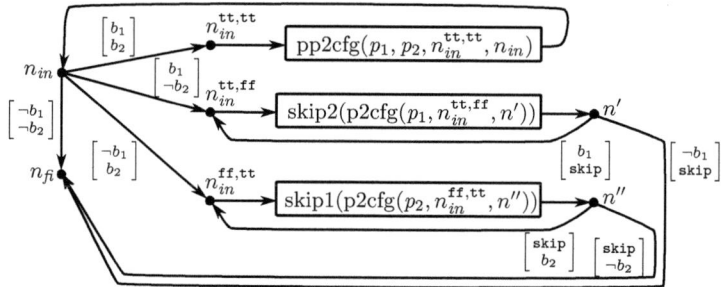

Figure 3.2: The compositions of CFGs corresponding to branching constructs

3.2. SELF-COMPOSITIONS OF CONTROL FLOW GRAPHS

- $c = d = x := e$ or $c = d = \mathtt{skip}$, i.e., in case of assignments the commands need to be identical including the variable on the left and the expression on the right.

- $c = \mathtt{if}\ b_1\ \mathtt{then}\ \{p^1_{tt}\}\ \mathtt{else}\ \{p^1_{ff}\}$ and $d = \mathtt{if}\ b_2\ \mathtt{then}\ \{p^2_{tt}\}\ \mathtt{else}\ \{p^2_{ff}\}$.

- $c = \mathtt{while}\ b_1\ \mathtt{do}\ \{p_1\}$ and $d = \mathtt{while}\ b_2\ \mathtt{do}\ \{p_2\}$

In case the roots of the ASTs of the commands c and d are not composable, then we put them in sequence. This is achieved by means of two additional functions. The function skip1(G) replaces each label f of the edges of the graph G with $\left[\begin{smallmatrix}\mathtt{skip}\\f\end{smallmatrix}\right]$, and similarly, skip2($G$) replaces these labels with $\left[\begin{smallmatrix}f\\\mathtt{skip}\end{smallmatrix}\right]$. In order to compute pc2cfg(c, d, n_{in}, n_{fi}) in this case, we instantiate a fresh node n' and compute skip2(c2cfg(c, n_{in}, n')) and skip1(c2cfg(d, n', n_{fi})).

It remains to consider a pair of commands c and d where the roots of the corresponding ASTs are composable. If they are not branching constructs, then pc2cfg(c, d, n_{in}, n_{fi}) = $(n_{in}, \left[\begin{smallmatrix}c\\d\end{smallmatrix}\right], n_{fi})$.

Now consider a pair of branching constructs. Their composition is defined in Figure 3.2. The idea is to compose the CFGs of the bodies of the branching constructs according to all possible valuations of the conditional expressions, and then to connect them with edges so that they fulfill the conditions of compositions of CFGs stated in Definition 8. In particular, the composition of two loops results in three. One loop handles the case when the bodies are executed simultaneously, the other two execute the body of only one original loop. This way we handle the situation when the two original loops execute a different number of times.

Note that the functions pp2cfg and pc2cfg are mutually recursive. Accordingly, subprograms at each level of the ASTs are aligned separately.

The following theorem states the correctness of the given construction.

Theorem 5. *Consider a program p together with its CFG G as constructed by the call p2cfg(p, n_{in}, n_{fi}). In this case, the CFG constructed by the function call pp2cfg(p, p, n'_{in}, n'_{fi}) is a self-composition of G according to Definition 8.*

Proof. The statement follows from Lemma 16 in Section 6.2. □

For the following theorem, assume that the size of a CFG is defined as the sum of the number of its nodes and its edges.

Theorem 6. *Given that the CFG of program p as computed by the function p2cfg(p, n_{in}, n_{fi}) has size K, the self-composition computed by the function pp2cfg(p, p, n_{in}, n_{fi}) has size $O(K^2)$.*

Proof. The statement follows from Lemma 19 in Section 6.2. □

According to Theorem 6, the size of the self-composition of a CFG is at most quadratic in terms of its original size. In none of our practical experiments, though, the theoretical upper bound was ever attained (see Section 3.4). In all of our results presented in Section 3.4, the sizes of the self-compositions are strictly less than ten times that of the original CFGs.

3.3 Proving Noninterference

In this section we show how to apply the developments of Sections 3.1 and 3.2 in order to verify the compliance of tree-manipulating programs with end-to-end information flow policies.

In order to verify an information flow policy, our analysis maintains abstract states $d : \mathcal{X} \to \mathcal{P}(\mathfrak{B}_{\Sigma_2,\{\#,bv,\star\}})$, which are mappings from variables to sets of trees possibly containing occurrences of dedicated leaves bv and $\star$. A pair of states $\begin{bmatrix} s \\ t \end{bmatrix}$ is in the concretization $\begin{bmatrix} s \\ t \end{bmatrix} \in \gamma(d)$ of d, if for all variables x, $\begin{bmatrix} s(x) \\ t(x) \end{bmatrix} \in \gamma(d(x))$ holds. Here, we overload the notation γ by applying it to the concretization of abstract states as well as to the concretization of abstract sets of trees. A pair of trees $\begin{bmatrix} \tau_1 \\ \tau_2 \end{bmatrix}$ is in the concretization of a set Λ of abstract trees, if Λ contains a tree τ such that both τ_1 and τ_2 can be obtained from τ by replacing the occurrences of bv with identical basic values, and the occurrences of $\star$ with any, possibly different subtrees. Consider, e.g., the language $\Lambda = \{\texttt{a(}\star\texttt{,}bv\texttt{)}, \texttt{b(}bv\texttt{,}\star\texttt{)}\}$. Then $\begin{bmatrix} \tau_1 \\ \tau_2 \end{bmatrix} \in \gamma(\Lambda)$ for $\tau_1 = \texttt{a('Top secret!','42')}$, and $\tau_2 = \texttt{a('Top secret, too!', '42')}$. Accordingly, if $\begin{bmatrix} \tau_1 \\ \tau_2 \end{bmatrix} \in \gamma(\Lambda)$, then the elements of Λ can be considered as potential public views of the trees τ_1 and τ_2, where the occurrences of $\star$ identify the positions of secrets. A public view is a piece of relational information on two trees in the sense that it determines their common upper parts and the locations of potential secrets. Therefore, information flow policies that can be verified by our method need to be given in the form of sets of public views for each variable in the initial abstract state of the analysis. In this chapter, abstract values d do not record precise information on basic values. Leaves labeled bv only mark the positions of basic values having secrecy level *low*.

For our analysis, we assume that the given set of public views for each program variable in the initial abstract state is regular, and thus can be described by a *nondeterministic finite tree automaton* [22]. A nondeterministic finite tree automaton $\mathcal{A}$ is a tuple $\mathcal{A} = (Q, \Sigma_2, \Sigma_0, Q_f, \Delta)$ with the following members:

- Q is a finite set of states;
- Σ_2 and Σ_0 are the finite sets of binary and nullary alphabet elements respectively;
- Q_f is a finite set of accepting states;
- Δ is a finite set of rules of the form:

$$q \leftarrow \sigma_0$$
$$q \leftarrow \sigma_2(q_1, q_2)$$

Above, we have that $q, q_1, q_2 \in Q$, $\sigma_0 \in \Sigma_0$ and $\sigma_2 \in \Sigma_2$.

A run of a tree automaton computes a final state for a tree by replacing its subtrees by the members of Q bottom up according to the rules. An automaton accepts a tree, if there is a run that results in an accepting state $q_f \in Q_f$.

In our analysis we use Horn clauses to define regular sets of trees. By identifying the set of states Q with names of predicates, we can construct implications describing the functionality of the rules the following way:

3.3. PROVING NONINTERFERENCE

- Rules of the form p ← σ_0 are represented by predicates of the form p(σ_0) stating that a leaf labeled σ_0 is accepted by state p.

- Rules of the form p ← σ_2(q,r) are represented by implications of the form p($\sigma_2(X_1,X_2)$) ⇐ q(X_1),r(X_2). The implication states that if the children of a node labeled σ_2, are accepted by states q and r then the corresponding subtree should be accepted by state p.

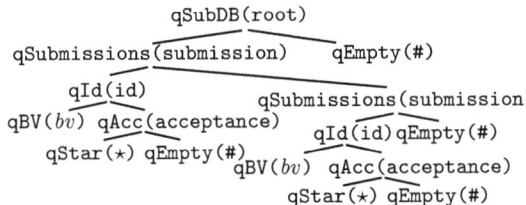

Figure 3.3: The public view of the database of submissions shown in Figure 2.1 accepted by the predicate qSubDB defined by the implications of (3.4).

In our running example the acceptance state of submissions is confidential. In (3.4) we give implications defining the public views of all possible databases, and thus formalizing the corresponding information flow policy.

$$
\begin{aligned}
&\text{qSubDB(root(L,R))} \Leftarrow \text{qSubmissions(L),qEmpty(R)}.\\
&\text{qSubmissions(submission(L,R))} \Leftarrow \text{qId(L),qSubmissions(R)}\\
&\text{qSubmissions(\#)}.\\
&\qquad \text{qId(id(L,R))} \Leftarrow \text{qBV(L),qAcc(R)}.\\
&\text{qAcc(acceptance(L,R))} \Leftarrow \text{qStar(L),qEmpty(R)}.\\
&\text{qBV}(bv). \qquad\qquad \text{qStar}(\star). \qquad\qquad \text{qEmpty(\#)}.
\end{aligned}
\qquad(3.4)
$$

As Figure 3.3 illustrates, the public view of a database accepted by the predicate qSubDB is a tree with root labeled root having a first child accepted by qSubmissions and a second child accepted by qEmpty. The other predicates can be understood similarly. In particular, the predicate qAcc accepts only trees, the first child of which is a leaf labeled $\star$, specifying that the corresponding value is confidential.

Given an initial abstract state d_0 describing the set of public views of pairs of potential initial states, we are interested in computing the sets of potential public views for every pair of jointly reachable program points. In our analysis, the sets of public views for variables x occurring at nodes n of the CFG are described by means of unary predicates $\text{var}_{x,n}$, which are defined by means of Horn clauses. Formally, $\tau \in d(x)$ at node n if $\text{var}_{x,n}(\tau)$ holds. There are two kinds of Horn clauses. The first group is used for specifying the set of initial public views for each variable at the initial node n_{in}. In our running example the variable subDB contains the database in the initial state of our program, therefore, the corresponding information for the initial node n_{in} is defined by: $\text{var}_{\text{subDB},n_{in}}(X) \Leftarrow \text{qSubDB}(X)$. The second group of clauses describes how the public views at different program points are related to each other. These clauses are obtained from the self-composition of the CFG.

In order to deal with program errors as well, we additionally provide Boolean values $B_{\text{\textnormal{\textwon}}}$ and $B_\star$ in abstract states. If $B_{\text{\textnormal{\textwon}}}$ holds in the abstract state for a program point, then $\begin{bmatrix}\text{\textwon}\\\text{\textwon}\end{bmatrix}$ can be a member of the concretization. If $B_\star$ holds, then it is also possible that only one of component of a pair of concrete states is \text{\textwon}. This means that the occurrence of an error may depend on the secret. The values of $B_{\text{\textwon}}$ and $B_\star$ at node n are represented by means of the nullary predicates $\texttt{public\_error}_n$ and $\texttt{secret\_error}_n$ respectively.

In the following, we describe how the abstract state transformers $\mathcal{S}\left[\!\!\left[\begin{smallmatrix}f\\g\end{smallmatrix}\right]\!\!\right]^\sharp$ of edges $(n, \left[\begin{smallmatrix}f\\g\end{smallmatrix}\right], n')$ are formalized by means of Horn clauses. In order to do so we need that the set of binary alphabet elements Σ_2 potentially occurring in the variables of a program is finite and a priori known. This information can be extracted from the interface descriptions of web services, and needs to be provided for the analysis. Therefore, in this chapter we extend the assembly language for tree manipulation so that programs begin with the following declaration:

$$\texttt{binary\_alphabet:} \sigma_1, \ldots, \sigma_n;$$

It suffices to provide only those binary alphabet elements explicitly that do not occur in the program text.

Recall that, due to our alignment procedure, edges either correspond to assignments or to Boolean expressions, but never to both.

Assignments as Horn Clauses

First, we discuss the case of assignments, i.e., transformers of edges of the form:

$$(n, \begin{bmatrix} x\texttt{:=}e_1(x_1, \ldots, x_n)\\ y\texttt{:=}e_2(y_1, \ldots, y_m)\end{bmatrix}, n') \tag{3.5}$$

If no error occurs, then x and y are updated, the values of other variables remain unchanged. Error propagation is discussed later. Accordingly, for all variables $z \neq x$ and $z \neq y$ the following clauses are defined, which propagate their values without modification:

$$\texttt{var}_{z,n'}(\texttt{X}) \Leftarrow \texttt{var}_{z,n}(\texttt{X}).$$

Note that according to the construction of compositions of CFGs described in Section 3.2, it holds in (3.5) that $x = y$, $e_1 = e_2$ and for all i we have that $x_i = y_i$, or one of the assignments is $\texttt{skip}$. The reason is that only equivalent assignments are composable.

Now we discuss the abstract transformers of edges with assignments that can occur in compositions of CFGs. Values of variables on the left hand sides of the assignments are defined by the following clauses.

- For edges with label $\begin{bmatrix}x\texttt{:=\#}\\x\texttt{:=\#}\end{bmatrix}$ we define $\texttt{var}_{x,n'}(\texttt{\#}) \Leftarrow \texttt{var}_{y,n}(\_)$ for all variables y occurring in the program, where '$\_$' denotes an anonymous logic variable. The implication is required to ensure that $\texttt{\#}$ is added to the predicate $\texttt{var}_{x,n'}$ only if node n may be reachable. We consider a node n as unreachable, if there is no variable x and tree τ so that $\texttt{var}_{x,n}(\tau)$ holds.

- For edges with $\begin{bmatrix}x\texttt{:=}y\\x\texttt{:=}y\end{bmatrix}$ we define: $\texttt{var}_{x,n'}(\texttt{X}) \Leftarrow \texttt{var}_{y,n}(\texttt{X}).$

3.3. PROVING NONINTERFERENCE

- For edges with $\begin{bmatrix} x:=\sigma_2(y,z) \\ x:=\sigma_2(y,z) \end{bmatrix}$ we define:

$$\text{var}_{x,n'}(\sigma_2(\texttt{L},\texttt{R})) \Leftarrow \text{var}_{y,n}(\texttt{L}), \text{var}_{z,n}(\texttt{R}).$$

- For edges with $\begin{bmatrix} x:=y/1 \\ x:=y/1 \end{bmatrix}$ we define $\text{var}_{x,n'}(\texttt{L}) \Leftarrow \text{var}_{y,n}(\sigma_2(\texttt{L},\_))$ for all $\sigma_2 \in \Sigma_2$. As an example, let us suppose that the abstract value of variable subDB at node n is a model of the predicate qSubDB according to the implications in (3.4). Using the command submissions := subDB/1 we can assign the list of submissions into variable submissions. The implication defining the abstract value of submissions after the assignment is:

$$\text{var}_{\texttt{submissions},n'}(\texttt{L}) \Leftarrow \text{var}_{\texttt{subDB},n}(\texttt{root}(\texttt{L},\_))$$

However, the state transformer needs to be able to carry out this modification for all possible abstract values having a binary root. Therefore, the implication is repeated for all possible binary alphabet elements $\sigma_2 \in \Sigma_2$.

An error is caused by an expression of the form $x/1$, if the root of the content of x does not have children, i.e., it is a leaf. Therefore, in addition the following is defined:

$$\begin{aligned} \texttt{public\_error}_{n'} &\Leftarrow \text{var}_{y,n}(\#). \\ \texttt{public\_error}_{n'} &\Leftarrow \text{var}_{y,n}(bv). \\ \texttt{secret\_error}_{n'} &\Leftarrow \text{var}_{y,n}(\star). \end{aligned} \quad (3.6)$$

- For edges with $\begin{bmatrix} x:=y/2 \\ x:=y/2 \end{bmatrix}$ we define $\text{var}_{x,n'}(\texttt{R}) \Leftarrow \text{var}_{y,n}(\sigma_2(\_,\texttt{R}))$ for all $\sigma_2 \in \Sigma_2$. The implications handling errors are identical to those in (3.6).

- By edges with $\begin{bmatrix} f \\ f \end{bmatrix}$ where $f = x:=\lambda_t(x_1,x_2,\ldots,x_k)$ it needs to be examined whether the variables in the arguments contain secrets. The implications below are used for the purpose, where the second and third lines are defined for all $\sigma_2 \in \Sigma_2$:

$$\begin{aligned} &\texttt{secret}(\star). \\ &\texttt{secret}(\sigma_2(\texttt{L},\_)) \Leftarrow \texttt{secret}(\texttt{L}). \quad \forall \sigma_2 \in \Sigma_2 \\ &\texttt{secret}(\sigma_2(\_,\texttt{R})) \Leftarrow \texttt{secret}(\texttt{R}). \quad \forall \sigma_2 \in \Sigma_2 \end{aligned} \quad (3.7)$$

Concerning the resulting value of x we have:

$$\text{var}_{x,n'}(bv) \Leftarrow \text{var}_{x_1,n}(\_), \text{var}_{x_2,n}(\_), \ldots, \text{var}_{x_k,n}(\_). \quad (3.8)$$

$$\begin{aligned} \text{var}_{x,n'}(\star) \Leftarrow\ & \text{var}_{x_i,n}(X_i), \texttt{secret}(X_i), \\ & \text{var}_{x_1,n}(\_), \ldots, \\ & \text{var}_{x_k,n}(\_). \quad \forall x_i \in \{x_1,\ldots,x_k\} \end{aligned} \quad (3.9)$$

According to implication (3.8), the value of x at node n' will contain bv if all of the input variables of the function λ_t are defined. Furthermore, according to implication (3.9), if any of the input variables depends on the secret, then the resulting abstract value will also contain $\star$. Implications of the form (3.9) are defined for all input variables x_i of the function λ_t.

Since the evaluation of λ_t can result in the error state, we need in addition:

$$\texttt{public\_error}_{n'} \Leftarrow \texttt{var}_{x_1,n}(\_), \texttt{var}_{x_2,n}(\_), \ldots, \texttt{var}_{x_k,n}(\_). \quad (3.10)$$

However, the occurrence of an error can also depend on secret values. In order to handle this we need:

$$\begin{aligned}\texttt{secret\_error}_{n'} \Leftarrow\ & \texttt{var}_{x_i,n}(X_i), \texttt{secret}(X_i),\\ & \texttt{var}_{x_1,n}(\_), \ldots,\\ & \texttt{var}_{x_k,n}(\_). \quad \forall x_i \in \{x_1, \ldots, x_k\}\end{aligned} \quad (3.11)$$

An implication of the form (3.11) needs to be defined for each input variable x_i of the function λ_t.

By defining implications (3.10) and (3.11), our only assumption about the semantics of λ_t is that it is deterministic. However, it is possible to enhance the precision of the analysis, if further conditions for the occurrence of an error can be captured using Horn clauses. Given that conditions like that are available, we can restrict the set of cases when the occurrence of an error is considered by appending those conditions to the tails of implications (3.10) and (3.11).

- For edges of the form $\begin{bmatrix} x:=e(x_1,\ldots,x_k) \\ \texttt{skip} \end{bmatrix}$ and $\begin{bmatrix} \texttt{skip} \\ x:=e(x_1,\ldots,x_k) \end{bmatrix}$ we define:

$$\texttt{var}_{x,n'}(\star) \Leftarrow \texttt{var}_{x_1,n}(\_), \ldots, \texttt{var}_{x_k,n}(\_).$$

If the effect of an edge consists of an assignment and a skip command, then in the resulting abstract state the value of the variable on the left hand side becomes $\star$, indicating that its value might be different in the corresponding two concrete states. This happens independently of the values of input variables of expressions on the right hand side. If the expression is of the form $y/1$, $y/2$ or $\lambda_t(x_1, x_2, \ldots, x_k)$, then we define in addition $\texttt{secret\_error}_{n'} \Leftarrow \texttt{var}_{x_i,n}(\star)$ for all input variables y and x_i in order to indicate that an error may occur only in one of the pair of states. Again, depending on the semantics of the specific interpreted function λ_t, it is possible to pose further conditions for the inclusion of the secret-dependent error state in the resulting abstract value.

Boolean Expressions as Horn Clauses

We now discuss the abstract transformers for Boolean expressions. In our implementation we treat two branching constructs composable only if their conditional expressions are syntactically equivalent in addition to the conditions discussed in Section 3.2.

- By edges labeled $\begin{bmatrix} b \\ b \end{bmatrix}$, $\begin{bmatrix} b \\ \texttt{skip} \end{bmatrix}$ or $\begin{bmatrix} \texttt{skip} \\ b \end{bmatrix}$, where $b = \lambda_b(x_1, x_2, \ldots, x_k)$, the values of all variables y occurring in the program are propagated using the following implication generated for all $y \in \mathcal{X}$:

$$\texttt{var}_{y,n'}(X) \Leftarrow \texttt{var}_{y,n}(X), \texttt{var}_{x_1,n}(\_), \ldots, \texttt{var}_{x_k,n}(\_).$$

In other words, it is checked whether the values of input variables of the conditional expression have been defined, in order to ensure that the node n is reachable. The actual values of variables are propagated without modification.

3.3. PROVING NONINTERFERENCE

- In case the label of the root of a tree is tested using an edge having a label of the form $\left[\begin{smallmatrix}\text{top}(x)=\sigma\\ \text{top}(x)=\sigma\end{smallmatrix}\right]$, then the following clauses are defined to propagate the values of variables $y \neq x$ if $\sigma \in \Sigma_2$:

$$\begin{aligned}\text{var}_{y,n'}(\text{X}) &\Leftarrow \text{var}_{y,n}(\text{X}),\\ & \text{var}_{x,n}(\sigma(\_,\_)).\\ \text{var}_{y,n'}(\text{X}) &\Leftarrow \text{var}_{y,n}(\text{X}), \text{var}_{x,n}(\star).\end{aligned} \quad (3.12)$$

The value of the variable x is propagated as well:

$$\text{var}_{x,n'}(\sigma(\text{L},\text{R})) \Leftarrow \text{var}_{x,n}(\sigma(\text{L},\text{R})). \quad (3.13)$$

$$\text{var}_{x,n'}(\sigma(\star,\star)) \Leftarrow \text{var}_{x,n}(\star). \quad (3.14)$$

If $\sigma = \#$ then $\sigma(X,Y)$ is exchanged with $\#$ in (3.12), (3.13) and (3.14).

- For edges with $\left[\begin{smallmatrix}\text{top}(x)=\sigma\\ \text{skip}\end{smallmatrix}\right]$ or $\left[\begin{smallmatrix}\text{skip}\\ \text{top}(x)=\sigma\end{smallmatrix}\right]$ implications (3.12) and (3.13) need to be repeated and in addition $\text{var}_{x,n'}(\star) \Leftarrow \text{var}_{x,n}(\star)$ defined.

- By edges with $\left[\begin{smallmatrix}\neg\text{top}(x)=\sigma\\ \neg\text{top}(x)=\sigma\end{smallmatrix}\right]$, $\left[\begin{smallmatrix}\neg\text{top}(x)=\sigma\\ \text{skip}\end{smallmatrix}\right]$ or $\left[\begin{smallmatrix}\text{skip}\\ \neg\text{top}(x)=\sigma\end{smallmatrix}\right]$, the values of variables are only propagated in the case when the root of the value of x is not equal to σ. Therefore, the following implication is defined for all variables y other than x and for all alphabet elements $\delta \in \Sigma_2 \setminus \{\sigma\}$:

$$\text{var}_{y,n'}(\text{X}) \Leftarrow \text{var}_{y,n}(\text{X}), \text{var}_{x,n}(\delta(\_,\_)). \quad (3.15)$$

In order to handle the value of x as well, the following implication is defined for all $\delta \in \Sigma_2 \setminus \{\sigma\}$:

$$\text{var}_{x,n'}(\delta(\text{L},\text{R})) \Leftarrow \text{var}_{x,n}(\delta(\text{L},\text{R})). \quad (3.16)$$

Additionally, we need to define (3.15) and (3.16) so that $\delta(X,Y)$ is replaced by $\star$ and bv, and if $\sigma \neq \#$ then by $\#$ too.

- In case the two components of the label of an edge are the negations of each other, e.g., $\left[\begin{smallmatrix}\neg b(x_1,x_2,...,x_k)\\ b(x_1,x_2,...,x_k)\end{smallmatrix}\right]$, then the values of variables need to be propagated only in the case, when at least one of the variables in the argument depends on the secret. Assuming that a Boolean expression is a deterministic function, it can only return different values for different arguments. Therefore, considering two concrete states s and t, $\left[\begin{smallmatrix}\neg b(x_1,x_2,...,x_k)\\ b(x_1,x_2,...,x_k)\end{smallmatrix}\right]\left[\begin{smallmatrix}s\\ t\end{smallmatrix}\right] = \left[\begin{smallmatrix}s\\ t\end{smallmatrix}\right]$ is only possible if $s(x_i) \neq t(x_i)$ at least for one variable x_i of the argument. Furthermore, $\left[\begin{smallmatrix}s(x_i)\\ t(x_i)\end{smallmatrix}\right] \in \gamma(d(x_i))$ is only possible in this case, if there is at least one leaf labeled $\star$ in $d(x_i)$. Accordingly, the following is defined for all variables y occurring in the program and for all variables $x_i \in \{x_1,...,x_k\}$:

$$\begin{aligned}\text{var}_{y,n'}(\text{X}) &\Leftarrow \text{var}_{y,n}(\text{X}), \text{var}_{x_i,n}(\text{X}i),\\ & \text{secret}(\text{X}i).\end{aligned} \quad (3.17)$$

Propagating the Error

Finally, in order to propagate the error state, for all edges we define:

$$\texttt{public\_error}_{n'} \Leftarrow \texttt{public\_error}_n.$$
$$\texttt{secret\_error}_{n'} \Leftarrow \texttt{secret\_error}_n.$$

This concludes the description of Horn clauses formalizing abstract state transformers.

Discussion

We observe the following:

Theorem 7. *The abstract transformer* $\mathcal{S}\left[\begin{smallmatrix}f\\g\end{smallmatrix}\right]^{\sharp}$ *for a pair* $\left[\begin{smallmatrix}f\\g\end{smallmatrix}\right]$ *as defined by Horn clauses is a correct abstract transformer, i.e., it satisfies the conditions of (3.1). In other words, if* $[\![f]\!](s_0) = s$, $[\![g]\!]t_0 = t$ *where* $\left[\begin{smallmatrix}s_0\\t_0\end{smallmatrix}\right] \in \gamma(d_0)$ *and* $\mathcal{S}\left[\begin{smallmatrix}f\\g\end{smallmatrix}\right]^{\sharp} d_0 = d$, *then* $\left[\begin{smallmatrix}s\\t\end{smallmatrix}\right] \in \gamma(d)$.

Proof. The statement follows by a comparison of the concrete transformers in Section 2.1.2 and the implications defined for pairs of labels of edges. □

Because of Theorem 7, the least solution of the set of Horn clauses defined for a program overapproximates the MTC solution. Therefore, for example, noninterference for a particular output variable x holds at program exit n_{fi}, if the predicate $\texttt{var}_{x,n_{fi}}$ does not accept trees containing $\star$.

Algorithmically, therefore, the analysis boils down to computing (or approximating) the model of the set of Horn clauses defined for the program. The head of each clause possibly generated by our analysis is of one of the forms

$$h \quad ::= \quad \texttt{p} \mid \texttt{p}(X) \mid \texttt{p}(\sigma_0) \mid \texttt{p}(\sigma_2(X_1, X_2)),$$

where X_1, X_2 are distinct. Therefore, all of them belong to the class of Horn clauses $\mathcal{H}_1$ [60, 79]. Finite sets of clauses of this class are known to have least models consisting of regular sets. Moreover, finite automata characterizing these regular sets, can be effectively computed.

3.3.1 Case Study

Let us come back to our running example, the document submission system, which updates the acceptance status of papers depending on the average of the scores given by reviewers. Now we demonstrate the functionality of the analysis by proving an end-to-end information flow policy on the program in Listing 2.1, the implementation of the database updating routine. Note that the program has been extended with the declaration of binary alphabet elements as it is required by the analysis. Our goal is to prove that the confidential value of $\texttt{averageScore}$ in the initial state may only affect the acceptance state of submissions, and nothing else. In order to do so, we need to construct an initial abstract state d_0 for the analysis reflecting the desired information flow policy. Therefore, we set $d_0(\texttt{averageScore}) = \{\star\}$. Since the identifier of the submission, the acceptance state of which is to be updated, is public, we set

$d_0(\texttt{paperId}) = \{bv\}$. Furthermore, we also suppose that there is a database of submissions similar to that in Figure 2.1 in the initial value of variable subDB. Therefore, we assign the set of public views of all possible databases to $d_0(\texttt{subDB})$ by specifying that all trees τ for which $\texttt{qSubDB}(\tau)$ holds are also members of $d_0(\texttt{subDB})$. Finally, because we would like to investigate the case when the acceptance value of a submission is updated in the "review" phase, we set $d_0(\texttt{phase}) = \{\texttt{review(\#,\#)}\}$.

```
1  binary_alphabet: review, root, submission, id, acceptance;
2
3  // 1. Selecting the phase:
4    if top(phase)=notify then {
5      toAuthors := subDB;
6    }
7    else {
8
9  // 2. Initialization:
10     empty := #;
11     submissionsRev := #;
12       // var_submissionsRev,(13,13)(X) <= qSubmissions(X).
13     submissions := subDB/1;
14       // var_submissions,(17,17)(X) <= qSubmissions(X).
15
16  // 3. Branching based on conditional value:
17     if averageScore < '1.5' then {
18
19  // 4/tt. Searching the elements to be modified:
20         found := false(empty,empty);
21         while top(found)=false do {
22           id := submissions/1;
23             // var_id,(24,73)(X) <= qId(X).
24           idVal := id/1;
25             // var_idVal,(26,75)(X) <= qBV(X).
26           if idVal = paperId then {
27             found := true(empty,empty);
28           } else {
29             submissionsRev := submission(id,submissionsRev);
30               // var_submissionsRev,(31,80)(X) <= qSubmissions(X).
31             submissions := submissions/2;
32               // var_submissions,(21,70)(X) <= qSubmissions(X).
33           };
34         };
35
36  // 5/tt. Modifying the acceptance value depending on
37  //        averageScore:
38         acceptanceVal := 'rejected';
39           // var_acceptanceVal,(42,91)(X) <= qStar(X).
40
41  // 6/tt. Reconstructing the data structure of the submission:
42         acceptance := acceptance(acceptanceVal,empty);
43           // var_acceptance,(44,93)(X) <= qAcc(X).
44         id := id(idVal,acceptance);
45           // var_id,(46,95)(X) <= qId(X).
46         submissions := submissions/2;
```

```
47         // var_{submissions,(48,97)}(X) ⇐ qSubmissions(X).
48         submissions := submission(id,submissions);
49         // var_{submissions,(52,101)}(X) ⇐ qSubmissions(X).
50
51 // 7/tt. Reconstructing the data structure of the database:
52         stop := false(empty,empty);
53         while top(stop)=false do {
54           if top(submissionsRev)=submission then {
55             id := submissionsRev/1;
56             // var_{id,(57,106)}(X) ⇐ qId(X).
57             submissions := submission(id,submissions);
58             // var_{submissions,(59,108)}(X) ⇐ qSubmissions(X).
59             submissionsRev := submissions/2;
60             // var_{submissionsRev,(53,101)}(X) ⇐ qSubmissions(X).
61           } else {
62             stop := true(empty,empty);
63           };
64         };
65
66       } else {
67
68 // 4/ff. Searching the elements to be modified:
69         found := false(empty,empty);
70         while top(found)=false do {
71           id := submissions/1;
72           // var_{id,(24,73)}(X) ⇐ qId(X).
73           idVal := id/1;
74           // var_{idVal,(26,75)}(X) ⇐ qBV(X).
75           if idVal = paperId then {
76             found := true(empty,empty);
77           } else {
78             submissionsRev := submission(id,submissionsRev);
79             // var_{submissionsRev,(31,80)}(X) ⇐ qSubmissions(X).
80             submissions := submissions/2;
81             // var_{submissions,(21,70)}(X) ⇐ qSubmissions(X).
82           };
83         };
84
85 // 5/ff. Modifying the acceptance value depending on
86 //        averageScore:
87         acceptanceVal := 'accepted';
88         // var_{acceptanceVal,(42,91)}(X) ⇐ qStar(X).
89
90 // 6/ff. Reconstructing the data structure of the submission:
91         acceptance := acceptance(acceptanceVal,empty);
92         // var_{acceptance,(44,93)}(X) ⇐ qAcc(X).
93         id := id(idVal,acceptance);
94         // var_{id,(46,95)}(X) ⇐ qId(X).
95         submissions := submissions/2;
96         // var_{submissions,(48,97)}(X) ⇐ qSubmissions(X).
97         submissions := submission(id,submissions);
98         // var_{submissions,(52,101)}(X) ⇐ qSubmissions(X).
99
100 // 7/ff. Reconstructing the data structure of the database:
```

3.4. PRACTICAL EXPERIMENTS   43

```
101         stop := false(empty,empty);
102         while top(stop)=false do {
103           if top(submissionsRev)=submission then {
104             id := submissionsRev/1;
105             // var_id,(57,106)(X) ⇐ qId(X).
106             submissions := submission(id,submissions);
107             // var_submissions,(59,108)(X) ⇐ qSubmissions(X).
108             submissionsRev := submissions/2;
109             // var_submissionsRev,(53,102)(X) ⇐ qSubmissions(X).
110           } else {
111             stop := true(empty,empty);
112           };
113         };
114       };
115
116  // 8. Presenting the result.
117       subDB := root(submissions,empty);
118           // var_subDB,(119,119)(X) ⇐ qSubDB(X).
119       subDB_Output := subDB;
120           // var_subDB_Output,(121,121)(X) ⇐ qSubDB(X).
121     };
```

Listing 3.1: The results of the analysis of the program in Listing 2.1 extended with the declaration of binary alphabet elements.

In order to illustrate the functionality of the analysis on the program in Listing 2.1, we identify the nodes of the self-composition of the corresponding CFG with pairs of numbers standing for the lines in the code before their execution. Accordingly, we specify the initial analysis information for the initial node $(2,2)$ of the self-composition of the CFG using the following implications:

$$\begin{aligned}
\text{var}_{\text{averageScore},(2,2)}(X) &\Leftarrow \text{qStar}(X). \\
\text{var}_{\text{paperId},(2,2)}(X) &\Leftarrow \text{qBV}(X). \\
\text{var}_{\text{subDB},(2,2)}(X) &\Leftarrow \text{qSubDB}(X). \\
\text{var}_{\text{phase},(2,2)}(\text{review}(\#,\#)).
\end{aligned}$$

The actual code that has been analyzed is shown in Listing 3.1, where the result of the analysis is indicated in comments for each relevant assignment. The result of the analysis reveals that the final abstract value of the variable subDB_Output equals to the initial one defined by the predicate qSubDB. In other words, the secret remains in the variable averageScore and in the acceptance values of submissions in the variable subDB, and does not interfere with other values.

3.4 Practical Experiments

We have implemented a prototype to carry out the analysis described in this chapter. We have implemented the function $\text{pp2cfg}(p, r, n_{in}, n_{fi})$ in OCaml, where the *Robust Tree Edit Distance* algorithm [62] is used to compute the distance between the ASTs of commands. The set of Horn clauses generated from the self-compositions of CFGs is solved using the $\mathcal{H}_1$ solver of Nielson et al. [60]. We have carried out the analysis on five examples.

- **Joining Tables.** This program implements the join of two tables as published in [29] and in [11]. An array of payment data of employees is joined together with an array storing their personal information. According to the privacy policy, this join can only take place for the employees that have explicitly agreed to it.
- **Submission Database.** This program is our running example shown in Listing 3.1.
- **Medical Records.** This example implements the benchmark of [2], where a list of medical records is manipulated. Here we address the situation when there are separate updating and query routines for the confidential and the public data in one program. We demonstrate that the manipulation of the confidential information of patients does not influence public data.
- **Bayes Classifier.** This program is an implementation of the second example in [29], which demonstrates how to verify the noninterference of a data-mining algorithm, the *Naive Bayes classifier*. The classifier predicts the class of records based on statistics compiled from a training set. We prove that the data of only those individuals is going to influence the statistics who have explicitly agreed to it.

Experiment	# of lines	$|G|$	$|GG|$	# of implications
Joining Tables	26	45	237	3510
Submission Database	64	109	751	14008
Medical Records	97	163	859	22532
Bayes Classifier	133	241	1561	89720

Experiment	running time	peak memory usage
Joining Tables	4.839 sec	19.17 MiB
Submission Database	10.371 sec	21.03 MiB
Medical Records	12.590 sec	21.82 MiB
Bayes Classifier	131.980 sec	89.85 MiB

Table 3.1: Summary of the runtime behavior of the analysis.

For all four examples, our analysis succeeded to infer noninterference automatically. Table 3.1 summarizes some quantitative details of our experiments. The experiments have been carried out in a 32 bit virtual machine on a laptop having a 2 GHz Intel® Core™ i7 processor. For each experiment Table 3.1 lists the following information: a) the number of lines of the code without comment and empty lines; b) the size of the CFG $|G|$ as the sum of the number of nodes and edges; c) the size of the self-composition of the CFG $|GG|$; d) the number of implications generated; e) the complete running time of the analysis including the computation of the self-composition of the CFG, and the computation of models of predicates; f) the peak memory consumption during the verification process involving the computation of self-compositions of CFGs and models of predicates.

3.5 Combining the Results of Multiple Analyses

Intuitively, if a CFG has multiple self-compositions delivering different analysis results, then one could suspect that it should be possible to combine these results in order to obtain a more precise overapproximation for the MTC solution. Let us now demonstrate through an example that this is indeed the case.

```
1  if sec = '0' then {
2      x := '1';
3      y := '2';
4  } else {
5      y := '2';
6      x := '1';
7  };
```

Listing 3.2: A branching construct.

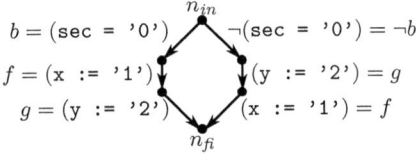

Figure 3.4: The CFG of the program in Listing 3.2, where assignments and Boolean expressions are abbreviated with f, b, etc.

Self-composition 1.   Self-composition 2.

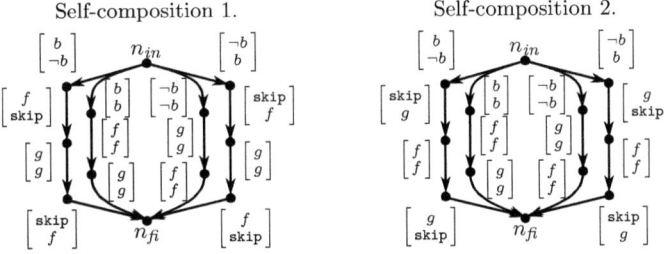

Figure 3.5: Two possible self-compositions of the CFG in Figure 3.4. For the meaning of f, g and b please refer to Figure 3.4.

Listing 3.2 shows a branching construct with a Boolean expression depending on a secret value stored in the variable `sec`. The corresponding CFG is illustrated in Figure 3.4. It is easy to see that in the final state of the computation the values of the variables `x` and `y` do not depend on the secret, because their values are identical at the end of the branches. At the same time, we cannot prove this using the developments of the previous sections of this chapter. The reason is that using one self-composition we can either prove the independence of `x` or `y` from the secret, but not both in the same time. Figure 3.5 illustrates two different self-compositions of the CFG in Figure 3.4. As it is indicated by the figures, it is impossible to align both of f and g in all of the paths. Therefore, given that the initial abstract state is so that $d_{in}(\textsf{sec}) = \{\star\}$, the results d of the analyses on the self-compositions will either be so that $\{\star\} \subseteq d(\mathbf{x})$ or $\{\star\} \subseteq d(\mathbf{y})$.

Let us examine the analyses corresponding to the two CFGs in Figure 3.4 closer. We have that $\mathcal{S}\left[\begin{smallmatrix} \textsf{sec = '0'} \\ \neg\textsf{sec = '0'} \end{smallmatrix}\right]^{\#} d_{in} = d_{in}$ and $\mathcal{S}\left[\begin{smallmatrix} \neg\textsf{sec = '0'} \\ \textsf{sec = '0'} \end{smallmatrix}\right]^{\#} d_{in} = d_{in}$, because there are pairs of states $\left[\begin{smallmatrix} s \\ t \end{smallmatrix}\right] \in \gamma(d_{in})$ so that $s(\textsf{sec}) \neq t(\textsf{sec})$. Therefore, those paths of the CFGs in Figure 3.5 need to be evaluated as well that begin with $\left[\begin{smallmatrix} b \\ \neg b \end{smallmatrix}\right]$ or $\left[\begin{smallmatrix} \neg b \\ b \end{smallmatrix}\right]$. The resulting abstract value d_1 of the analysis on self-composition 1 is so that:

$$d_1(\mathbf{x}) = \{\star, bv\}$$
$$d_1(\mathbf{y}) = \{bv\}$$

$d_1(\mathbf{y}) = \{bv\}$ holds, because on all paths of self-composition 1 the variable y is only manipulated by edges having label $\left[\begin{smallmatrix} \textsf{y:='2'} \\ \textsf{y:='2'} \end{smallmatrix}\right]$. However, the labels of edges manipulating x are not aligned well on some paths, therefore, $\star \in d_1(\mathbf{x})$. Similarly, the resulting abstract value of the analysis on self-composition 2 is so that:

$$d_2(\mathbf{x}) = \{bv\}$$
$$d_2(\mathbf{y}) = \{\star, bv\}$$

Accordingly, if $\left[\begin{smallmatrix} s_1 \\ t_1 \end{smallmatrix}\right] \in \gamma(d_1)$ then $s_1(\mathbf{y}) = t_1(\mathbf{y})$ and similarly, if $\left[\begin{smallmatrix} s_2 \\ t_2 \end{smallmatrix}\right] \in \gamma(d_2)$ then $s_2(\mathbf{x}) = t_2(\mathbf{x})$. By taking the intersection of the two concretizations $\gamma(d_1) \cap \gamma(d_2)$, we can conclude that neither of the final values of x and y depends on the initial value of sec.

Theorem 8. *Given that we have multiple results $d_1, ..., d_n$ for an analysis, where for each d_i it holds that $d_i \sqsupseteq MTC(G, d_0)$, then $\bigsqcap_i d_i$ is also a sound result so that:*

$$\bigsqcap_i d_i \sqsupseteq MTC(G, d_0)$$

Proof. The statement trivially follows from the properties of lattices. □

Theorem 8 assures us that in the case, when a CFG has multiple self-compositions yielding different analysis results, then the greatest lower bound of the results is a sound result too. Furthermore, as the example above shows, there could be cases, when desired properties can only be proved by computing the greatest lower bound of the analysis results of multiple self-compositions of the CFG corresponding to the program.

3.6 Related Work

This work relies on the observation [21, 13, 25] that the verification of k-hypersafety properties of programs can be reduced to the verification of safety properties of the k-fold self-compositions of the programs.

3.6. RELATED WORK

Several authors have used self-compositions of programs for the analysis of hyperproperties, i.e., [13, 59, 71, 25]. In [71] a type-system based transformation is presented to construct the self-composition. The self-composition of branching constructs with low-security conditionals results in one branching construct with the same condition expression. In [59] the same idea is applied for object-oriented languages. Differently from our approach, these solutions cannot take advantage of similarities in the code of different branches. Their motivation is to apply already existing techniques of proving safety properties for the purpose of proving hypersafety properties.

Barthe et al. [11] offer a variety of possibly conditional rewritings of the original program to achieve appropriate alignments. Such conditions may enforce, e.g., that two loops are iterated equally often. These conditions must be later discarded by the theorem prover or remain and then restrict the admissible input values. Furthermore, no algorithm or heuristics is provided how these rules should be applied. In our solution no extra conditions are imposed. Instead, skip instructions are inserted where needed. In case the conditions of two different loops are equal, we are still able to infer equal numbers of iterations and thus achieve a perfect alignment. In [12] notions of compositions of CFGs similar to ours are applied for proving relational properties of potentially dissimilar programs with the help of theorem provers. However, no algorithm is provided for the construction of the self-compositions. Here, we presented an algorithm for the purpose, which is completely deterministic and well tailored for the application of relational abstract interpretation. In particular, our solution uses the Robust Tree Edit Distance [62] algorithm in order to align similar program fragments with each other. Furthermore, similarly to [12], our approach can also deal with dissimilar programs. This capability is taken advantage of when different branches of a branching construct are analyzed.

While our method is based on self-compositions of control flow graphs, other people apply type systems for the verification of noninterference properties, e.g., [78, 57, 56, 17]. An other alternative is to use program dependence graphs [41]. Generally, though, the above solutions consider the program counter to have a security level implying that all data possibly manipulated in secret-dependent branches are declared secret. Accordingly, they would have difficulties with some of our benchmarks, e.g., the data-base of paper submissions.

A non-relational abstract interpretation has been presented in [34], where the security of programs is investigated depending on the observational capabilities of attackers. If the public input values are handled as constants in the initial state, then no information leaks to public variables in the final state, if the property that the attackers can observe can be proved to be constant. A different way of applying abstract interpretation for proving the information flow security of programs is presented in [83] and in [10], where the security labels [26, 27] are treated as abstractions of values, and a consistent labeling is computed according to the abstract semantics. The approaches of [34, 83, 27, 10] do not consider self-compositions of the programs, and therefore cannot take advantage of similarities in different branches of branching constructs.

Abstract interpretation of tree-manipulating programs is described, e.g., in [53], where Møller et al. summarize their experiences using XML Graphs as an abstract domain. Our analysis is similar to that, in the sense that the trees generated by the grammars or automata correspond to public views. Each public view, though, represents a relational piece of information, namely, the common part of two tree-structured values.

There are also papers focusing on proving hyperproperties of programs manipulating complex data structures. In [11, 12, 58] the authors present potentially interactive approaches using theorem provers, which are also capable of dealing with our examples. In contrast to these techniques, our static analysis based on abstract interpretation is fully automatic.

Since XML is a standard format for hierarchically organizing and communicating data, security here is a major concern. Several authors therefore, have investigated how to enforce access control policies on XML documents by computing "user views", i.e., fragments of the documents accessible for certain users [1, 24, 33, 54]. These approaches however, do not consider self-compositions.

Chapter 4
Model Checking

Complex workflow systems, as frequently used by organizations, bear the risk of revealing critical information through software bugs, attacks, or simple misconfiguration. Their thorough analysis can prevent costly security incidents and helps building trust in the system. However, the verification of information flow properties is beyond the scope of classical automatic verification methods for functional properties, as it requires the comparison of different execution paths [5]. On the other hand, verification techniques for information flow properties (e.g. type systems motivated by [78]) may lack the flexibility to express that requirements may change over time in response to events in the environment. The temporal logic Restricted SecLTL [28] combines both worlds and allows to precisely characterize under which temporal conditions and until which point in time a piece of information needs to be considered secret.

Web-based applications and enterprise systems perform their jobs mainly by manipulating semi-structured data like XML documents (or data structures such as linked lists and hash maps), which results in a potentially infinite state space. The model checking approach presented in [28], however, can only deal with systems having a finite state space.

Here, we develop a technique to verify temporal information flow properties of transition systems modeling tree-manipulating processes that exchange an unbounded number of tree-shaped data values with the environment during an execution. These transition systems are defined using programs written in an extension of the assembly language for tree manipulation shown in Figure 2.2.

Policies to be verified need to be composed in the logic Restricted SecLTL [28]. Restricted SecLTL extends the positive fragment of the Linear Temporal Logic [75] (LTL) with an additional modal operator, the so-called *hide* operator $\mathcal{H}$. Using the hide operator we can express that the values of specific output variables are independent of the introduced secret values until a specific event occurs. The secrecy of data is specified using regular sets of public views of documents as it has been discussed in Section 3.3.

Our solution is motivated by the automata theoretic model checking approach of [75, 28]. The product of the negated formula corresponding to the policy specification and the model is constructed, and then checked for emptiness. Since we are analyzing classical functional properties combined with information flow properties, unlike standard abstraction-based model checkers (cf. [30]), our model checker tracks multiple states of the same system simultaneously. An extended transition system is constructed, which tracks an additional execution of the system in parallel to the original one for each hide operator occurring in the policy specification. The extended transition system is nondeterministic. Each time a hide operator is evaluated, there is a successor state for each possible confidential input value. Therefore, it is possible to compare the output values of the original execution with that of the alternative runs corresponding to each potential secret value. Still, the extended transition system has an infinite state space. The abstraction techniques developed in Chapter 3 are applied in order to construct a finite overapproximation of the extended transition system. In particular, relational abstract values are used to describe the relation between the original execution and an alternative execution of the system corresponding to a secret value.

This chapter is structured in the following way. In Section 4.1 we discuss how to identify a transition system with a tree-manipulating program, and in Section 4.2 we introduce the policy specification language. In Section 4.3 we discuss how to construct extended transition systems, and show how to model-check information flow properties using these systems. In Section 4.4 we construct abstract models for extended transition systems using the program analysis techniques of Chapter 3, which endows us with the capability of checking information flow properties of systems having an infinite state space. In Section 4.5 we describe the implementation of the model checker, and in Section 4.6 we demonstrate its applicability. Finally, in Section 4.7 we relate our work to others.

4.1 Transition Systems

Here, we model tree-manipulating processes like web services and enterprise workflows using transition systems (or otherwise called state machines) having a potentially infinite state space. Therefore, we define now the concept of transition systems. Given that $a : X \to Z$ is a mapping from set X to set Z, we denote its projection to the subset $Y \subseteq X$ by $a|_Y$.

Definition 9 (Transition Systems). *A transition system M is a tuple $M = (\mathcal{X}_\mathcal{I}, \mathcal{X}_\mathcal{O}, \mathcal{V}, S, s_0, \delta)$, where S is a set of states including the initial state $s_0 \in S$, $\mathcal{X}_\mathcal{I}$ is the set of input variables, and $\mathcal{X}_\mathcal{O}$ is the set of output variables. The members of the alphabet $\mathcal{A} = \{a \mid a : \mathcal{X}_\mathcal{I} \cup \mathcal{X}_\mathcal{O} \to \mathcal{V}\}$ are mappings from the set of variables $\mathcal{X}_\mathcal{I} \cup \mathcal{X}_\mathcal{O}$ to the set of values $\mathcal{V}$, and $\delta : S \times \mathcal{A} \nrightarrow S$ is a partial transition function. Furthermore, $\mathcal{X}_\mathcal{I} \cap \mathcal{X}_\mathcal{O} = \emptyset$ needs to hold. We consider input enabled systems, that is, we require for every $s \in S$ and $a \in \mathcal{A}$ that there exists an $a' \in \mathcal{A}$ with $a'|_{\mathcal{X}_\mathcal{I}} = a|_{\mathcal{X}_\mathcal{I}}$ so that $\delta(s, a')$ is defined.*

Now we identify the members of the tuple describing a transition system with the objects of the semantics of the assembly language for tree manipulation. We extend the language defined in Figure 2.2 so that programs declare the set of input and output variables, furthermore the set of binary alphabet elements occurring in the values. Therefore, here, programs begin with the following declaration:

```
input:     x_1^i,...,x_l^i;
output:    x_1^o,...,x_m^o;
alphabet:  σ_1,...,σ_n;
```

4.1. TRANSITION SYSTEMS

Accordingly, the sets of input and output variables are defined as $\mathcal{X}_\mathcal{I} = \{x_1^i, ..., x_l^i\}$ and $\mathcal{X}_\mathcal{O} = \{x_1^o, ..., x_m^o\}$ respectively. Furthermore, the set of binary alphabet elements required by the abstract interpretation is defined by the elements σ_i in addition to those occurring in the program text. For the sake of simplicity, we suppose in the rest that the set of variables occurring a program is $\mathcal{X} = \mathcal{X}_\mathcal{I} \cup \mathcal{X}_\mathcal{O}$.

Since the values of variables in our programs are binary trees, the set of values $\mathcal{V}$ equals to the set $\mathfrak{B}_{\Sigma_2, \Sigma_0}$. Similarly, each member s of the set of states S is a mapping $s : \mathcal{X} \to \mathfrak{B}_{\Sigma_2, \Sigma_0}$ from the set of variables occurring in the program to the set of binary trees. We define the initial state so that $s_0(x) = \#$ for each variable $x \in \mathcal{X}$ occurring in the program. In other words, the initial values of the variables are the binary equivalents of empty forests.

We suppose that the execution of a program generated by nonterminal p in Figure 2.2 always terminates. In this work we regard the non-termination of a program as an error, the absence of which the presented techniques do not seek to prove. Furthermore, our programs are deterministic. In other words, for each initial state s there is at most one resulting state s'. Therefore, we will use the notation $[\![p]\!]s = s'$ in order to express that the execution of the program p on the initial state s results in the final state s'.

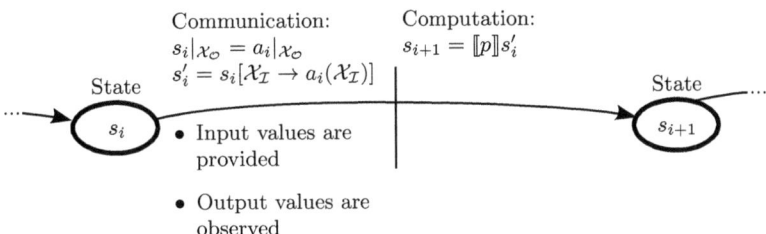

Figure 4.1: A transition of the state machine specified by a tree-manipulating program.

Transitions $\delta(s_i, a_i) = s_{i+1}$ of the transition system M specified by a program p are defined the following way as it is illustrated by Figure 4.1:

- First, it is checked whether the values of the output variables of the alphabet element are equal to the values of the output variables of the actual state. Accordingly, the transition can only take place if $s_i|_{\mathcal{X}_\mathcal{O}} = a_i|_{\mathcal{X}_\mathcal{O}}$ holds.

- The next state $s_{i+1} = [\![p]\!]s_i'$ is the result of the computation of the program p on the state $s_i' = s_i[\mathcal{X}_\mathcal{I} \mapsto a_i(\mathcal{X}_\mathcal{I})]$, where the values of the input variables of s_i are replaced with the values of the corresponding variables in a_i. Accordingly, the notation $s_i[\mathcal{X}_\mathcal{I} \mapsto a_i(\mathcal{X}_\mathcal{I})]$ is an abbreviation for $s_i[x_1^i \mapsto a(x_1^i)][x_2^i \mapsto a(x_2^i)]...[x_n^i \mapsto a(x_n^i)]$, where each $x_j^i \in \mathcal{X}_\mathcal{I}$.

In order to handle erroneous configurations, we extend the set of variables $\mathcal{X}$ with an implicit output variable $err \in \mathcal{X}_\mathcal{O}$. In case $err = \#$, then no error has occurred during the execution. On the other hand, if $err \neq \#$, then an error occurred during the execution. In this case the values of other variables are unspecified. Furthermore, whenever $s(err) \neq \#$, then we have that $s'(err) \neq \#$ for any a where $s' = \delta(s, a)$.

4.2 Temporal Information Flow Policies

Temporal information flow policies enable the specification of conditional secrecy and declassification based on the occurrences of events at the interfaces of reactive systems. In this work temporal information flow policies are defined using an extension of the positive fragment of the Linear Temporal Logic [76] called Restricted SecLTL [28], which is generated by the nonterminal φ using the grammar below:

$$\begin{aligned} \varphi &::= x \vartriangle L \mid \varphi \vee \varphi \mid \varphi \wedge \varphi \mid \bigcirc \varphi \mid \varphi \mathcal{U} \psi \mid \psi \mathcal{R} \varphi \mid \mathcal{H}_{H,O}\psi \\ \psi &::= x \vartriangle L \mid \psi \vee \psi \mid \psi \wedge \psi \mid \bigcirc \psi \mid \psi \mathcal{U} \psi \mid \psi \mathcal{R} \psi \end{aligned} \quad (4.1)$$

Atomic propositions are of the form $x \vartriangle L$ specifying that the value of the variable x is described by the regular tree language $L \subseteq \mathfrak{B}_{\Sigma_2, \{\#, bv\}}$. These constructs are atomic propositions from the point of view of the temporal logic. However, since they make statements about the properties of trees stored in variables, they are also predicates. Still, for the sake of clarity, we will call them atomic propositions. A tree τ is described by a language L, denoted $\tau \vartriangle L$, if there is a $\tau' \in L$, so that τ' can be constructed from τ by replacing its leaves having basic values with leaves labeled with bv.

Formulae are composed by the Boolean connectives except for negation and the LTL operators next $\bigcirc$, release $\mathcal{R}$ and until $\mathcal{U}$. We additionally introduce the common abbreviations $\text{tt} = (x \vartriangle L \vee x \vartriangle \overline{L})$, $\text{ff} = (x \vartriangle L \wedge x \vartriangle \overline{L})$, $\Diamond\varphi = \text{tt}\mathcal{U}\varphi$, $\Box\varphi = \text{ff}\mathcal{R}\varphi$, and $\varphi_1 \mathcal{W} \varphi_2 = (\varphi_1 \mathcal{U} \varphi_2) \vee \Box \varphi_1$, where $\overline{L}$ denotes the complement of the regular language L. Restricted SecLTL introduces the additional *hide* operator $\mathcal{H}_{H,O}\psi$ in order to specify noninterference properties. In $\mathcal{H}_{H,O}\psi$, $H : I \to \mathcal{P}(\mathfrak{B}_{\Sigma_2, \{\#, bv, \star\}})$ is a mapping from the set of variables $I \subseteq \mathcal{X}_\mathcal{I}$ to regular sets of binary trees over the binary alphabet Σ_2 and nullary alphabet $\{\#, bv, \star\}$. O is a set of output variables, and ψ is a positive LTL formula. The formula $\mathcal{H}_{H,O}\psi$ specifies the secrecy of certain subtrees of the values of variables $x_i \in \text{dom}(H)$ assigned by the environment at the time of evaluation. The requirement is that it must not be possible to make inferences on the secret subtrees based on the values in variables O until ψ holds. The positions of the secret subtrees of the input value in x_i are specified by the regular language $H(x_i)$, which defines a regular set of public views with respect to the security lattice element *low*.

The semantics of the logic Restricted SecLTL is defined in terms of the runs of the transition systems being examined.

Definition 10 (Runs and Executions of a Transition System). *Runs of a transition system M are infinite sequences of letters: $\vec{a} = a_0, a_1, \ldots$, with all $a_i \in \mathcal{A}$. Given a state $s \in S$, each run $\vec{a}$ is associated with a unique finite or infinite sequence of states, $s_0, \ldots, s_n$ or $s_0, s_1, \ldots$, called execution of M from s on $\vec{a}$ and denoted $\text{Exec}_M(s, \vec{a})$, such that $s_0 = s$ and $s_{i+1} = \delta(s_i, a_i)$ for all $0 \leq i < n$ or $i \geq 0$, respectively. Given a state s, we denote the set of runs on which M*

4.2. TEMPORAL INFORMATION FLOW POLICIES

has an infinite execution by $\mathsf{Runs}_{s,M}$. For a run/execution π and $i \in \mathbb{N}$, $\pi[i]$ is the $(i+1)^{th}$ element of π, $\pi[0,i)$ is the prefix of π up to (excluding) position i and, if π is infinite, $\pi[i,\infty)$ is its infinite suffix starting at i. The length of a finite execution π is $|\pi|$.

Now we extend the concretization function γ as it has been defined in Section 3.3 to letters of the alphabet $\mathcal{A}$, sets of variables $X \subseteq \mathcal{X}$ and functions $H : I \to \mathcal{P}(\mathfrak{B}_{\Sigma_2,\{\#,bv,\star\}})$. $\begin{bmatrix} a_1 \\ a_2 \end{bmatrix} \in \gamma_X(H)$ holds, if for all $x \in X$ where $x \in \mathsf{dom}(H)$ it holds that $\begin{bmatrix} a_1(x) \\ a_2(x) \end{bmatrix} \in \gamma(H(x) \cup \mathfrak{B}_{\Sigma_2,\{\#,bv\}})$, furthermore, for all other variables $y \in X$, where $y \notin \mathsf{dom}(H)$ it holds that $a_1(y) = a_2(y)$. There is no restriction on the values of variables $z \notin X$. Furthermore, we apply the notation $a_1 =_X a_2$ in order to abbreviate that for all variables $x \in X$ it holds that $a_1(x) = a_2(x)$. We apply the notation $=_X$ also to sequences of letters. Accordingly, $\vec{a}_1 =_X \vec{a}_2$ means that for all j it holds that $\vec{a}_1[j] =_X \vec{a}_2[j]$.

Definition 11 (Alternative Runs). *The set of alternative runs of a transition system for a given run $\vec{a}$ and initial state s is the set of runs such that on each of them each letter except for the first one agrees with the corresponding letter on $\vec{a}$ in the input variables, and the values of the input variables of the first letter may differ in the secret subtrees specified by H. Formally, for $\vec{a} \in \mathcal{A}^\omega$ and $s \in S$,*

$$\mathsf{AltRuns}_M(s,\vec{a},H) = \{\vec{a}' \in \mathsf{Runs}_{s,M} \mid \begin{bmatrix} a[0] \\ \vec{a}'[0] \end{bmatrix} \in \gamma_{\mathcal{X}_\mathcal{I}}(H) \text{ and } \vec{a}[1,\infty) =_{\mathcal{X}_\mathcal{I}} \vec{a}'[1,\infty)\}$$

Now we define the semantics of the logic Restricted SecLTL.

Definition 12 (Semantics of Restricted SecLTL [28]). *Let $M = (\mathcal{X}_\mathcal{I}, \mathcal{X}_\mathcal{O}, \mathfrak{B}_{\Sigma_2,\Sigma_0}, S, s_0, \delta)$ be a transition system. An infinite run $\vec{a} \in \mathsf{Runs}_{s,M}$ for some state $s \in S$ and the state s satisfy a formula φ of the logic Restricted SecLTL, denoted $M, s, \vec{a} \models \varphi$ if the following conditions are satisfied:*

1. *if $\varphi = x \vartriangle L$ for some $x \in \mathcal{X}$, then $M, s, \vec{a} \models \varphi$ iff $\vec{a}[0](x) \vartriangle L$ holds;*

2. *if $\varphi = \varphi_1 \vee \varphi_2$, then $M, s, \vec{a} \models \varphi$ iff $M, s, \vec{a} \models \varphi_1$ or $M, s, \vec{a} \models \varphi_2$;*

3. *if $\varphi = \varphi_1 \wedge \varphi_2$, then $M, s, \vec{a} \models \varphi$ iff $M, s, \vec{a} \models \varphi_1$ and $M, s, \vec{a} \models \varphi_2$;*

4. *if $\varphi = \bigcirc \varphi'$, then $M, s, \vec{a} \models \varphi$ iff $M, s', \vec{a}[1,\infty) \models \varphi'$ where $s' = \delta(s, \vec{a}[0])$;*

5. *if $\varphi = \varphi_1 \mathcal{U} \varphi_2$, then $M, s, \vec{a} \models \varphi$ holds iff for some $i \geq 0$ we have that $M, \vec{s}[i], \vec{a}[i,\infty) \models \varphi_2$ and for all j with $0 \leq j < i$ we have that $M, \vec{s}[j], \vec{a}[j,\infty) \models \varphi_1$, where $\vec{s} = \mathsf{Exec}_M(s, \vec{a})$;*

6. *if $\varphi = \varphi_1 \mathcal{R} \varphi_2$, then $M, s, \vec{a} \models \varphi$ iff either $M, \vec{s}[i], \vec{a}[i,\infty) \models \varphi_2$ holds for all $i \geq 0$, or there is a $j \geq 0$ such that $M, \vec{s}[j], \vec{a}[j,\infty) \models \varphi_1$ and for all $0 \leq k \leq j$ we have $M, \vec{s}[k], \vec{a}[k,\infty) \models \varphi_2$, where $\vec{s} = \mathsf{Exec}_M(s, \vec{a})$;*

7. *if $\varphi = \mathcal{H}_{H,O}\varphi'$, then $M, s, \vec{a} \models \varphi$ iff for every $\vec{a}' \in \mathsf{AltRuns}_M(s, \vec{a}, H)$ it holds that $\vec{a} =_O \vec{a}'$ or there exists $i \in \mathbb{N}$ such that $M, \vec{s}[i], \vec{a}[i,\infty) \models \varphi'$ and it holds that $\vec{a}[0,i) =_O \vec{a}'[0,i)$, where $\vec{s} = \mathsf{Exec}_M(s, \vec{a})$.*

We say that a transition system M satisfies a formula φ denoted $M \models \varphi$, iff $M, s_0, \vec{a} \models \varphi$ for every $\vec{a} \in \mathsf{Runs}_{s_0, M}$.

As an example, let us compose a Restricted SecLTL formula formalizing the informal requirement of (1.1) for the state machine defined by the program in Listing 2.1:

> "The scores of the papers may not be revealed to the authors before the notification phase." (1.1)

The formalization is:

$$\Box \left(\mathcal{H} \left\{ \begin{array}{l} \mathtt{averageScore} \mapsto \mathtt{secret} \\ \mathtt{subDB} \mapsto \mathtt{qSubDB} \end{array} \right\}, \{\mathtt{toAuthors}\} \left(\mathtt{phase} \mathrel{\triangle} \mathtt{notify} \right) \right) \quad (4.2)$$

In the formula (4.2) languages are defined using names of predicates as they have been applied in Section 3.3. Accordingly, the language corresponding to the predicate `secret` has been defined in (3.7), and `qSubDB` is the predicate defining the set of public views of databases according to (3.4). The language corresponding to `notify` is the set of trees with roots labeled `notify`. The informal meaning of (4.2) is the following. At each point of time it is a requirement that the value of the input variable `averageScore`, and the acceptance values stored in the database `subDB` do not influence the value of the output variable `toAuthors` until the value of the input variable `phase` does not have root labeled `notify`. This is enforced by the semantics in Definition 12 so that the value of `toAuthors` in each alternative run needs to equal to that on the original one until the value of `phase` becomes `notify`.

In the next sections we elaborate on how to verify specifications composed in Restricted SecLTL using automaton-based model checking techniques combined with relational abstract interpretation.

4.3 Model Checking Systems with Finite State Space

In this section we describe an algorithm that can verify state machines having a finite state space, and in the next section we extend this algorithm for systems with infinite state space using relational abstract interpretation.

Similarly to the automata-theoretic model checking techniques of [75], the main idea here is to construct a nondeterministic Büchi automaton accepting the set of runs violating the specification and check its intersection with the set of runs generated by the model for emptiness. However, the verification of a subformula $\mathcal{H}_{H,O}\varphi$ requires the comparison of the actual run of the state machine with the alternative runs. Therefore, it does not suffice to construct the product of the automata corresponding to the formula and the state machine. In order to verify whether the formula φ holds on the state machine M, we will apply the model checking techniques of [75] to the corresponding extended model M_k and a modified formula $\mathsf{tr}(\mathsf{NNF}(\neg\varphi))$, where k is the number of hide operators in φ, and $\mathsf{NNF}(\neg\varphi)$ is the negation normal for of $\neg\varphi$. M_k and $\mathsf{tr}(\mathsf{NNF}(\neg\varphi))$ are constructed so that the validity of $\mathsf{tr}(\mathsf{NNF}(\neg\varphi))$ on M_k entails the validity of $\neg\varphi$ on M.

4.3. MODEL CHECKING SYSTEMS WITH FINITE STATE SPACE

Definition 13 (Extended Transition Systems). *An extended transition system is a nondeterministic transition system defined by a tuple $M_k = (\mathcal{X}_\mathcal{I}, \mathcal{X}_\mathcal{O}, \mathfrak{B}_{\Sigma_2, \Sigma_0}, k, S^*, s_0^*, \delta^*)$ with the following components:*

- $\mathcal{X}_\mathcal{I}$ is the set of input variables, and $\mathcal{X}_\mathcal{O}$ is the set of output variables so that $\mathcal{X}_\mathcal{I} \cap \mathcal{X}_\mathcal{O} = \emptyset$ holds.

- The elements of the alphabet $\mathcal{A}^*$ are of the form $a^* = (a, \vartheta)$, where $a : \mathcal{X} \to \mathfrak{B}_{\Sigma_2, \Sigma_0}$ is a mapping from variables to binary trees, and ϑ is a subset of $\{start^i, leak^i \mid 1 \leq i \leq k\}$.

- S^* is a set of states.

- s_0^* is the initial state so that $s_0^* \in S^*$.

- $\delta^* : S^* \times \mathcal{A}^* \to \mathcal{P}(S^*)$ is a transition function, which maps a state and an alphabet element to a set of states.

Since extended transition systems are nondeterministic, we need an additional definition.

Definition 14 (Runs and Executions of a Nondeterministic Transition System). *Runs of a nondeterministic transition system M_k are infinite sequences of letters: $\vec{a}^* = a_0^*, a_1^*, \ldots$, so that each $a_j^* \in \mathcal{A}^*$. Given a state $s^* \in S^*$, each run $\vec{a}^*$ is associated with the set of finite or infinite sequences of states, $s_0^*, \ldots, s_n^*$ or $s_0^*, s_1^*, \ldots$, called executions of M_k from s^* on $\vec{a}^*$ denoted $\mathsf{Exec}_{M_k}(s^*, \vec{a}^*)$, where $s_0^* = s^*$ and $s_{j+1}^* \in \delta(s_j^*, a_j^*)$ for each $j \geq 0$. Given a state s^*, we denote the set of runs on which M_k has at least one infinite execution from s^* by Runs_{s^*, M_k}.*

In order to verify whether φ holds on the state machine $M = (\mathcal{X}_\mathcal{I}, \mathcal{X}_\mathcal{O}, \mathfrak{B}_{\Sigma_2, \Sigma_0}, S, s_0, \delta)$, we need to construct the corresponding extended state machine M_k, where k is the number of hide operators $\mathcal{H}^i_{H^i, O^i} \psi$ in φ. Accordingly, we need an arbitrary but fixed indexing of these operators in φ beginning with 1. We define $M_k = (\mathcal{X}_\mathcal{I}, \mathcal{X}_\mathcal{O}, \mathfrak{B}_{\Sigma_2, \Sigma_0}, k, S^*, s_0^*, \delta^*)$ based on M and φ the following way:

- The states of M_k are $k+1$ long tuples of the states of M:

$$S^* = \{(s^0, ..., s^k) \mid \forall s^i \in S\}$$

The member s^0 of a state $s^* = (s^0, s^1, ..., s^k)$ corresponds to the state of the original system, and each s^i with $i > 0$ represents an alternative run corresponding to the hide operator $\mathcal{H}^i$ having index i.

- The initial state $s_0^* = (s_0, ..., s_0)$ is a $k+1$ long tuple, where each member is the initial state of M.

- The alphabet $\mathcal{A}^*$ of M_k consists of tuples of the form $a^* = (a, \vartheta)$, where $a \in \mathcal{A}$ is a member of the alphabet of M, and ϑ is a subset of the set $\{start^i, leak^i \mid 1 \leq i \leq k\}$ where i is an index of a hide operator in φ. For the sake of simplicity, by writing $a^*(x)$ we mean $a(x)$ for some variable $x \in \mathcal{X}$, and $a^*(\vartheta)$ means ϑ, where $a^* = (a, \vartheta)$. Therefore, the semantics of LTL formulae remains valid on the runs of M_k, except for point 7. We are not going to verify formulae containing hide operators explicitly on an extended machine.

- M_k is a nondeterministic transition system. Therefore, its transition function $\delta^* : S^{k+1} \times \mathcal{A}^* \to \mathcal{P}(S^{k+1})$ is a function from the set of states and alphabet elements to the powerset of states. If $s^{*\prime} \in \delta^*(s^*, (a, \vartheta))$, where $s^* = (s^0, ..., s^i, ...)$ and $s^{*\prime} = (s^{0\prime}, ..., s^{i\prime}, ...)$, then $s^{0\prime} = \delta(s^0, a)$. Furthermore, each $s^{i\prime}$ is an arbitrary state satisfying the following constraints:

    - If $start^i \notin \vartheta$, then $\delta(s^i, b) = s^{i\prime}$ for some $b \in \mathcal{A}$ so that $a|_{\mathcal{X}_\mathcal{I}} = b|_{\mathcal{X}_\mathcal{I}}$. Further constraints on b are:
        * If $leak^i \notin \vartheta$ then $b =_{O^i} a$.
        * If $leak_i \in \vartheta$ then $b \neq_{O^i} a$.
    - If $start^i \in \vartheta$, then $s^{i\prime} = \delta(s^0, b)$ where $\begin{bmatrix} a \\ b \end{bmatrix} \in \gamma_{\mathcal{X}_\mathcal{I}}(H^i)$. Here, H^i is the function specifying public views for input variables corresponding to the operator $\mathcal{H}^i_{H^i, O^i}\psi$ with index i in the formula φ. This constraint is responsible for starting the alternative runs corresponding to the hide operator. Further constraints on b are:
        * If $leak^i \notin \vartheta$ then $b =_{O^i} a$.
        * If $leak_i \in \vartheta$ then $b \neq_{O^i} a$.

In order to verify the validity of $M \models \varphi$ using the extended machine M_k, we also need to transform the specification φ. The first step is to negate φ and construct its negation normal form $\mathsf{NNF}(\neg\varphi)$ by pushing the negation to propositions using the following equalities:

- $\neg(x \vartriangle L) = x \vartriangle \overline{L}$
- $\neg(\varphi_1 \vee \varphi_2) = \neg\varphi_1 \wedge \neg\varphi_2$
- $\neg(\varphi_1 \wedge \varphi_2) = \neg\varphi_1 \vee \neg\varphi_2$
- $\neg \bigcirc \varphi = \bigcirc \neg\varphi$
- $\neg(\varphi_1 \mathcal{U} \varphi_2) = \neg\varphi_1 \mathcal{R} \neg\varphi_2$
- $\neg(\varphi_1 \mathcal{R} \varphi_2) = \neg\varphi_1 \mathcal{U} \neg\varphi_2$
- $\neg \mathcal{H}_{H,O}\psi = \mathcal{L}_{H,O}\neg\psi$

Since L is a regular set of trees, it can be represented using a regular tree automaton [22]. Regular tree automata can be complemented, and $\overline{L}$ denotes the set of trees accepted by the complemented automaton. Because of the last equality, a negated Restricted SecLTL formula is not a Restricted SecLTL formula. The operator $\mathcal{L}_{H,O}\psi$ is called the *leak* operator [28]. It enforces information leakage meanwhile ψ holds.

Definition 15 (Semantics of the Leak Operator). *Let M be a transition system. An infinite run $\vec{a} \in \mathsf{Runs}_{s,M}$ for some state $s \in S$ and the state s satisfy a SecLTL formula φ with leak operators, denoted $M, s, \vec{a} \models \varphi$, if the following condition is satisfied in addition to points 1-7 in Definition 12:*

8. *if $\varphi = \mathcal{L}_{H,O}\psi$, then $M, s, \vec{a} \models \varphi$ iff for at least one $\vec{a}\,' \in \mathsf{AltRuns}_M(s, \vec{a}, H)$ there exists $j \in \mathbb{N}$ such that $\vec{a}[j](x_o) \neq \vec{a}\,'[j](x_o)$ for some $x_o \in O$, meanwhile for all $0 \leq l \leq j$ it holds that $M, \vec{s}[l], \vec{a}[l, \infty) \models \psi$ where $\vec{s} = \mathsf{Exec}_M(s, \vec{a})$.*

4.3. MODEL CHECKING SYSTEMS WITH FINITE STATE SPACE   57

The second step of transforming φ succeeds by applying the function tr on NNF($\neg\varphi$), which replaces each subformula of the form $\mathcal{L}^i_{H^i,O^i}\psi$ by the following:

$$start^i \wedge \psi \wedge \left[leak^i \vee \bigcirc\Big((\neg start^i \wedge \psi)\mathcal{U}(\neg start^i \wedge \psi \wedge leak^i)\Big)\right] \quad (4.3)$$

Intuitively, (4.3) enforces the initialization of the alternative runs corresponding to the leak operator $\mathcal{L}^i$ by $start_i$, and enforces the occurrence of an information leakage by $leak_i$. Accordingly, the semantics of the logic needs to be extended as well in order to handle the new propositions $start^i$, and $leak^i$:

Definition 16 (Semantics of $start^i$ and $leak^i$). *Let M_k be an extended transition system. An infinite run $\vec{a}^* \in \mathsf{Runs}_{s^*,M_k}$ for some state $s^* \in S^*$ and the state s^* satisfy an LTL formula φ, denoted $M_k, s^*, \vec{a}^* \models \varphi$, if the following conditions are satisfied in addition to points 1-6 in Definition 12:*

- *if $\varphi = P$ for some $P \in \{start^i, leak^i\}$, then $M_k, s^*, \vec{a}^* \models \varphi$ iff $P \in \vec{a}^*[0](\vartheta)$ holds;*

- *if $\varphi = \neg P$ for some $P \in \{start^i, leak^i\}$, then $M_k, s^*, \vec{a}^* \models \varphi$ iff $P \notin \vec{a}^*[0](\vartheta)$ holds;*

In the rest we denote a tuple of states with $\underline{s}$. Accordingly, if there is a state $s^* = (s^0, s^1, ..., s^k)$ of M_k, then sometimes we abbreviate s^* with $(s^0, \underline{s})$. We observe the following about the relation between a transition system and the corresponding extended transition system:

Theorem 9. *Let us consider the state machine $M = (\mathcal{X}_\mathcal{I}, \mathcal{X}_\mathcal{O}, \mathfrak{B}_{\Sigma_2, \Sigma_0}, S, s_0, \delta)$, an arbitrary state of it $s \in S$, an arbitrary run $\vec{a} = a_0, a_1, ... \in \mathsf{Runs}_{s,M}$ and an arbitrary formula φ of the logic Restricted SecLTL having k hide operators. In this case, $M, s, \vec{a} \models \mathsf{NNF}(\neg\varphi)$ implies that for any $\underline{s} = s^1, ..., s^k$ there is a sequence $\vartheta_0, \vartheta_1, ...$ so that it holds for the run $\vec{a}^* = (a_0, \vartheta_0), (a_1, \vartheta_1), ...$ that $\vec{a}^* \in \mathsf{Runs}_{(s,\underline{s}),M_k}$ and $M_k, (s, \underline{s}), \vec{a}^* \models \mathsf{tr}(\mathsf{NNF}(\neg\varphi))$, where $M_k = (\mathcal{X}_\mathcal{I}, \mathcal{X}_\mathcal{O}, \mathfrak{B}_{\Sigma_2, \Sigma_0}, k, S^*, s_0^*, \delta^*)$ is the extended transition system corresponding to M.*

The proof can be found in Section 6.3.

According to [75] and [28], given an LTL formula in negation normal form ψ over the set of propositions *Prop* it is possible to construct a nondeterministic Büchi automaton $N_\psi = (S^N, \mathcal{P}(Prop), s_0^N, \rho, F)$, which accepts exactly the set of runs specified by ψ. In our setting a proposition is either of the form $x \triangle L$, $start^i$, $leak^i$, $\neg start^i$ or $\neg leak^i$. In the definition of N_ψ, S^N is a finite set of states, $\mathcal{P}(Prop)$ is the powerset of the set of propositions occurring in ψ, s_0^N is the initial state, and F is a set of accepting states. $\rho: S^N \times \mathcal{P}(Prop) \to \mathcal{P}(S^N)$ is the transition function mapping a state and a set of propositions to a set of successor states. Now, we define a transition function $\rho_0: S^N \times \mathcal{A}^* \to \mathcal{P}(S^N)$ on the alphabet of M_k too. $s^{N\prime} \in \rho_0(s^N, a^*)$ if and only if there is a $\Psi \in \mathcal{P}(Prop)$ so that $s^{N\prime} \in \rho(s^N, \Psi)$, where $a^* \models \bigwedge_{P \in \Psi} P$. $(a, \vartheta) \models x \triangle L$ if $a(x) \triangle L$, $(a, \vartheta) \models start^i$ if $start^i \in \vartheta$, and $(a, \vartheta) \models leak^i$ if $leak^i \in \vartheta$. And similarly, $(a, \vartheta) \models \neg start^i$ if $start^i \notin \vartheta$ and $(a, \vartheta) \models \neg leak^i$ if $leak^i \notin \vartheta$. The new transition function ρ_0 was necessary so that we can define the execution of N_ψ on runs of M_k. An execution of $N_\psi = (S^N, \mathcal{P}(Prop), s_0^N, \rho, F)$ on a run $\vec{a}^* = a_0^*, a_1^*, ...$ is a sequence of states $s_0^N, s_1^N, ...$ so that for each $j \geq 0$ it holds that $s_{j+1}^N \in \rho_0(s_j^N, a_j^*)$. An execution of N_ψ is accepting, if it is infinite, and there is an infinite number of accepting states $s^N \in F$ in it.

Now we can construct the product automaton N_{M_k, N_ψ} of an extended state machine M_k and a Büchi automaton N_ψ. Given that $N_\psi = (S^N, \mathcal{P}(Prop), s_0^N, \rho, F)$, and $M_k = (\mathcal{X}_\mathcal{I}, \mathcal{X}_\mathcal{O}, \mathfrak{B}_{\Sigma_2, \Sigma_0}, k, S^*, s_0^*, \delta^*)$, the product $N_{M_k, N_\psi} = (S^\times, A^*, s_0^\times, \delta^\times, F^\times)$ is a tuple having the following constituents:

- $S^\times$ is a set of states of the form (s^*, s^N), where $s^* \in S^*$ is a state of the extended machine, and $s^N \in S^N$ is a state of the Büchi automaton corresponding to the formula ψ.

- A^* is the alphabet of the extended automaton M_k.

- $s_0^\times = (s_0^*, s_0^N)$ is the initial state of the product automaton. It is a pair of the initial states of the extended automaton and the Büchi automaton corresponding to the formula.

- $F^\times$ is a set of states of the form (s^*, s^N), where $s^* \in S^*$ is a state of M_k, and $s^N \in F$ is an accepting state of N_ψ.

- $\delta^\times$ is the transition function. $(s^{*\prime}, s^{N\prime}) \in \delta^\times((s^*, s^N), a^*)$ whenever we have that $s^{*\prime} \in \delta^*(s^*, a^*)$ and $s^{N\prime} \in \rho_0(s^N, a^*)$.

Similarly to N_ψ, the acceptance condition of N_{M_k, N_ψ} is that its execution is infinite, and contains an infinite number of accepting states.

Theorem 9 yields a method to directly verify a property φ on a state machine M in case its state space and its alphabet are finite. First, we need to construct the corresponding extended machine M_k and the modified formula $\text{tr}(\text{NNF}(\neg\varphi))$. Then, we need to construct the Büchi automaton $N_{\text{tr}(\text{NNF}(\neg\varphi))}$ accepting the runs satisfying $\text{tr}(\text{NNF}(\neg\varphi))$. Finally, we need to construct the product automaton $N_{M_k, N_{\text{tr}(\text{NNF}(\neg\varphi))}}$ of $N_{\text{tr}(\text{NNF}(\neg\varphi))}$ and M_k, and check whether it is empty [76]. If the language accepted by $N_{M_k, N_{\text{tr}(\text{NNF}(\neg\varphi))}}$ is empty, it follows then that there is no run $\vec{a}^*$ for which it would hold that $M_k, s_0^*, \vec{a}^* \models \text{tr}(\text{NNF}(\neg\varphi))$. Taking the contrapositive of the statement of Theorem 9, it follows that there is no run $\vec{a}$ for which it would hold that $M, s_0, \vec{a} \models \neg\varphi$. From this we can then conclude that $M \models \varphi$.

However, our focus is on systems with infinite state space. Therefore, in the following sections we introduce a verification algorithm based on abstraction techniques, in order to verify information flow policies specified in the logic Restricted SecLTL on systems with infinite state space.

4.4 Model Checking Systems with Infinite State Space

In this section we apply the abstract interpretation techniques of Chapter 3 in order to model-check transition systems with infinite state space and alphabet. Therefore, we define now abstract transition systems that overapproximate the behavior of extended transition systems.

4.4. MODEL CHECKING SYSTEMS WITH INFINITE STATE SPACE

Definition 17 (Abstract Transition System). *The abstract transition system $\widehat{M}_k = (\mathcal{X}_\mathcal{I}, \mathcal{X}_\mathcal{O}, \mathcal{P}(\mathfrak{B}_{\Sigma_2,\{\#,bv\}}), k, \widehat{S}, \widehat{\underline{s_0}}, \widehat{\delta})$ is an abstraction of the extended transition system $M_k = (\mathcal{X}_\mathcal{I}, \mathcal{X}_\mathcal{O}, \mathfrak{B}_{\Sigma_2,\Sigma_0}, k, S^*, s_0^*, \delta^*)$ if the following conditions hold:*

- *The alphabet $\widehat{\mathcal{A}}$ consists of elements of the form $\widehat{\underline{a}} = (\widehat{a}, \vartheta)$. Each $\widehat{a} : \mathcal{X}_\mathcal{I} \cup \mathcal{X}_\mathcal{O} \to \mathcal{P}(\mathfrak{B}_{\Sigma_2,\{\#,bv\}})$ is a mapping from the set of input and output variables to regular sets of binary trees. The binary alphabet of these trees is Σ_2 and the nullary alphabet is $\{\#, bv\}$. Furthermore, ϑ is a subset of $\{start^i, leak^i \mid 1 \leq i \leq k\}$. We define the concretization function $\gamma^A : \widehat{\mathcal{A}} \to \mathcal{P}(\mathcal{A}^*)$ from the abstract alphabet to the powerset of the alphabet of the extended machine. $(a, \vartheta_2) \in \gamma^A(\widehat{a}, \vartheta_1)$ whenever $\vartheta_2 = \vartheta_1$, and for all $x \in \mathcal{X}_\mathcal{I} \cup \mathcal{X}_\mathcal{O}$ we have that $a(x) \triangle \widehat{a}(x)$.*

- *$\widehat{S}$ is a set of abstract states. We require the existence of a concretization function $\gamma^S : \widehat{S} \to \mathcal{P}(S^*)$ from the set of abstract states to the powerset of the set of states of the concrete transition system.*

- *$\widehat{\underline{s_0}} \in \widehat{S}$ is the initial state, so that $s_0^* \in \gamma^S(\widehat{\underline{s_0}})$.*

- *$\widehat{\delta} : \widehat{S} \times \widehat{\mathcal{A}} \to \widehat{S}$ is the abstract transition function. Whenever $s^{*\prime} \in \delta^*(s^*, a^*)$, where $s^* \in \gamma^S(\widehat{\underline{s}})$ and $a^* \in \gamma^A(\widehat{\underline{a}})$, then we have that $\widehat{\underline{s}}' = \widehat{\delta}(\widehat{\underline{s}}, \widehat{\underline{a}})$ so that $s^{*\prime} \in \gamma^S(\widehat{\underline{s}}')$.*

We want to reduce the verification problem of $M \models \varphi$ to proving that the language accepted by the Büchi automaton $N_{\widehat{M}_k, N_{tr(NNF(\neg\varphi))}}$ is empty. Here, $N_{\widehat{M}_k, N_{tr(NNF(\neg\varphi))}}$ is the product of the Büchi automaton $N_{tr(NNF(\neg\varphi))}$ corresponding to the specification φ and the abstract state machine $\widehat{M}_k$ corresponding to M_k. Therefore, we define now the product $N_{\widehat{M}_k, N_\psi}$ of an arbitrary abstract machine $\widehat{M}_k = (\mathcal{X}_\mathcal{I}, \mathcal{X}_\mathcal{O}, \mathcal{P}(\mathfrak{B}_{\Sigma_2,\{\#,bv\}}), k, \widehat{S}, \widehat{\underline{s_0}}, \widehat{\delta})$ and the nondeterministic Büchi automaton $N_\psi = (S^N, \mathcal{P}(Prop), s_0^N, \rho, F)$ corresponding to the LTL formula ψ. The Büchi automaton $N_{\widehat{M}_k, N_\psi} = (\widehat{S}^\times, \widehat{\mathcal{A}}, \widehat{s_0}^\times, \widehat{\delta}^\times, \widehat{F}^\times)$ is a tuple with the following constituents:

- *$\widehat{S}^\times$ is a set of states of the form $(\widehat{\underline{s}}, s^N)$, where $\widehat{\underline{s}} \in \widehat{S}$ and $s^N \in S^N$.*

- *$\widehat{\mathcal{A}}$ is the alphabet, which is identical to the alphabet of $\widehat{M}_k$.*

- *$\widehat{s_0}^\times = (\widehat{\underline{s_0}}, s_0^N)$ is the initial state, where $\widehat{\underline{s_0}}$ is the initial state of $\widehat{M}_k$ and s_0^N is the initial state of N_ψ.*

- *$\widehat{\delta}^\times$ is a nondeterministic transition function. $(\widehat{\underline{s}}', s^{N\prime}) \in \widehat{\delta}^\times((\widehat{\underline{s}}, s^N), (\widehat{a}, \vartheta))$, if it holds that $\widehat{\underline{s}}' = \widehat{\delta}(\widehat{\underline{s}}, (\widehat{a}, \vartheta))$, and there is a transition $s^{N\prime} \in \rho(s^N, \Psi)$ of N_ψ so that $(\widehat{a}, \vartheta) \models \bigwedge_{P \in \Psi} P$. $(\widehat{a}, \vartheta) \models x \triangle L$ holds if $\widehat{a}(x) \subseteq L$ holds. Furthermore, $(\widehat{a}, \vartheta) \models start^i$ if $start^i \in \vartheta$, $(\widehat{a}, \vartheta) \models leak^i$ if $leak^i \in \vartheta$, $(\widehat{a}, \vartheta) \models \neg start^i$ if $start^i \notin \vartheta$ and finally, $(\widehat{a}, \vartheta) \models \neg leak^i$ if $leak^i \notin \vartheta$. Since L is a regular language of trees, the question whether $\widehat{a}(x) \subseteq L$ holds is decidable.*

- *$\widehat{F}^\times$ is the set of tuples $(\widehat{\underline{s}}, s^N)$, where $\widehat{\underline{s}} \in \widehat{S}$ and $s^N \in F$.*

Theorem 10. *Let us consider the product $N_{M_k, N_{\text{tr}(\text{NNF}(\neg\varphi))}}$ of the extended state machine M_k and the Büchi automaton $N_{\text{tr}(\text{NNF}(\neg\varphi))}$ corresponding to the LTL formula $\text{tr}(\text{NNF}(\neg\varphi))$. Furthermore, let us consider the product $N_{\widehat{M}_k, N_{\text{tr}(\text{NNF}(\neg\varphi))}}$ of the abstract state machine $\widehat{M}_k$ and $N_{\text{tr}(\text{NNF}(\neg\varphi))}$. In this case the fact that $L(N_{\widehat{M}_k, N_{\text{tr}(\text{NNF}(\neg\varphi))}}) = \emptyset$ entails that $L(N_{M_k, N_{\text{tr}(\text{NNF}(\neg\varphi))}}) = \emptyset$.*

For the proof, please, refer to Section 6.3.

According to Theorem 10, the product automaton $N_{\widehat{M}_k, N_{\text{tr}(\text{NNF}(\neg\varphi))}}$ can be used for the verification of the model M. Together with Theorem 9, its emptiness entails that $M \models \varphi$.

4.4.1 Constructing the Abstract Transition System

Now, we construct the abstract transition system $\widehat{M}_k = (\mathcal{X}_\mathcal{I}, \mathcal{X}_\mathcal{O}, \mathfrak{B}_{\Sigma_2, \{\#, bv\}}, k, \widehat{S}, \widehat{s}_0, \widehat{\delta})$ corresponding to the extended transition system $M_k = (\mathcal{X}_\mathcal{I}, \mathcal{X}_\mathcal{O}, \mathcal{P}(\mathfrak{B}_{\Sigma_2, \{\#, bv\}}), k, S^*, s_0^*, \delta^*)$ using the abstract interpretation techniques introduced in Chapter 3. An abstract state $\widehat{\underline{s}} \in \widehat{S}$ is a tuple $(\widehat{s}^0, \widehat{s}^1, ..., \widehat{s}^k)$ so that its concretization $\gamma^S(\widehat{\underline{s}})$ consists of states of the extended transition system $s^* = (s^0, s^1, ..., s^k) \in S^*$. $(s^0, s^1, ..., s^k) \in \gamma^S(\widehat{s}^0, \widehat{s}^1, ..., \widehat{s}^k)$ holds, if $(s^0, s^1, ..., s^k)$ satisfies the following conditions:

- For each $x \in \mathcal{X}$, we have that $s^0(x) \triangle \widehat{s}^0(x)$. The member $\widehat{s}^0$ of the abstract state is used to overapproximate the original execution of the system. Therefore, there are no leaves labeled $\star$ here. For each x, we have that $\widehat{s}^0(x) \in \mathcal{P}(\mathfrak{B}_{\Sigma_2, \{\#, bv\}})$.

- For $i \geq 1$, abstract values $\widehat{s}^i$ carry relational information on the states s^0 and s^i in the form of sets of potential public views. For the concretization of abstract values having leaves labeled $\star$ we apply the concretization function γ as it has been defined in Section 3.3. Therefore, we have the requirement that for each $i > 0$ and each $x \in \mathcal{X}$ it holds that:

$$\begin{bmatrix} s^0(x) \\ s^i(x) \end{bmatrix} \in \gamma(\widehat{s}^i(x))$$

Since each variable in the initial state s_0^* of M_k carries the value #, we define $\widehat{\underline{s}}_0 = (\widehat{s}^0, \widehat{s}^1, ...\widehat{s}^k)$ so that for each i and x, $\widehat{s}^i(x) = \{\#\}$. It holds now trivially that $s_0^* \in \gamma^S(\widehat{\underline{s}}_0)$.

The transition function $\widehat{\delta}$ of the abstract machine is defined using the analysis technique of Section 3.3. In order to take a transition, we carry out a separate analysis for each member of the state of $\widehat{M}_k$. Given that we would like to compute $\widehat{\delta}(\widehat{\underline{s}}, (\widehat{a}, \vartheta))$, where $\widehat{\underline{s}} = (\widehat{s}^0, \widehat{s}^1, ..., \widehat{s}^k)$, we need to carry out the following steps:

Step 1. In this step we check whether the transition can take place at all.

- We need to check whether all information leakages are potentially present that are specified by ϑ. Let us suppose that we would like to verify the formula φ, which has subformulae $\mathcal{H}^i_{H^i, O^i} \psi$ for all $0 < i \leq k$. If $leak^i \in \vartheta$, then there must be at least one $x_o \in O^i$ so that there is at least one tree

4.4. MODEL CHECKING SYSTEMS WITH INFINITE STATE SPACE   61

having leaves labeled $\star$ in $\widehat{s}^i(x_o)$. If this is not the case, then $\widehat{\delta}(\widehat{\underline{s}}, (\widehat{a}, \vartheta))$ is undefined.

- We also need to check whether there is a concrete letter a and a concrete state $(s^0, ..., s^k)$ corresponding to $\widehat{a}$ and $\widehat{\underline{s}}$, so that their output variables agree. In other words we need that $a(x_o) = s^0(x_o)$ for all $x_o \in \mathcal{X}_\mathcal{O}$. Therefore, in case $\widehat{s}^0(x_o) \cap \widehat{a}(x_o) = \emptyset$ for some $x_o \in \mathcal{X}_\mathcal{O}$, then $\widehat{\delta}(\widehat{\underline{s}}, (\widehat{a}, \vartheta))$ is not defined either.

Step 2. We construct now the initial analysis information d_0^i for each member of the abstract state $\widehat{s}^i$, so that the corresponding analysis can take place. For the main run of the system we define $d_0^0(y) = \widehat{a}(y)$ for each $y \in \mathcal{X}_\mathcal{I}$, and $d_0^0(x) = \widehat{s}^0(x) \cap \widehat{a}(x)$ for each $x \in \mathcal{X}_\mathcal{O}$.

For the analyses of alternative runs regular sets of public views might need to be computed in case they are initialized by the transition. This happens if $start^i \in \vartheta$ for some i. Let us suppose that in the formula we verify φ, there is a subformula $\mathcal{H}^i_{H^i, O^i} \psi$, and that $y \in \mathcal{X}_\mathcal{I}$ is an input variable. The problem by the construction of the language $d_0^i(y)$ is the following. It is possible that $H^i(y)$ contains public views, which are not appropriate public views of any trees in $\widehat{a}(y)$. If there is a public view, for which there is no corresponding secret in $\widehat{a}(y)$, then its presence reduces the precision of the analysis without need. Therefore, we remove those. Now we construct a subset $h_{y,i}$ of $H^i(y)$, which contains only those public views, for which there are corresponding trees in $\widehat{a}(y)$.

For the sake of simplicity, we suppose that regular sets of trees are represented using regular tree grammars. This does not contradict the fact that the analysis of Section 3.3 is defined in terms of regular tree automata, because they are in one-to-one correspondence with regular tree grammars [22]. We construct the grammar describing the regular set $h_{y,i}$ based on the grammars corresponding to $\widehat{a}(y)$ and $H^i(y)$. Let us suppose that the grammar of $\widehat{a}(y)$ consists of rules of the following form:

$$\begin{aligned} A &\to \sigma(B, C) \\ D &\to \# \\ E &\to bv \end{aligned} \qquad (4.4)$$

In (4.4) capital letters are nonterminals, $\sigma \in \Sigma_2$, and **#** and bv are the only nullary alphabet elements. Furthermore, let us suppose that the regular set of trees in $H^i(y)$ is given by a grammar having rules of the following form:

$$\begin{aligned} U &\to \zeta(V, Z) \\ X &\to \# \\ Y &\to bv \\ W &\to \star \end{aligned} \qquad (4.5)$$

In (4.5) capital letters are nonterminals, $\zeta \in \Sigma_2$, and **#**, bv and $\star$ are the nullary alphabet elements.

Now we construct a new grammar for $h_{y,i}$ based on the rules of (4.4) and (4.5). Given that the initial nonterminal of the grammar of $\widehat{a}(y)$ is F, and the initial nonterminal of the grammar of $H^i(y)$ is Z, the initial nonterminal of the new grammar is $[F, Z]$. The rules of the new grammar are the following:

- Whenever there is a rule $A \to \sigma(B,C)$ in $\widehat{a}(y)$ and there is a rule $U \to \sigma(V,Z)$ in $H^i(y)$, then we add $[A,U] \to \sigma([B,V],[C,Z])$ to the new grammar.

- Whenever there is a rule $W \to \star$ in $H^i(y)$, then we add the new rule $[G,W] \to \star$ for all nonterminals G of the grammar of $\widehat{a}(x_i)$.

- For all rules $I \to \xi$ of $\widehat{a}(y)$ and all rules $J \to \xi$ of $H^i(y)$, where $\xi \in \{bv, \#\}$, we have the new rule $[I,J] \to \xi$.

The new grammar generates only those public views, the public parts of which can be generated by the grammar of $\widehat{a}(y)$. By public part we mean the upper prefix without leaves labeled $\star$.

Now we can define the initial analysis information for the alternative runs of the system. For all $i > 0$ the initial analysis information d_0^i is defined the following way. We have two cases now depending on whether $start^i \in \vartheta$ or not.

- $start^i \notin \vartheta$. In this case the output variables are simply copied from the previous state. Therefore, we define $d_0^i(x) = \widehat{s}^i(x)$ for each $x \in \mathcal{X}_\mathcal{O}$. Furthermore, for each input variable $y \in \mathcal{X}_\mathcal{I}$ we have that $d_0^i(y) = \widehat{a}(y)$.

- $start^i \in \vartheta$. Now, $d_0^i(y) = \widehat{a}(y) \cup h_{y,i}$ for all variables $y \in \mathsf{dom}(H^i)$, where $h_{y,i}$ is a subset of $H^i(y)$ defined above. Values of output variables are initialized with those of the original execution. Therefore, for each $x \in \mathcal{X}_\mathcal{O}$ we define $d_0^i(x) = \widehat{s}^0(x)$.

  For variables $y \in \mathcal{X}_\mathcal{I}$ that are not members of $\mathsf{dom}(H^i)$ we simply define $d_0^i(y) = \widehat{a}(y)$.

Step 3. Let us suppose that the transition system M has been defined by program p. In the successor state $(\widehat{s}^{0\prime}, \widehat{s}^{1\prime}, ..., \widehat{s}^{k\prime}) = \widehat{\delta}(\widehat{\underline{s}}, (\widehat{a}, \vartheta))$ each $\widehat{s}^{i\prime}$ is the result of the analysis described in Section 3.3 based on the corresponding initial value d_0^i and program p. We require that no variable in the resulting abstract values is the empty set. Formally, we need that for each i and x, $\widehat{s}^{i\prime}(x) \neq \emptyset$ holds. Otherwise, we consider that the transition does not exist.

Theorem 11. *The abstract machine* $\widehat{M_k} = (\mathcal{X}_\mathcal{I}, \mathcal{X}_\mathcal{O}, \mathcal{P}(\mathfrak{B}_{\Sigma_2,\{\#,bv\}}), k, \widehat{S}, \widehat{\underline{s}_0}, \widehat{\delta})$ *constructed based on* $M_k = (\mathcal{X}_\mathcal{I}, \mathcal{X}_\mathcal{O}, \mathfrak{B}_{\Sigma_2,\Sigma_0}, k, S^*, s_0^*, \delta^*)$ *using the abstract interpretation techniques of Section 3.3, is indeed an abstraction of* M_k *according to Definition 17.*

For the proof, please, refer to Section 6.3.

According to Theorem 11, abstract machines constructed using the abstraction techniques of Section 3.3 can be applied for verification as it has been suggested by Theorem 10. However, there is no guarantee, that the state space of $\widehat{M_k}$ will be finite. Therefore, in the next section we introduce techniques to construct an abstract transition system with finite state space.

4.4.2 Constructing an Abstract State Machine Having Finite State Space

There is no guarantee that the state space of $\widehat{M_k}$ is finite. In order to enforce finiteness, we construct a set of Horn clauses, the model of which is a state machine $\widehat{N_{\widehat{M_k},N_\psi}} = (\widehat{\widehat{S}}^\times, \widehat{A}, \widehat{\widehat{s}_0}^\times, \widehat{\widehat{\delta}}^\times, \widehat{\widehat{F}}^\times)$ overapproximating the state space of the

4.4. MODEL CHECKING SYSTEMS WITH INFINITE STATE SPACE

product automaton $N_{\widehat{M_k},N_\psi} = (\widehat{S}^\times, \widehat{A}, \widehat{s}_0^\times, \widehat{\delta}^\times, \widehat{F}^\times)$ corresponding to $\widehat{M_k}$ and N_ψ. The set of states $\widehat{\widehat{S}}^\times$ consists of pairs of the form $(\widehat{\widehat{s}}, s^N)$, where $\widehat{\widehat{s}}$ overapproximates all states of $\widehat{M_k}$ for which there is a state $(\widehat{s}, s^N)$ in $\widehat{S}^\times$. Formally, for all $s^N \in S^N$ there is exactly one $\widehat{\widehat{s}} = (\widehat{\widehat{s}}^0, \widehat{\widehat{s}}^1, ..., \widehat{\widehat{s}}^k)$ where $(\widehat{s}, s^N) \in \widehat{S}^\times$. Therefore, it holds on all $((\widehat{\widehat{s}}^0, \widehat{\widehat{s}}^1, ..., \widehat{\widehat{s}}^k), s^N) \in \widehat{\widehat{S}}^\times$, on all $((\widehat{s}^0, \widehat{s}^1, ..., \widehat{s}^k), s^N) \in \widehat{S}^\times$, on all $0 \leq i \leq k$ and all $x \in \mathcal{X}$ that:

$$\widehat{\widehat{s}}^i(x) \supseteq \widehat{s}^i(x) \tag{4.6}$$

The alphabet, and the initial state of $N_{\widehat{\widehat{M_k},N_\psi}}$ are equal to that of $N_{\widehat{M_k},N_\psi}$. The set of accepting states $\widehat{\widehat{F}}^\times$ is a set of tuples of the form $(\widehat{\widehat{s}}, s^N)$, where s^N is an accepting state of N_ψ.

Let us suppose that the Restricted SecLTL formula we would like to verify is φ, where the corresponding Büchi automaton is $N_{\text{tr}(\text{NNF}(\neg\varphi))} = (S^N, \mathcal{P}(Prop), s_0^N, \rho, F)$. Now we construct the corresponding product automaton:

$$N_{\widehat{M_k},N_{\text{tr}(\text{NNF}(\neg\varphi))}} = (\widehat{\widehat{S}}^\times, \widehat{A}, \widehat{s}_0^\times, \widehat{\widehat{\delta}}^\times, \widehat{\widehat{F}}^\times)$$

We represent the transition function[1] ρ as a set of tuples, where $(s^N, \Psi, s^{N'}) \in \rho$ if and only if $s^{N'} \in \rho(s^N, \Psi)$. Let us suppose that the transition system M we would like to analyze is defined by program p. Now we generate the implications corresponding to the analysis of program p for all transitions of $N_{\text{tr}(\text{NNF}(\neg\varphi))}$ and parallel executions of M_k separately. The original analysis of Section 3.3 consists of implications over predicates of the form $\text{var}_{x,n}$, where $x \in \mathcal{X}$ is a variable of the program and n is a node in the self-composition of the CFG of the program. Now we extend the names of the predicates to $\text{var}_{x,n,i,r}$, where $0 \leq i \leq k$ and $r \in \rho$. We generate the implications as described in Section 3.3 for all possible transitions $r \in \rho$, and $0 \leq i \leq k$.

In the next step we define a unary predicate state_{x,i,s^N} for each $x \in \mathcal{X}$, each execution in $\widehat{M_k}$ identified by i, and each $s^N \in S^N$. Let us suppose that the final node of the self-composition of the CFG of the program p is n_{fi}, and that the result of the analysis corresponding to transition r, execution i and variable x is represented by predicate $\text{var}_{x,n_{fi},i,r}$. In order to realize the overapproximation of the states of $\widehat{M_k}$ as it is specified for $N_{\widehat{M_k},N_{\text{tr}(\text{NNF}(\neg\varphi))}}$, we generate the following implication for all variables x, executions i, and transitions $r = (s^N, \Psi, s^{N'})$:

$$\text{state}_{x,i,s^{N'}}(X) \Leftarrow \text{var}_{x,n_{fi},i,(s^N,\Psi,s^{N'})}(X). \tag{4.7}$$

Intuitively, implication (4.7) unifies the results of the analyses corresponding to the transition $(s^N, \Psi, s^{N'})$ of $N_{\text{tr}(\text{NNF}(\neg\varphi))}$, and identifies the values by the state $s^{N'}$. Based on implication (4.7) we can define the states of $N_{\widehat{M_k},N_{\text{tr}(\text{NNF}(\neg\varphi))}}$. Accordingly, a state $\widehat{\widehat{s}}^\times = ((\widehat{\widehat{s}}^0, ..., \widehat{\widehat{s}}^k), s^N)$ is defined as follows:

$$\forall x \in \mathcal{X}, 0 \leq i \leq k: \quad \widehat{\widehat{s}}^i(x) = \{\tau \mid \text{state}_{x,i,s^N}(\tau)\}$$

---
[1] Here, we overload the notation ρ. It stands for a transition function, and also for the set of transitions it enables. The transitions are represented as tuples.

However, in order to generate the complete state space of $N_{\widehat{M_k}, \widetilde{N_{\text{tr(NNF}(\neg\varphi))}}}$, additional implications are needed.

We define now the initial state. Let us suppose that the initial abstract value for each variable x is defined as the model of the unary predicate $\texttt{init}_x$. Therefore we define the following implication:

$$\texttt{state}_{x,i,s_0^N}(\texttt{X}) \Leftarrow \texttt{init}_x(\texttt{X}).$$

In our case, in the initial state of M the content of each variable is #. Therefore, we define for all $x \in \mathcal{X}$:

$$\texttt{init}_x(\texttt{\#}).$$

We also need to define the initial analysis information for the transitions. Here we rely on the description of the transition function $\widehat{\delta}$ presented in Section 4.4.1. Let us suppose that we would like to compute the successor state $(\widehat{\underline{s}}', s^{N'})$ of the transition $(\widehat{\underline{s}}, s^{N'}) \in \widehat{\delta}^\times(((\widehat{s}^0, \widehat{s}^1, ..., \widehat{s}^k), s^N), (\widehat{a}, \vartheta))$, where $s^{N'} \in \rho(s^N, \Psi)$. Since we overapproximate, we need to take into consideration all letters for which $(\widehat{a}, \vartheta) \models \bigwedge_{P \in \Psi} P$.

First, let us treat propositions of the form $y \triangle L_m$ in Ψ where $y \in \mathcal{X}_\mathcal{I}$. These constraints refer to the main run only, and not to alternative runs corresponding to hide operators. Note that, there can be multiple languages constraining the same variable. Let us suppose that the set of trees L_m is given by means of the predicate $\texttt{lang}_{L_m}$. As usual, node n_{in} stands for the initial node of the self-composition of the CFG of program p. We initialize each variable $y \in \mathcal{X}_\mathcal{I}$ of the main run the following way:

$$\texttt{var}_{y,n_{in},0,(s^N,\Psi,s^{N'})}(\texttt{X}) \Leftarrow \overbrace{\texttt{lang}_{L_1}(\texttt{X}), ..., \texttt{lang}_{L_l}(\texttt{X})}^{\forall (y \triangle L_m) \in \Psi}. \quad (4.8)$$

We initialize output variables in a similar way. The only difference is that the predecessor state needs to be taken into consideration as well. Therefore, we define for all $x \in \mathcal{X}_\mathcal{O}$:

$$\texttt{var}_{x,n_{in},0,(s^N,\Psi,s^{N'})}(\texttt{X}) \Leftarrow \texttt{state}_{x,0,s^N}(\texttt{X}), \overbrace{\texttt{lang}_{L_1}(\texttt{X}), ..., \texttt{lang}_{L_l}(\texttt{X})}^{\forall (x \triangle L_m) \in \Psi}. \quad (4.9)$$

By means of implications (4.8) and (4.9) we define the initial analysis information $d_0^0(x)$ for the analysis corresponding to the main run and to the transition $(s^N, \Psi, s^{N'})$ of $N_{\text{tr(NNF}(\neg\varphi))}$.

Now we define initial values for the analyses of alternative runs. Here we treat two cases based on whether $start^i \in \Psi$ or $\neg start^i \in \Psi$.

The case when $start^i \notin \Psi$ or $\neg start^i \in \Psi$. In this case we define the input variables for alternative runs exactly as we did for the original run. Accordingly, for all $0 < i \leq k$ and all $y \in \mathcal{X}_\mathcal{I}$ we define:

$$\texttt{var}_{y,n_{in},i,(s^N,\Psi,s^{N'})}(\texttt{X}) \Leftarrow \overbrace{\texttt{lang}_{L_1}(\texttt{X}), ..., \texttt{lang}_{L_l}(\texttt{X})}^{\forall (y \triangle L_m) \in \Psi}.$$

Now we treat two additional subcases based on whether $leak^i$ is a member of Ψ or not. Note that, transitions of Büchi automata $N_{\text{tr(NNF}(\neg\varphi))}$ constructed based

4.4. MODEL CHECKING SYSTEMS WITH INFINITE STATE SPACE 65

on our formulae $\text{tr}(\text{NNF}(\neg\varphi))$ do not have propositions of the form $\neg leak^i$. This is due to the properties of the formula (4.3) replacing leak operators.

- $leak^i \notin \Psi$. In this case we define for all $x \in \mathcal{X}_\mathcal{O}$:

$$\text{var}_{x,n_{in},i,(s^N,\Psi,s^{N'})}(\text{X}) \Leftarrow \text{state}_{x,i,s^N}(\text{X}).$$

- $leak^i \in \Psi$. We define for all $x \in \mathcal{X}_\mathcal{O}$ the following implication:

$$\text{var}_{x,n_{in},i,(s^N,\Psi,s^{N'})}(\text{X}) \Leftarrow \text{state}_{x,i,s^N}(\text{X}), \text{secret}(\text{X}).$$

In this case we explicitly make sure that the value of x has at least one leaf labeled $\star$ using predicate secret as it has been defined by implication (3.7). This is a key implication of our analysis. In this case, the transition can only take place, if there are potentially confidential values in the variable. However, this transition is part of an automaton generated based on a negated formula having hide operators $\mathcal{H}^i_{H^i,O^i}\psi$. Therefore, if there are no leaves labeled $\star$, then no leakage can happen at this transition. Furthermore, if $leak^i$ can never be satisfied, then the corresponding hide operator is in turn satisfied.

The case when $start^i \in \Psi$ **or** $\neg start^i \notin \Psi$**.** We allow the initialization of a new alternative run also in the case, when it is not explicitly forbidden by Ψ. Let us suppose now that there is a hide operator $\mathcal{H}^i_{H^i,O^i}\psi$ in the formula we check. Now we treat input variables $y \in \mathcal{X}_\mathcal{I}$ that are in the domain of H^i. According to Step 2 in the description of the transition function $\hat{\delta}$ in Section 4.4.1, now we need to compute a value $h_{y,i}$. Let us suppose that there are multiple propositions $y \vartriangle L_m$ in Ψ constraining the value of y. The value $h_{y,i}$ is the set of public views for which there is a corresponding document in the concretization of the intersection of the languages L_m. We cannot use Horn clauses in order to compute this. Therefore, we compute the intersection of the languages L_m using the $\mathcal{H}_1$ solver [60] resulting in a finite tree automaton. Based on the tree automaton we construct a regular tree grammar [22], and carry out the algorithm described in Section 4.4.1 in order to compute the grammar for $h_{y,i}$. Finally, we define the set of implications, the model of which is exactly the set of trees $h_{y,i}$. Let us suppose that the result is presented by means of the predicate $\mathbf{h}_{y,i}$. Accordingly, the variable y in the alternative run i is defined by the following implications:

$$\begin{aligned}\text{var}_{y,n_{in},i,(s^N,\Psi,s^{N'})}(\text{X}) &\Leftarrow \overbrace{\text{lang}_{L_1}(\text{X}),...,\text{lang}_{L_l}(\text{X})}^{\forall(y\vartriangle L_m)\in\Psi}. \\ \text{var}_{y,n_{in},i,(s^N,\Psi,s^{N'})}(\text{X}) &\Leftarrow \mathbf{h}_{y,i}(\text{X}).\end{aligned} \qquad (4.10)$$

In case of variables $y \notin \text{dom}(H^i)$ no secret is introduced. Therefore we define:

$$\text{var}_{y,n_{in},i,(s^N,\Psi,s^{N'})}(\text{X}) \Leftarrow \overbrace{\text{lang}_{L_1}(\text{X}),...,\text{lang}_{L_l}(\text{X})}^{\forall(y\vartriangle L_m)\in\Psi}.$$

Again, we treat two additional subcases based on whether $leak^i$ is a member of Ψ or not. The difference to the previous case is, that output variables are now initialized based on the original run identified by index 0.

- $\textit{leak}^i \notin \Psi$. In this case we define for all $x \in \mathcal{X}_\mathcal{O}$:

$$\texttt{var}_{x,n_{in},i,(s^N,\Psi,s^{N'})}(\texttt{X}) \Leftarrow \texttt{state}_{x,0,s^N}(\texttt{X}).$$

- $\textit{leak}^i \in \Psi$. We define for all $x \in \mathcal{X}_\mathcal{O}$ the following implication:

$$\texttt{var}_{x,n_{in},i,(s^N,\Psi,s^{N'})}(\texttt{X}) \Leftarrow \texttt{state}_{x,0,s^N}(\texttt{X}),\texttt{secret}(\texttt{X}).$$

In this case we explicitly make sure that the considered values have leaves labeled $\star$ using predicate $\texttt{secret}$ as it has been defined by implication (3.7). Note that, the condition of the implication above never holds. In our model there are no values having label $\star$ in the original run.

The models of predicates $\texttt{state}_{x,i,s^N}$ yield the state space of $N_{\widehat{\widehat{M_k},N_{\text{tr(NNF}(\neg\varphi))}}}$. However, we still need to identify the transitions. We define the nullary predicate $\texttt{trans}_{(s^N,\Psi,s^{N'})}$ that holds if the transition of $N_{\widehat{\widehat{M_k},N_{\text{tr(NNF}(\neg\varphi))}}}$ corresponding to the transition $(s^N,\Psi,s^{N'})$ of $N_{\text{tr(NNF}(\neg\varphi))}$ can take place using the following implication:

$$\texttt{trans}_{(s^N,\Psi,s^{N'})} \Leftarrow \overbrace{\texttt{var}_{x,n_{in},i,(s^N,\Psi,s^{N'})}(\texttt{X}_{x,in,i})}^{\forall x \in \mathcal{X} \text{ and } 0 \leq i \leq k},\dots, \overbrace{\texttt{var}_{x,n_{fi},i,(s^N,\Psi,s^{N'})}(\texttt{X}_{x,fi,i})}^{\forall x \in \mathcal{X} \text{ and } 0 \leq i \leq k},\dots \quad (4.11)$$

According to implication (4.11), $\texttt{trans}_{(s^N,\Psi,s^{N'})}$ holds if all variables are defined for the original run and all alternative runs modeled by $\widehat{M_k}$ at the initial n_{in} and final n_{fi} nodes of the corresponding analyses. Now we can define the transition function $\widehat{\widehat{\delta}}^\times$ of the automaton $N_{\widehat{\widehat{M_k},N_{\text{tr(NNF}(\neg\varphi))}}}$. $(\widehat{\widehat{\underline{s}}}',s^{N'}) \in \widehat{\widehat{\delta}}^\times((\widehat{\widehat{\underline{s}}},s^N),(\widehat{a},\vartheta))$ holds, if and only if $\texttt{trans}_{(s^N,\Psi,s^{N'})}$ holds and for all $x \in \mathcal{X}$ we have that $\widehat{a}(x) = \bigcap_{(x \triangle L_m) \in \Psi} L_m$

Theorem 12. $L(N_{\widehat{\widehat{M_k},N_{\text{tr(NNF}(\neg\varphi))}}}) = \emptyset$ *entails that* $L(N_{\widehat{\widehat{M_k},N_{\text{tr(NNF}(\neg\varphi))}}}) = \emptyset$.

For the proof, please refer to Section 6.3.

Theorem 12 assures us that abstract machines $N_{\widehat{\widehat{M_k},N_{\text{tr(NNF}(\neg\varphi))}}}$ possess the property, which is needed for verification.

4.4.3 Computing the Result

The goal is to construct a Büchi automaton based on $N_{\widehat{\widehat{M_k},N_{\text{tr(NNF}(\neg\varphi))}}}$, the emptiness of which entails the emptiness of $N_{\widehat{\widehat{M_k},N_{\text{tr(NNF}(\neg\varphi))}}}$, and which can be checked with an already implemented algorithm. This automaton, the "distilled" automaton, is constructed based on $N_{\text{tr(NNF}(\neg\varphi))}$ and $N_{\widehat{\widehat{M_k},N_{\text{tr(NNF}(\neg\varphi))}}}$. Given the implications in Section 4.4.2, we "distill" the automaton $N_{\text{tr(NNF}(\neg\varphi))} = (S^N, \mathcal{P}(Prop), s_0^N, \rho, F)$ by removing those transitions from ρ, the corresponding transition of which cannot be taken in $N_{\widehat{\widehat{M_k},N_{\text{tr(NNF}(\neg\varphi))}}}$. A transition of $N_{\widehat{\widehat{M_k},N_{\text{tr(NNF}(\neg\varphi))}}}$ cannot take place if the corresponding predicate $\texttt{trans}_{(s^N,\Psi,s^{N'})}$ does not hold.

4.5. IMPLEMENTATION

Now we define the distilled automaton $N^*_{\text{tr}(\text{NNF}(\neg\varphi))} = (S^N, \mathcal{P}(Prop), s_0^N, \rho^*, F)$ based on $N_{\text{tr}(\text{NNF}(\neg\varphi))} = (S^N, \mathcal{P}(Prop), s_0^N, \rho, F)$. The only difference between the two automata is in their transition functions. $s^{N\prime} \in \rho^*(s^N, \Psi)$ holds if $s^{N\prime} \in \rho(s^N, \Psi)$ and $\text{trans}_{(s^N, \Psi, s^{N\prime})}$ hold. Now we enumerate the transitions in $N_{\text{tr}(\text{NNF}(\neg\varphi))}$ and remove those on which $\text{trans}_{(s^N, \Psi, s^{N\prime})}$ does not hold. Now $N^*_{\text{tr}(\text{NNF}(\neg\varphi))}$ is the usual nondeterministic Büchi automaton, the emptiness of which can be checked according to [72].

Theorem 13. *Let us consider the transition system M and the formula φ of the logic Restricted SecLTL. We suppose that $N^*_{\text{tr}(\text{NNF}(\neg\varphi))}$ is the corresponding "distilled" automaton. In this case $L(N^*_{\text{tr}(\text{NNF}(\neg\varphi))}) = \emptyset$ entails that $M \models \varphi$.*

For the proof, please, refer to Section 6.3.

According to Theorem 13, the emptiness of the distilled automaton entails that the system adheres to the corresponding information flow policy. Furthermore, there are already implemented tools, e.g, GOAL [72] for deciding whether the language of a Büchi automaton is empty.

In the next sections we describe the practical implementation of the model checker and demonstrate its usability.

4.5 Implementation

This section describes the practical implementation of the model checking approach introduced in Section 4.4.

4.5.1 Transforming Formulae into Büchi Automata

We have extended the LTL2Buchi translator implemented at the NASA Ames research Center [35], in order to transform formulae of the logic Restricted SecLTL into nondeterministic Büchi automata. In the previous sections, a formula was negated first, then its negation normal form was constructed, and then leak operators have been replaced with a dedicated LTL subformula (4.3). For practical reasons, in the implementation we do it differently. First, hide operators are replaced with an other subformula. Therefore, if we would like to check the validity of the formula φ on a model, then each subformula of the form $\mathcal{H}^i_{H^i, O^i} \psi'$ is replaced by the following:

$$\neg start^i \vee (\neg leak^i \mathcal{W} \psi') \tag{4.12}$$

By negating (4.12) we obtain:

$$start^i \wedge \left((\neg leak^i \wedge \neg \psi') \mathcal{U} (leak^i \wedge \neg \psi') \right) \tag{4.13}$$

Essentially, therefore, leak operators of the form $\mathcal{L}^i_{H_i, O_i} \psi$ are replaced in the implementation with:

$$start^i \wedge \left((\neg leak^i \wedge \psi) \mathcal{U} (leak^i \wedge \psi) \right) \tag{4.14}$$

From now on, we denote the transformation of the implementation by tr'. It replaces leak operators of the form $\mathcal{L}^i_{H^i, O^i}(\psi)$ in $\text{NNF}(\neg\varphi)$ with (4.14). The application of tr′ is correct because of the following reasons. In the implementation, the construction of the product automaton $N_{M_k, N_{\text{tr}(\text{NNF}(\neg\varphi))}}$ corresponding to the model M and the formula φ differs to some extent to that discussed in Section 4.3. Let us regard the transition $(s^{*\prime}, s^{N\prime}) \in \delta^\times((s^*, s^N), (a, \vartheta))$ of $N_{M_k, N_{\text{tr}(\text{NNF}(\neg\varphi))}}$, where the corresponding transition of $N_{\text{tr}(\text{NNF}(\neg\varphi))}$ is $s^{N\prime} \in \rho(s^N, \Psi)$. In the implementation, $start^i \notin \vartheta$ if $start^i \notin \Psi$. In other words, M_k does not start a new alternative run corresponding to a hide operator nondeterministically, if it is not explicitly prescribed by the Büchi automaton $N_{\text{tr}(\text{NNF}(\neg\varphi))}$. As a result, each $\neg start^i$ can be removed from the replacement of leak operators. Let us denote the product automaton with the new semantics by $N'_{M_k, N_{\text{tr}'(\text{NNF}(\neg\varphi))}}$. The following theorem indicates that we can use the product automaton $N'_{M_k, N_{\text{tr}'(\text{NNF}(\neg\varphi))}}$ for verification.

Theorem 14. $L(N'_{M_k, N_{\text{tr}'(\text{NNF}(\neg\varphi))}}) = \emptyset$ *entails that* $L(N_{M_k, N_{\text{tr}'(\text{NNF}(\neg\varphi))}}) = \emptyset$.

For the proof, please, refer to Section 6.3.

4.5.2 The Verification Procedure

We have implemented the model checker in OCaml. It was possible to decompose the model checking procedure into many subproblems, for the majority of which there has already been an implementation. Therefore, the model checker integrates many already existing tools and contains the implementation of missing functionalities.

For the verification of a model, a dedicated directory needs to be opened. This directory will contain several files describing the model, the property to be verified, the regular grammars corresponding to sets of documents, the Horn clauses implementing the analysis of Section 3.3, etc. Now we go over the verification process, and discuss the emerging subproblems with their solutions. We refer to the Restricted SecLTL formula to be verified by φ.

1. In this step we construct the Büchi automaton for the formula to be verified. The formula needs to be stored in the file `property.ltl`. In the first step of the verification, hide operators are replaced with (4.12), and then the formula is negated. Next, the corresponding Büchi automaton is constructed. We have used an extension of the LTL2Buchi translator implemented at the NASA Ames research Center [35] in order to carry out this step. The XML representation of the resulting automaton is written into the file `property.xml`. We denote this automaton by $N_{\text{tr}'(\text{NNF}(\neg\varphi))}$.

2. In this step additional grammars are generated. The program to be verified needs to be stored in the file `workflow.wf`. This file contains the set of binary alphabet elements Σ_2 that can possible occur in the values too. In this step, two grammars are constructed. One generates the universal language, and the other generates the set of secret-dependent documents over the binary alphabet Σ_2 and nullary alphabet $\{bv, \star, \#\}$. The first grammar is stored in the file `anything.inputLang`, and the second is stored in `secret_dep.inputLang`. The purpose of these languages is the following. There are cases, when a transition of the Büchi automaton $N_{\text{tr}'(\text{NNF}(\neg\varphi))}$ does not pose constraints on an input variable. Still a grammar for the corresponding value needs to be defined. The corresponding language is

4.5. IMPLEMENTATION

going to be the intersection of the universal language and the complement of the set of secret-dependent documents.

3. In this step all grammars are complemented. The languages that the user refers to in φ need to be represented in the form of Horn clauses, and need to be stored in files having extension inputLang. In this step we complement all grammars stored in files with extension inputLang. The Binary Tree Automata Library written by Emmanuel Filiot [32] is used for the purpose. The complemented grammars are output in the form of Horn clauses into files having the same names as the original ones with the postfix .complemented appended to them.

4. In this step the input grammars for transitions are computed. The transitions of $N_{\text{tr}'(\text{NNF}(\neg\varphi))}$ are enumerated and the conditions examined that they pose. For each transition of the form $s^{N'} \in \rho(s^N, \Psi)$, and for each variable $x \in \mathcal{X}$ occurring in the program, we compute the intersection of the grammars L, where $x \vartriangle L \in \Psi$ occurs. The constraints of transitions Ψ are always extended with the universal language and the complement of the language of secret-dependent documents. This resulting intersection language is the effective input language of the variable x in the original run. The result is written into a file with extension intersection. The computation is carried out by the $\mathcal{H}_1$ solver [60].

5. In this step, input grammars for alternative runs are computed. Let us suppose that there are subformulae of the form $\mathcal{H}^i_{H^i, O^i} \psi$ in φ. Now, the transitions of $N_{\text{tr}'(\text{NNF}(\neg\varphi))}$ are examined again. For each transition having constraints of the form $start^i \in \Psi$, grammars are constructed describing the input values of variables of the corresponding alternative runs. The subset $h_{x,i}$ of $H^i(x)$ is computed[2] for each input variable x which is a member of $\text{dom}(H^i)$. $h_{x,i}$ contains public views only for trees that are contained by the effective input language as computed by the previous step. Note that in Section 4.4, two implications (4.10) have been used to assign the effective input language and the corresponding set of public views to a variable. In the implementation, we unify the corresponding languages separately. In the next step, therefore, the grammar of $h_{x,i}$ is unified with the effective input language for x. The resulting grammar is called *combined grammar*. It is required that the grammar of $H^i(x)$ is stored in a file having extension secGram. The combined grammar is stored in a file having extension combined. This step of the model checking process is carried out by the OCaml implementation.

6. A separate set of Horn clauses implementing the program analysis of Section 3.3 is generated for the original run of the system and for each of the alternative runs corresponding to hide operators. This set of clauses is written into the file called h1.p. Additionally, the contents of all files describing grammars are copied into this file. Because there could be name clashes among the predicates of grammar descriptions, the actual file names are prepended to them. An additional implication of the form

---

[2] $h_{x,i}$ is computed according to Step 2. of the construction of the abstract transition system as it is described in Section 4.4.1.

of (4.11) is generated for each transition of $N_{tr'(\mathsf{NNF}(\neg\varphi))}$ in order to check its fireability. These implications are also written into h1.p.

7. In this step, the "distilled" automaton is constructed. The transitions of $N_{tr'(\mathsf{NNF}(\neg\varphi))}$ are enumerated and their fireability is determined based on the corresponding implication of the form (4.11). The models of predicates in h1.p are computed by the $\mathcal{H}_1$ solver described in [60]. The transitions of $N_{tr'(\mathsf{NNF}(\neg\varphi))}$ are removed that cannot fire, and the distilled automaton is written into the file properties_processed.xml. The XML manipulation is carried out using the XML-Light library [70].

8. The distilled automaton $N^*_{tr'(\mathsf{NNF}(\neg\varphi))}$ is checked for emptiness using the GOAL tool [72].

The last step delivers the final result of the analysis as well. If GOAL reports $N^*_{tr'(\mathsf{NNF}(\neg\varphi))}$ to be empty, then $M \models \varphi$ is proved. In the other case we have no answer. One reason is that abstract interpretation is involved in the verification process. In this case it is possible that the property does not hold. However, it is also possible that the property holds, but the verification algorithm was too imprecise to prove it.

4.6 Case Studies

In this section we describe two examples that we used to test the implementation of the model checker. First, we verified the information flow policy (4.2) on the model corresponding to the program in Listing 2.1 extended with the description of variables and the alphabet. Note that it is impossible to verify the program without taking the temporal aspect into consideration, or restricting the value of variable toAuthors as it has been done in Section 3.3.1. The reason is that the database containing secrets is assigned to the public variable toAuthors at line 3. Therefore, either the value of variable phase needs to be chosen so that the conditional expression at line 2 is always false, or when it is true, then the temporal information flow policy needs to have released the secret by that time. Considering the policy in (4.2) the latter is the case. In (4.2) the condition of information release is that the value of variable phase has root labeled notify, which coincides with the branching condition at line 2.

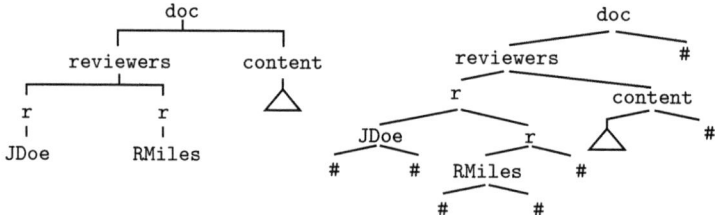

Figure 4.2: A document submission in unranked form on the left and in binary form on the right.

Now we discuss an other case study, on which we tested the model checking algorithm. We consider an other module of the imaginary conference manage-

4.6. CASE STUDIES

ment system. Using this module, submissions are uploaded together with the list of reviewers who are allowed to read the submission. Figure 4.2 illustrates a submission like that in unranked and in binary form. The submissions are then assigned to reviewers that appear in the list. In our example there are three reviewers, John Doe (abbreviated `JDoe`), John Styles (abbreviated `JStyles`) and Richard Miles (abbreviated `RMiles`).

```
1   input: phase, indoc;
2   output: toJDoe, toRMiles, toJStyles;
3   alphabet: upload, release, doc, reviewers,
4            JDoe, RMiles, r, content;
5
6      empty:=#;
7      if top(phase) = init then {
8         toJDoe := listElement(empty,empty);
9         toRMiles := listElement(empty,empty);
10        toJStyles := listElement(empty,empty);
11        allSubmissions := listElement(empty,empty);
12     } else {
13        if top(phase) = release then {
14           toJDoe := allSubmissions;
15           toRMiles := allSubmissions;
16           toJStyles := allSubmissions;
17        } else {
18           // top(phase) = upload
19           // Here are the submissions uploaded together
20           // with the list of reviewers, who are allowed to
21           // read them.
22           allSubmissions := listElement(indoc,allSubmissions);
23           reviewers := indoc/1;
24           r := reviewers/1;
25           last :=false(empty,empty);
26           while top(last) = false do {
27              allowedRev := r/1;
28              if top(allowedRev) = JDoe then {
29                 toJDoe := listElement(indoc,toJDoe);
30              } else {
31                 skip;
32              };
33              if top(allowedRev) = RMiles then {
34                 toRMiles := listElement(indoc,toRMiles);
35                 ///////////////////////////////////
36                 // Uncomment the line below
37                 // to make the property invalid.
38                 // toJStyles := listElement(indoc,toJStyles);
39              } else {
40                 skip;
41              };
42              if top(allowedRev) = JStyles then {
43                 toJStyles := listElement(indoc,toJStyles);
44              } else {
45                 skip;
46              };
47              r:=r/2;
```

```
48                if top(r)=# then {
49                    last:=true(empty,empty);
50                } else {
51                    skip;
52       }; }; }; };
```
Listing 4.1: A module of the conference management system where submissions are uploaded.

The program implementing the module is shown by Listing 4.1. Similarly to the previous example, the functionality of the module is governed by *phases*. The actual phase is given by the label of the root of the tree in variable **phase**. An execution of the system consists of three phases. First, an initialization step is needed, where the phase is **init**. Then, several transitions in the phase **upload** follow, and finally, a **release** phase is expected with a single step. During the upload phase documents are uploaded and assigned to reviewers. In the final release phase all of the uploaded documents are disclosed to all reviewers. We suppose that the discussion about the acceptance of the papers takes place before the release phase, and therefore, the potential conflicts of interest between authors and reviewers becomes irrelevant after that.

The piece of code in Listing 4.1 works the following way. During the upload phase, the relevant part of the execution of each transition starts at line 22. First, the input document in variable **indoc** is appended to the list in variable **allSubmissions** containing all of the submissions uploaded so far. The loop at line 26 assigns the document to the allowed reviewers. There is an iteration for each element of the list of allowed reviewers, where the document is appended to the lists of the appropriate reviewer. In the release phase on the other hand, all of the uploaded submissions stored in variable **allSubmissions** are copied to the output variables of the reviewers.

We would like to verify that a document only gets sorted into the list of a specific reviewer, if his name appears in the list of allowed reviewers. For the formalization of the requirement we need to be able to express that the contents of submissions are secret. In this example this is done by the predicate **contentSec**, which accepts binary trees similar to that in Figure 4.2, where the subtree of the content is exchanged with a single leaf labeled $\star$. The requirement from the point of view of John Styles can be formalized by the following formula:

$$\Box\Big[\texttt{indoc} \mathbin{\triangle} \texttt{allowedJS} \lor \mathcal{H}_{\{\texttt{indoc}\mapsto\texttt{contentSec}\},\{\texttt{toJStyles}\}}(\texttt{phase} \mathbin{\triangle} \texttt{release})\Big]$$
(4.15)

Let us suppose that the predicate **allowedJS** accepts document trees, where John Styles is among the allowed reviewers. The formula (4.15) is an example, where secrecy is specified conditionally based on the value of a variable. The formula holds on the model in two cases. One of the cases is when the secret does not influence the variable **toJStyles**. The other case is when John Styles is among the allowed reviewers as it is specified by the predicate **allowedJS**. In the latter case, of course, the noninterference specified by the hide operator does not need to hold.

However, as it is the case by many practical applications, in order to execute the program in Listing 4.1 successfully, the environment also has to satisfy some conditions. The program in Listing 4.1 is not prepared to handle an arbitrary sequence of input values. It assumes, that the first phase of the execution consists

4.6. CASE STUDIES

of an initialization step, and that the value of variable indoc is always a valid input document. Using Restricted SecLTL we can also incorporate assumptions of the verified model regarding the environment into the specification. These assumptions can be formalized as implications as the formula below exemplifies:

$$\texttt{phase} \mathbin{\triangle} \texttt{init} \Rightarrow \Box \Big[\texttt{indoc} \mathbin{\triangle} \texttt{doc} \Rightarrow$$
$$\Big(\texttt{indoc} \mathbin{\triangle} \texttt{allowedJS} \lor \mathcal{H}_{\{\texttt{indoc} \mapsto \texttt{contentSec}\}, \{\texttt{toJStyles}\}} (\texttt{phase} \mathbin{\triangle} \texttt{release}) \Big) \Big]$$
(4.16)

Here, we assume that the predicate doc accepts the set of valid documents, and init holds on values having root labeled with init. The intuitive meaning of the formula (4.16) is that the desired secrecy only needs to hold in case the value of the variable indoc is a valid input document. Additionally, we are only interested in the behavior of the system, when it is initialized first. This is expressed by the first implication, the left hand side of which constrains the value of variable phase. However, a formula $a \Rightarrow b$ equals to $\neg a \lor b$, and Restricted SecLTL does not support negation. Since regular tree grammars can be complemented, we can still express the requirements of (4.16) in Restricted SecLTL:

$$\varphi = \texttt{phase} \mathbin{\triangle} \overline{\texttt{init}} \lor \Box \Big[\texttt{indoc} \mathbin{\triangle} \overline{\texttt{doc}} \lor$$
$$\Big(\texttt{indoc} \mathbin{\triangle} \texttt{allowedJS} \lor \mathcal{H}_{\{\texttt{indoc} \mapsto \texttt{contentSec}\}, \{\texttt{toJStyles}\}} (\texttt{phase} \mathbin{\triangle} \texttt{release}) \Big) \Big]$$
(4.17)

Figure 4.3 illustrates the Büchi automaton constructed by GOAL based on φ in (4.17). The distilled automaton corresponding to the model and the formula is shown in Figure 4.4. As the figure illustrates, the accepting state is unreachable. Therefore, the automaton has no accepting run, and the specification is proved to be valid. We also carried out an experiment to find out what happens, if the instruction at line 38 is commented out. In this case the program violates the property of (4.17), because John Styles can receive documents also in the situation e.g., when only Richard Miles is entitled to read. The corresponding distilled automaton is shown in Figure 4.5. As we can see, this automaton has accepting runs, therefore, the property φ could not be proved on the system.

Note that, the labels of edges of the automata in Figures 4.3, 4.4 and 4.5 have been modified for the sake of readability. It is necessary for the implementation that these labels are machine-readable. The machine-readable labels have the same meanings as the ones in the Figures, but they are much more difficult to comprehend.

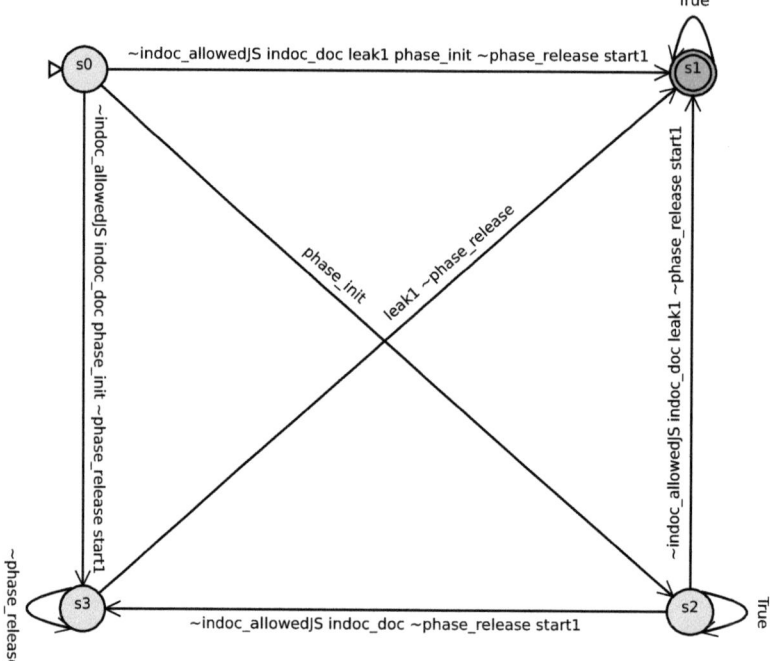

Figure 4.3: The Büchi automaton $N_{tr'(\textsf{NNF}(\neg\varphi))}$ constructed by GOAL based on the formula in (4.17). The initial state s0 is marked with a triangle, and the accepting state s1 is marked with two rings. Propositions of the form variable △ grammar are written as variable_grammar, and ∼ stands for negation.

4.6. CASE STUDIES

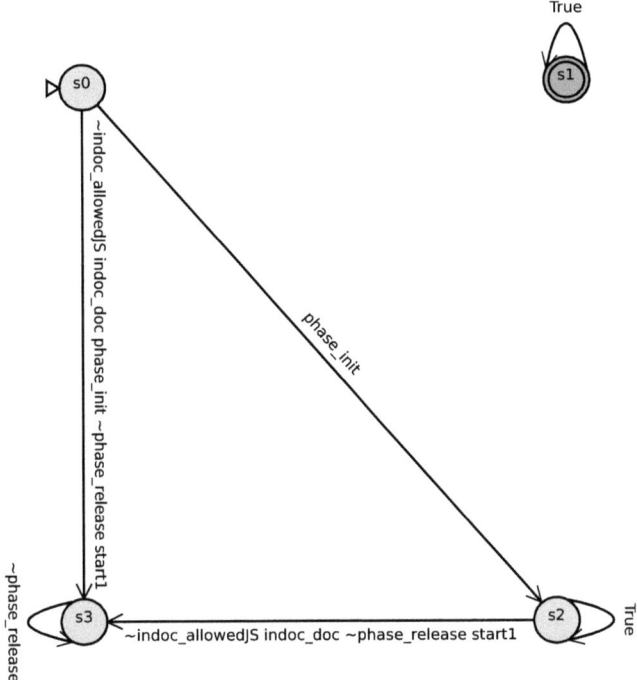

Figure 4.4: The distilled automaton corresponding to the formula (4.17) and the model on Listing 4.1.

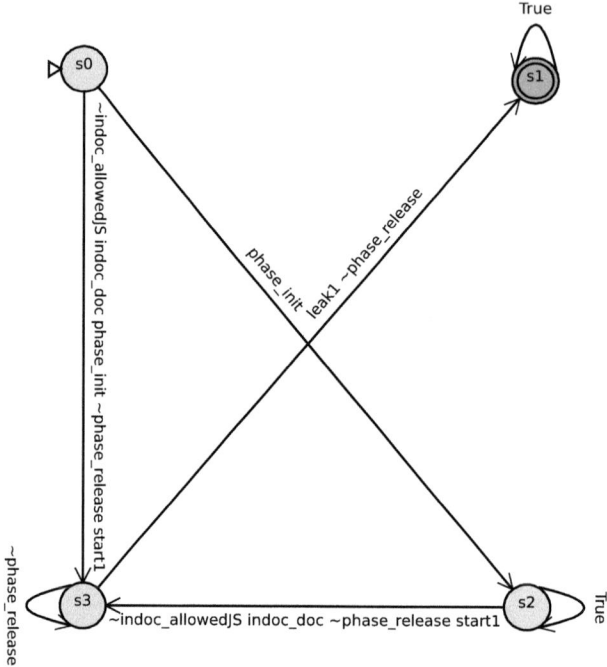

Figure 4.5: The distilled automaton corresponding to the formula (4.17) and the model in Listing 4.1, when an error is injected by the instruction at line 38.

4.7 Related Work

In [28] an automata-theoretic approach was presented for the verification of finite-state systems against temporal information flow properties specified in SecLTL. The logic Restricted SecLTL used in this work is a modification of SecLTL, where negation is not allowed. Therefore, Restricted SecLTL is a minimalistic extension of positive LTL specifically oriented towards information flow. It thus provides a more natural specification framework than previous approaches to combining information flow and temporal properties. These include the usage of epistemic logic to specify noninterference [31, 9] and the characterization of observational determinism in CTL* and in the polyadic modal μ-calculus[44] using the self-composed system. Our model checking algorithm can be seen as an extension of the idea to reduce the information flow analysis to the analysis of the self-composition of the model [13, 71, 8, 21]. Unlike previous works however, our technique is not bound to *two* (or any fixed number of) copies of the system, but can be applied to properties over an arbitrary amount of copies (specified via multiple hide operators). Sabelfeld et al. [67] investigate the principles and dimensions of declassification. Restricted SecLTL addresses the dimensions "What" and "When" among others, because the conditional declassification of specific pieces of information can be specified.

Chapter 5
Conclusion

In this work we have shown three methods to analyze information flow properties of tree-manipulating programs. Information flow properties are composed in terms of public views, which are the public upper parts of trees not containing confidential values. Therefore, our algorithms can cope with information flow properties that assign different security levels to different subtrees in a single document.

Chapter 2 introduced a runtime monitor that can enforce the secrecy of subtrees during the execution. The key idea of the approach is to apply a generalized constant propagation in order to compute the public views of the results of branching constructs depending on secret.

In Chapter 3 we have presented a general approach for statically analyzing 2-hypersafety properties. The approach is based on finding appropriate self-compositions of control flow graphs. Our algorithm to construct quality self-compositions is completely deterministic and uses the Robust Tree Edit Distance [62] measure in order to align similar program fragments with each other. We have applied our technique to analyze information flow properties of programs manipulating semi-structured data.

Our results open many directions for further research, e.g.:

- In our analysis, different program variables are treated separately. Extra precision, perhaps may be obtained by using predicates that relate the contents of different variables in states. The resulting clauses then may no longer be members of the class $\mathcal{H}_1$. Still, one may apply a Horn clause based approach, but use a first order theorem prover such as, e.g., SPASS [80] as a back-end, instead of an $\mathcal{H}_1$ solver.

- The language we have considered in this work does not support procedure calls. It still remains an open question, how the Horn clause formulation of the analysis can be optimally extended also to recursive procedures.

- As the theory of the merge over all twin computations solution and the construction of self-compositions of control flow graphs is independent of specific programming languages and semantics, it is possible to apply our framework to additional programming languages as well.

The solutions in Chapter 2 and Chapter 3 do not consider information flow policies changing in time. Therefore, in Chapter 4 we have presented a method for verifying reactive systems with possibly infinite state space against requirements specified in Restricted SecLTL. We have integrated the abstract interpretation technique of Chapter 3 with the model checking algorithm for SecLTL [28], which yields a powerful verification method. The resulting model checker is applicable to infinite state reactive systems manipulating document trees and specifications capturing the interplay between information flow and functional properties in a temporal context.

Chapter 6

Proofs

6.1 Proofs for Chapter 2

Lemma 1. *Let us consider the program $c_1;...;c_n$, where $n \geq 0$. If for each i and D_i there exists a D_{i+1} so that $\langle c_i(m), D_i \rangle \to_\mu^* D_{i+1}$ then $\langle (c_1;...;c_n)(m), D_1 \rangle \to_\mu^* D_{n+1}$.*

Proof. If $n = 0$, then $p = \varepsilon$ and the result follows. If $n > 0$, we prove inductively on the number of steps the rule MS is applied. About c_1 we know that there exists a D_2 so that $\langle c_1(m), D_1 \rangle \to_\mu^* D_2$. So for this reason we can apply rule MS on program $c_1;...;c_n$. We have $\langle (c_1;...;c_n)(m), D_1 \rangle \to_\mu \langle (c_2;...;c_n)(m), D_2 \rangle$.
We suppose that there is a D_{i-1} so that:

$$\langle (c_1;...;c_n)(m), D_1 \rangle \to_\mu^* \langle c_{i-1};...;c_n, D_{i-1} \rangle$$

We know that for each D_{i-1} there exists a D_i so that $\langle c_{i-1}(m), D_{i-1} \rangle \to_\mu^* D_i$. Using rule MS, we have: $\langle (c_{i-1};...;c_n)(m), D_{i-1} \rangle \to_\mu \langle (c_i;...;c_n)(m), D_i \rangle$. So we have $\langle (c_1;...;c_n)(m), D_1 \rangle \to_\mu^* \langle (c_i;...;c_n)(m), D_i \rangle$. This reasoning is valid for any i and specifically for n too, so the statement is proved. □

Lemma 2. *The preorder of trees has the ascending chain condition.*

Proof. In this proof the set Σ_2 stands for the binary alphabet elements, and Σ_0 for the nullary ones without $\star$. Furthermore τ/π denotes the subtree of the tree τ at position π.

Let us suppose that $\tau_1 \sqsubseteq \tau_2$, $\tau_1 \neq \tau_2$ and there is no τ_3 such that $\tau_1 \sqsubseteq \tau_3 \sqsubseteq \tau_2$. In this case there are the following possible differences between τ_1 and τ_2:

1. There is one position π for which $\tau_1(\pi) \neq \tau_2(\pi)$ but in all other positions ν it is true that $\tau_1(\nu) = \tau_2(\nu)$. In this case, $\tau_1(\pi) \in \Sigma_0$ and $\tau_2(\pi) = \star$.

2. There is one position π among those positions ν for which $\tau_1(\nu) \in \Sigma_2$ so that $\tau_1(\pi) \neq \tau_2(\pi)$. For all other ν like that it is true that $\tau_1(\nu) = \tau_2(\nu)$. Furthermore, $\tau_1/\pi = \alpha(\star, \star)$ for some alphabet element α, and $\tau_2/\pi = \star$.

Our statement is that if there is an ascending sequence of trees $\tau_0 \sqsubseteq \tau_1 \sqsubseteq ...$ then there exists a finite number n so that for each $i \geq n$ it is true that $\tau_i = \tau_n$.

Let us collect the information on the number of different node types in a tree τ into a tuple $(n_b, n_u, n_\star)$, where the members are the number of binary nodes, the number of nullary nodes, and the number of nodes labeled $\star$ respectively. n_u does not contain nodes labeled $\star$. Because of the properties of a binary tree we know, that for each tree $n_b + 1 = n_u + n_\star$.

So if there are two trees τ_1 and τ_2 for which it is true that $\tau_1 \sqsubseteq \tau_2$, $\tau_1 \neq \tau_2$, and there is no τ_3 such that $\tau_1 \sqsubseteq \tau_3 \sqsubseteq \tau_2$ then we can say the following about the tuples belonging to them:

1) $n_b^{\tau_2} = n_b^{\tau_1}$, $n_u^{\tau_2} - 1 = n_u^{\tau_1}$ and $n_\star^{\tau_2} = n_\star^{\tau_1} + 1$. Or

2) $n_b^{\tau_2} = n_b^{\tau_1} - 1$, $n_u^{\tau_2} = n_u^{\tau_1}$ and $n_\star^{\tau_2} = n_\star^{\tau_1} - 1$.

The top element of the preorder is the tree $\tau = \star$, with tuple $(0, 0, 1)$. Accordingly, if we have a tree τ_0 with tuple $(n_b^{\tau_0}, n_u^{\tau_0}, n_\star^{\tau_0})$, it takes at the most $n = n_u + n_b$ steps for an ascending chain to arrive at the tree $\star$.

$\square$

Lemma 3. *For all programs p and monitor states D there exists another monitor state D' so that $\langle p(m), D \rangle \rightarrow_\mu^* D'$. In other words, the generalized constant propagation always terminates.*

Proof. First we prove the statement on commands of the form while b do $\{p\}$ and if b then $\{p_{tt}\}$ else $\{p_{ff}\}$ inductively on the maximal number of such commands on any root-leaf path of the abstract syntax tree.

0 In this case the program is either one assignment, or a sequence of assignments.

Let us consider one assignment. If $D \in \{\top, \bot, \notmid\}$ then the rule MCE is applied on the monitor state and $D = D'$. If $D \notin \{\top, \bot, \notmid\}$ then the rule MA is applied. Since the denotation function $\mathcal{M}[\![x\!:=\!e]\!]^\sharp$ is a total function, the assignment always has a resulting monitor state.

If the program is a sequence of assignments then termination follows from Lemma 1 and from the above statement.

i In this case we suppose that in the programs p, p_{tt} and p_{ff} there are maximally $i - 1$ if and while constructs on any root-leaf path of the abstract syntax tree. We suppose that these programs terminate. In other words there exists a D' for any D so that $\langle p(m), D \rangle \rightarrow_\mu^* D'$, $\langle p_{tt}(m), D \rangle \rightarrow_\mu^* D'$ and $\langle p_{ff}(m), D \rangle \rightarrow_\mu^* D'$. There are two cases: Either the program is a command if b then $\{p_{tt}\}$ else $\{p_{ff}\}$ or while b do $\{p\}$. We treat these cases separately.

– if: The program is of the form if b then $\{p_{tt}\}$ else $\{p_{ff}\}$. If $D \in \{\top, \bot, \notmid\}$ the the rule MCE is applied, and the termination is trivial, the resulting state is D' for which $D' = D$ holds.
If $D \notin \{\top, \bot, \notmid\}$ then the rule MI is applied. The denotation function $\mathcal{M}[\![b]\!]^\sharp$ is a total function, therefore, $\mathcal{M}[\![b]\!]^\sharp D$ and $\mathcal{M}[\![\neg b]\!]^\sharp D$ always exist. According to the inductive assumption, there exist D_1 and D_2 so that $\langle p_{tt}(m), \mathcal{M}[\![b]\!]^\sharp D \rangle \rightarrow_\mu^* D_{tt}$ and $\langle p_{ff}(m), \mathcal{M}[\![\neg b]\!]^\sharp D \rangle \rightarrow_\mu^* D_{ff}$. According to rule MI, the result D' is $D_{tt} \sqcup D_{ff}$, which always exists too.

6.1. PROOFS FOR CHAPTER 2

- while: We consider two cases. In case 1 the rules MWT and MWF are used by the monitor semantics to execute the program, in case 2 MWH and MWX are used to execute the program.

  1. In this case we suppose that in the execution

     $$\langle \text{while}(n) \ b \ \text{do} \ \{p(n)\}, D\rangle \rightarrow^*_\mu D'$$

     only the rules MWT and MWF are used. Let us look closer at this execution, which looks the following:

     $$\langle \text{while}(n) \ b \ \text{do} \ \{p(n)\}, D_0\rangle \quad \rightarrow_\mu$$
     $$\langle \text{while}(n-1) \ b \ \text{do} \ \{p(n)\}, D_1\rangle \quad \rightarrow_\mu \ ...$$
     $$\rightarrow_\mu \quad \langle \text{while}(n-i) \ b \ \text{do} \ \{p(n)\}, D_i\rangle$$

     Because of the condition $n > 0$ in rule MWT, $i < n$ in all configurations. But because the application of MWT increments i, it can be applied at most n times. By the application of the rule MWF the execution of the command terminates. If the condition of the rule MWF cannot be satisfied along the execution, then sooner or later the conditions of the rule MWT are going to be unsatisfiable too, and case 2 will apply.

  2. In this case we suppose that one of the rules, MWH or MWX is applied on the monitor state $D = D_0$. The execution of the while loop looks the following:

     $$\langle \text{while}(n) \ b \ \text{do} \ \{p(n)\}, D_0\rangle \quad \rightarrow_\mu$$
     $$\langle \text{while}(n-1) \ b \ \text{do} \ \{p(n)\}, D_1\rangle \quad \rightarrow_\mu \ ...$$
     $$\rightarrow_\mu \quad \langle \text{while}(n-i) \ b \ \text{do} \ \{p(n)\}, D_i\rangle$$

     Because of the condition of rule MWH, it is true for each i in the above execution that $D_i \sqsubseteq D_{i+1}$. Furthermore, if the condition $(\mathcal{M}[\![\neg b]\!]^\sharp D \neq \bot \wedge \mathcal{M}[\![b]\!]^\sharp D \neq \bot) \vee n \leq 0$ once holds for a monitor state D it is always going to hold in the rest of the execution. Accordingly, it is not possible for an execution, that once MWH or MWX has been executed, MWT or MWF is executed afterwards for the same while instance.

     The execution of the while instance terminates, when the rule MWX is applied. This is the case if the condition $D_{i+1} \sqsubseteq D_i$ holds. But because we know that $D_i \sqsubseteq D_{i+1}$ always holds, in reality, MWX is applied if $D_i = D_{i+1}$. Lemma 2 assures us that there exists an i for which this is the case.

Until now we have proved that our statement holds for commands of the form while b do $\{p\}$, if b then $\{p_{tt}\}$ else $\{p_{ff}\}$, and for assignments. It follows then from Lemma 1 that any sequence of these commands also terminates. □

Lemma 4. *If $s \sqsubseteq D$, then for each assignment or Boolean expression f it holds that if $[\![f]\!]s = s'$ then $\mathcal{M}[\![f]\!]^\sharp D = D'$ so that $s' \sqsubseteq D'$.*

Proof. First we treat the case when $s = \frac{1}{4}$. In this case we know that $D = \frac{1}{4}$ or $D = \top$ because of the assumptions of the lemma that $s \sqsubseteq D$. According to the rules in Figure 2.3 $[\![f]\!]\frac{1}{4} = \frac{1}{4}$ for all possible f, and according to rule (2.7)

$\mathcal{M}[\![f]\!]^\sharp D = D$ for all possible f if $D \in \{\natural, \top\}$. Therefore, the statement follows because $\natural \sqsubseteq \natural$ and $\natural \sqsubseteq \top$.

Now we treat the case when $s : \mathcal{X} \to \mathfrak{B}_{\Sigma_2, \Sigma_0}$. According to the assumptions of the lemma, it is possible now that $D = \top$. Since according to rule (2.7) $\mathcal{M}[\![f]\!]^\sharp \top = \top$ for all f and there is no s^* for which $s^* \not\sqsubseteq \top$, the statement follows.

Now we treat the case when $s : \mathcal{X} \to \mathfrak{B}_{\Sigma_2, \Sigma_0}$ and $D : \mathcal{X} \to \mathfrak{B}_{\Sigma_2, \Sigma_0 \cup \{\top, \bot, \natural\}}$. Since there are finitely many Boolean and tree expressions, we prove the statement of the lemma for each one in a separate case.

- x:=y. It follows from Definition 3 that $s(y) \sqsubseteq D(y)$. Similarly, we know that for all variables z it holds that $s(z) \sqsubseteq D(z)$. Putting all together, $s[x \mapsto s(y)] \sqsubseteq D[x \mapsto D(y)]$.

- x:=#. Trivial.

- x:=$\sigma_2(x_1, x_2)$. From the assumptions of the lemma follows that $s(x_1) \sqsubseteq D(x_1)$ and $s(x_2) \sqsubseteq D(x_2)$. From Definition 2 and the fact that for all other variables the statement holds, the result follows.

- x:=y/1. Regarding the value of $D(y)(\varepsilon)$ we have the following possibilities:

    - $\star$. In this case $\mathcal{M}[\![x\mathbin{:=}y/1]\!]^\sharp D = \top$. Because for any state s^* it holds that $s^* \sqsubseteq \top$ the statement is proved.

    - #. In this case because of our assumption, $s(y)(\varepsilon) = \#$ and the result of the transformers on both, s and D is $\natural$. Because $\natural \sqsubseteq \natural$ the statement holds.

    - $\sigma_2 \in \Sigma_2$. Because of the assumptions of the lemma and Definition 3 we know that in this case $s(y) = \sigma_2(\tau_1, \tau_2)$ for some τ_1 and τ_2, and $D(y) = \sigma_2(\tau_1^\sharp, \tau_2^\sharp)$ for some $\tau_1^\sharp$ and $\tau_2^\sharp$, where $\tau_1 \sqsubseteq \tau_1^\sharp$ and $\tau_2 \sqsubseteq \tau_2^\sharp$. It follows now that $s'(x) = \tau_1$ and $D'(x) = \tau_1^\sharp$, for which our statement holds.

- x:=y/2. It can be shown similarly to the previous case.

- x:=$\lambda_t(x_1, x_2, \ldots)$. For this case the statement follows directly from the definition of the monitor state transformer in (2.6).

- top(x)=σ. In this case if $[\![\mathtt{top(x)}=\sigma]\!]s = s$, then the assumptions of the lemma entail that $D(x)(\varepsilon) \in \{\sigma, \star\}$. According to rule (2.1) in this case the statement holds.

- ¬top(x)=σ. In this case if $[\![\neg\mathtt{top(x)}=\sigma]\!]s = s$, then the assumptions of the lemma entail that $D(x)(\varepsilon) \in (\Sigma_2 \cup \Sigma_0 \cup \{\star\}) \setminus \{\sigma\}$. Therefore, the statement holds according to (2.2).

- $\lambda_b(x_1, x_2, \ldots)$. In this case the statement follows directly from (2.5).

$\square$

Lemma 5. *Let us suppose that the program p is of the form $c_1; \ldots; c_n$ so that $n \geq 0$, and that for all c_i it holds that if $\langle c_i, s_i \rangle \to_\rho^* s_{i+1}$ and $s_i \sqsubseteq D_i$, then $\langle c_i(m), D_i \rangle \to_\mu^* D_{i+1}$ so that $s_{i+1} \sqsubseteq D_{i+1}$. In this case if $s_1 \sqsubseteq D_1$ and*

$\langle c_1;...;c_n, s_1\rangle \to_\rho^* s_{n+1}$, then $\langle(c_1;...;c_n)(m), D_1\rangle \to_\mu^* D_{n+1}$ so that $s_{n+1} \sqsubseteq D_{n+1}$.

Proof. We prove inductively on the number of times the rules MS and RS are executed:

0 In this case the statement trivially holds.

i We suppose that the statement holds for $i-1$ applications of the rules RS and MS. In this case the program p is of the form $c_1;...;c_n$ and we know that $s_1 \sqsubseteq D_1$. Because of the inductive assumption it follows that if $\langle c_1;...;c_n, s_1\rangle \to_\rho^* \langle c_i;...;c_n, s_i\rangle$ then $\langle(c_1;...;c_n)(m), D_1\rangle \to_\mu^* \langle(c_i;...;c_n)(m), D_i\rangle$ so that $s_i \sqsubseteq D_i$. According to Lemma 4 we know that if furthermore $\langle c_i, s_i\rangle \to_\rho^* s_{i+1}$, then $\langle c_i(m), D_i\rangle \to_\mu^* D_{i+1}$ so that $s_{i+1} \sqsubseteq D_{i+1}$. So after applying the rules the ith time it follows that $\langle c_i;...;c_n, s_i\rangle \to_\rho \langle c_{i+1};...;c_n, s_{i+1}\rangle$ and similarly, $\langle(c_i;...;c_n)(m), D_i\rangle \to_\mu \langle(c_{i+1};...;c_n(m), D_{i+1}\rangle$, where of course $s_{i+1} \sqsubseteq D_{i+1}$ holds.

□

Lemma 6. *If $s \sqsubseteq D$ and $\langle p, s\rangle \to_\rho^* s'$ then $\langle p(m), D\rangle \to_\mu^* D'$ so that $s' \sqsubseteq D'$.*

Proof. First we prove the statement on programs of the form while b do $\{p\}$; and if b then $\{p_{\tt tt}\}$ else $\{p_{\tt ff}\}$; inductively on the number of commands of these forms to be found on any root-leaf path of the abstract syntax tree. In other words, on the number of if and while constructs embedded into each other.

0 In this case there are no if and while constructs in the program. So the program is either one assignment, or a sequence of assignments. Let us treat first the case of one single assignment. In this case the statement directly follows from Lemma 4. If the program is a sequence of assignments, then our statement follows from Lemma 5.

i Let us first suppose that the program is if b then $\{p_{\tt tt}\}$ else $\{p_{\tt ff}\}$;. We suppose that in the abstract syntax trees of the programs $p_{\tt tt}$ and $p_{\tt ff}$ there are maximally $i-1$ pieces of if and while constructs embedded into each other, and that if $s \sqsubseteq D$ and $\langle p_{\tt tt}, s\rangle \to_\rho^* s'$ then $\langle p_{\tt tt}(m), D\rangle \to_\mu^* D'$ so that $s' \sqsubseteq D'$. We suppose that this statement also holds for the program $p_{\tt ff}$.

If $s = \frac{\ell}{\ell}$ then $D \in \{\frac{\ell}{\ell}, \top\}$ and our statement follows from the rule E in Figure 2.4 and rule MCE in Figure 2.10. If $s \neq \frac{\ell}{\ell}$ and $D = \top$ then according to rule MCE in Figure 2.10 $\langle$if b then $\{p_{\tt tt}\}$ else $\{p_{\tt ff}\}, \top\rangle \to_\mu \top$. Furthermore, we suppose that according to rules IT and IF there is an s' so that $\langle$if b then $\{p_{\tt tt}\}$ else $\{p_{\tt ff}\}, s\rangle \to_\rho s'$. From Definition 3 it follows that $s' \sqsubseteq \top$, and the statement is proved.

If $D : (\mathcal{X} \to \mathfrak{B}_{\Sigma_2, \Sigma_0 \cup \{\star\}})$ then it is true for the corresponding execution state s that $s : (\mathcal{X} \to \mathfrak{B}_{\Sigma_2, \Sigma_0})$. Accordingly, exactly one of the rules IT or IF is applied on s by the real semantics. We investigate the two cases separately.

IT In this case $[\![b]\!]s = s$. Because of Lemma 4 we know that $\mathcal{M}[\![b]\!]^\sharp D = D'$ so that $s \sqsubseteq D'$. the rest follows from the inductive assumption.

IF In this case $\llbracket \neg b \rrbracket s = s$. Because of Lemma 4 we have $\mathcal{M} \llbracket \neg b \rrbracket^\sharp D = D'$ so that $s \sqsubseteq D'$. the rest follows from the inductive assumption.

We now come to the point where the program p is while b do $\{p\}$;. If $s = \xi$ then $D \in \{\xi, \top\}$ and our statement follows from the rule E in Figure 2.4 and rule MCE in Figure 2.10. If $s \neq \xi$ and $D = \top$ then according to rule MCE in Figure 2.10 $\langle \text{while}(n)\ b\ \text{do}\ \{p\}, \top \rangle \rightarrow_\mu \top$. Furthermore, we suppose that according to rules WT and WF there is an s' so that $\langle \text{while}\ b\ \text{do}\ \{p\}, s \rangle \rightarrow_\rho^* s'$. From Definition 3 it follows that $s' \sqsubseteq \top$, and the statement is proved.

Now we investigate the case when $s : (\mathcal{X} \rightarrow \mathfrak{B}_{\Sigma_2, \Sigma_0})$ and $D : (\mathcal{X} \rightarrow \mathfrak{B}_{\Sigma_2, \Sigma_0 \cup \{\star\}})$. We investigate two cases depending on whether the rules MWH and MWX are applied or not.

1. The rules MWH and MWX are not applied, only the rules MWT and MWF are applied during the execution of the while instance.

   The real configuration is $\langle \text{while}\ b\ \text{do}\ \{p\}, s \rangle$ and the monitor configuration is $\langle \text{while}(n)\ b\ \text{do}\ \{p\}, D \rangle$, so that $s \sqsubseteq D$.

   If $\llbracket \neg b \rrbracket s = s$ then from Lemma 4 it follows that $\mathcal{M} \llbracket \neg b \rrbracket^\sharp D = D'$ so that $s \sqsubseteq D'$. In this case our statement trivially follows, only the rule MWF is applied on the monitor state and the rule WF on the real execution state.

   However, if $\llbracket b \rrbracket s = s$ it means that the rule WT is applied on the real configuration, and because of Lemma 4 it follows that $\mathcal{M} \llbracket b \rrbracket^\sharp D = D^*$, where $s \sqsubseteq D^*$, so the rule MWT is applied on the monitor configuration. In this case the program p is executed on the real state s and on the monitor state D^*. Based on the inductive assumption we see that on the resulting states s' and D' it holds that $s' \sqsubseteq D'$. (Please refer to the rules in order to see what s' and D' mean.) The resulting configurations are $\langle \text{while}\ b\ \text{do}\ \{p\}, s' \rangle$ and $\langle \text{while}(n - 1)\ b\ \text{do}\ \{p\}, D' \rangle$ after executing p. So if along the execution of the while loop a monitor configuration $\langle \text{while}(n - i)\ b\ \text{do}\ \{p\}, D^{**} \rangle$ is never reached where $i = n$ or $\mathcal{M} \llbracket b \rrbracket^\sharp D^{**} \neq \bot$ and $\mathcal{M} \llbracket \neg b \rrbracket^\sharp D^{**} \neq \bot$ in the same time, then inductively applying the above arguments we can see that at the point where $\mathcal{M} \llbracket b \rrbracket^\sharp D^{**} = \bot$ holds and the rule MWF is applied on the monitor configuration, WF is going to be applied on the real configuration, and our statement holds.

   On the other hand, if a state is reached where either $i = n$ or $\mathcal{M} \llbracket b \rrbracket^\sharp D^{**} \neq \bot$ and $\mathcal{M} \llbracket \neg b \rrbracket^\sharp D^{**} \neq \bot$ in the same time, then one of the rules MWH or MWX is applied, and case 2 applies.

2. In this case the monitor rules MWH and MWX are applied on the monitor configuration.

   Let us define a sequence of real states $s_0, s_1, \ldots$ and a sequence of monitor states $D_0, D_1, \ldots$ so that for each i it holds that $\langle p, s_i \rangle \rightarrow_\rho^* s_{i+1}$ and $\langle p(m), D_i \rangle \rightarrow_\mu^* D'_i$ so that $D_{i+1} = D_i \sqcup D'_i$. We regard these two sequences as the states at the time the configurations to be executed are $\langle \text{while}\ b\ \text{do}\ \{p\}, s_i \rangle$ and $\langle \text{while}(n - i)\ b\ \text{do}\ \{p\}, D_i \rangle$.

   We know that $s_0 \sqsubseteq D_0$. Let us suppose $s_i \sqsubseteq D_i$. In this case because of the inductive assumption we know that $s_{i+1} \sqsubseteq D'_i \sqsubseteq (D'_i \sqcup D_i) =$

D_{i+1}. Let us suppose that we have reached an i where $D_{i+1} \sqsubseteq D_i$. Because $D_{i+1} = D_i \sqcup D'_i$ it follows that $D_i \sqsubseteq D_{i+1}$ for each i. So if $D_{i+1} \sqsubseteq D_i$, then $D_{i+1} = D_i$. It means that for each $j > i$ $D_j = D_i$. So we can just as well finish the computation and apply MWX to return D_i as the result.

Until this point we have proved for all commands c of the programming language that if $s \sqsubseteq D$ and $\langle c, s \rangle \to_\rho^* s'$, then $\langle c(m), D \rangle \to_\mu^* D'$ and $s' \sqsubseteq D'$ hold. Because of Lemma 5 it is also true for programs which are sequences of such commands. □

Lemma 7. *Let us consider the program $p = c_1;...;c_n$. If for all commands c_i, it follows from $s \sqsubseteq D$ and $\langle c_i, m, (s, D) \rangle \to_\gamma^* (s', D')$ that $s' \sqsubseteq D'$, then if $s \sqsubseteq D$ and $\langle c_1;...;c_n, m, (s, D) \rangle \to_\gamma^* (s', D')$ then $s' \sqsubseteq D'$.*

Proof. We prove inductively on the number of applications of the rule CS in Figure 2.8, that if $\langle c_i;...;c_n, m, (s, D) \rangle \to_\gamma \langle c_{i+1};...;c_n, m, (s', D') \rangle$ so that $s \sqsubseteq D$ then $s' \sqsubseteq D'$. Specifically, if $\langle c_n; \varepsilon, m, (s, D) \rangle \to_\gamma \langle \varepsilon, m, (s', D') \rangle$ so that $s \sqsubseteq D$ then $s' \sqsubseteq D'$.

We have a case splitting now according to the number of applications of the rule CS:

0 The statement trivially holds.

i We have the configuration $\langle c_i;...;c_n, m, (s, D) \rangle$. The inductive assumption is that $s \sqsubseteq D$. From the assumption of the lemma we know that if $\langle c_i, m, (s, D) \rangle \to_\gamma^* (s', D')$ so that $s \sqsubseteq D$ then $s' \sqsubseteq D'$. We can now apply the rule CS:

$$\langle c_i;...;c_n, m, (s, D) \rangle \to_\gamma \langle c_{i+1};...;c_n, m, (s', D') \rangle$$

The statement of the lemma follows.

□

Lemma 8. *If we have*

$$\langle p, m, (s_1, D) \rangle \to_\gamma^* (s'_1, D'_1) \text{ and } \langle p, m, (s_2, D) \rangle \to_\gamma^* (s'_1, D'_2)$$

so that $s_1, s_2 \sqsubseteq D$ then $D'_1 = D'_2$.

Proof. By looking at the monitored semantics in Figure 2.8 and the rules of the generalized constant propagation in Figure 2.10 one can observe that the monitor state never depends on the real state, and the final monitor state can be computed independently of the real state. Because of this reason the statement holds. □

Lemma 9. *If $\langle p, m, (s, D) \rangle \to_\gamma^* (s', D')$ so that $s \sqsubseteq D$, and for all variables x we have that $s(x) \in \mathfrak{B}_{\Sigma_2, \Sigma_0}$ and $D(x) \in \mathfrak{B}_{\Sigma_2, \Sigma_0 \cup \{*\}}$ then both of the following holds:*

1. *If $s' \neq \natural$, then for all variables x we have that $s'(x) \in \mathfrak{B}_{\Sigma_2, \Sigma_0}$ and;*

2. *$s' \sqsubseteq D'$*

Proof. The transition rules having names beginning with C are the rules of the monitored semantics as they are shown in Figure 2.8.

1. Considering the tree expression semantics in Figure 2.3, it is easy to see that if there are no positions in the variables of the execution state s labeled $\star$ then there aren't any in $[\![f]\!]s$ either, because the semantics does not introduce them. So no sequence of assignments executed by the rule CA will introduce these labels.

2. First, we prove the lemma on programs of the form while b do $\{p\}$; and if b then $\{p_{\mathtt{tt}}\}$ else $\{p_{\mathtt{ff}}\}$;. If $D \in \{\xi, \top\}$ then the rule CCE is applied and the result follows trivially, because the states are not modified. If this is not the case then we prove inductively on the maximal number of occurrences of if and while constructs on any root-leaf path of the the abstract syntax tree of the program.

    0 Let us first investigate the case when the program is a single assignment $x\mathtt{:=}e$. If $D \in \{\xi, \top\}$ then the rule CCE is applied. If $D = \xi$ then $s = \xi$ too because of our assumption. Since the application of the rule does not modify the states, our result follows. If $D = \top$ then our result follows from the fact that for any mapping $s : \mathcal{X} \to \mathfrak{B}_{\Sigma_2,\Sigma_0}$ it is true that $s \sqsubseteq \top$.

    If $D \notin \{\top, \xi\}$ then D is the mapping $D : \mathcal{X} \to \mathfrak{B}_{\Sigma_2,\Sigma_0 \cup \{\star\}}$. In this case the rule CA is applied and the result follows from Lemma 4.

    If the program is a sequence of assignments, the statement follows from the proof above and Lemma 7.

    i We investigate the case of the if and while commands in separate cases:

    if In this case the program is if b then $\{p_{\mathtt{tt}}\}$ else $\{p_{\mathtt{ff}}\}$ where $p_{\mathtt{tt}}$ and $p_{\mathtt{ff}}$ contain $i-1$ levels of embedded if and while constructs at the maximum. Our inductive assumption is that if $s \sqsubseteq D$ and $\langle p_{\mathtt{tt}}, m, (s, D) \rangle \to_\gamma^* (s', D')$ or $\langle p_{\mathtt{ff}}, m, (s, D) \rangle \to_\gamma^* (s', D')$ then $s' \sqsubseteq D'$. Here, we have 3 cases according to the result of $\mathcal{M}[\![b]\!]^\sharp D$ and $\mathcal{M}[\![\neg b]\!]^\sharp D$.

    * $\mathcal{M}[\![\neg b]\!]^\sharp D = \bot$. In this case the rule CIT is applied. According to our inductive assumption if $\langle p_{\mathtt{tt}}, m, (s, D) \rangle \to_\gamma^* (s', D')$ then $s' \sqsubseteq D'$. Based on this and the rule CIT we can conclude the validity of the lemma.

    * $\mathcal{M}[\![b]\!]^\sharp D = \bot$. In this case the rule CIF is applied. According to our inductive assumption if $\langle p_{\mathtt{ff}}, m, (s, D) \rangle \to_\gamma^* (s', D')$ then $s' \sqsubseteq D'$. Based on this and the rule CIF we can conclude the validity of the lemma.

    * $\mathcal{M}[\![\neg b]\!]^\sharp D \neq \bot \wedge \mathcal{M}[\![b]\!]^\sharp D \neq \bot$. In this case the rule CIH is applied, and our statement follows from Lemma 6.

    while Our inductive assumption is that $s \sqsubseteq D$ and $\langle p, m, (s, D) \rangle \to_\gamma^* (s', D')$ entail that $s' \sqsubseteq D'$. If the rule CWF is used, our statement trivially follows, because this rule does not modify the real and monitor states.

6.1. PROOFS FOR CHAPTER 2

In order to prove our statement on the rule CWT let us look at a sequence of applications of it:

$$\langle \texttt{while } b \texttt{ do } p, m, (s_0, D_0)\rangle \to_\gamma$$
$$\langle \texttt{while } b \texttt{ do } p, m, (s_1, D_1)\rangle \to_\gamma \ldots \to_\gamma$$
$$\langle \texttt{while } b \texttt{ do } p_t, m, (s_i, D_i)\rangle$$

Next, we prove inductively that if we have a sequence of applications of the rule CWT as shown above, then the property $s_j \sqsubseteq D_j$ is an invariant along the transitions. For the initial configuration $s_0 \sqsubseteq D_0$ holds because of the assumption of the lemma.

Let us suppose that the property holds after executing the transition CWT $i-1$ times. So we have the configuration:

$$\langle \texttt{while } b \texttt{ do } \{p\}, m, (s_{i-1}, D_{i-1})\rangle$$

We know about the configuration above that $s_{i-1} \sqsubseteq D_{i-1}$ because of the inductive assumption. Based on the assumption on the program p we know that if $s_{i-1} \sqsubseteq D_{i-1}$ and

$$\langle p, m, (s_{i-1}, D_{i-1})\rangle \to_\gamma^* (s_i, D_i)$$

then $s_i \sqsubseteq D_i$. Accordingly, our statement holds for each i.

In case CWH is applied, the validity of our statement is guaranteed by Lemma 6.

Until this point we have proved our statement on programs, which are either assignments, or are of the form `while` b `do` $\{p\}$; or `if` b `then` $\{p_{tt}\}$ `else` $\{p_{ff}\}$;. The validity of the lemma for any program, i.e., any sequence of commands, is assured by Lemma 7. □

6.2 Proofs for Chapter 3

Lemma 10. *If $(\mathbb{A}, \alpha, \gamma, \mathbb{B})$ is a Galois connection then the following holds:*

$$a \sqsubseteq_\mathbb{A} \gamma(b_1) \sqcap_\mathbb{A} \ldots \sqcap_\mathbb{A} \gamma(b_n) \Rightarrow a \sqsubseteq_\mathbb{A} \gamma(b_1 \sqcap_\mathbb{B} \ldots \sqcap_\mathbb{B} b_n)$$

Proof. From the precondition follows:

$$a \sqsubseteq_\mathbb{A} \gamma(b_1)$$
$$\vdots$$
$$a \sqsubseteq_\mathbb{A} \gamma(b_n)$$

Therefore, for each i it follows from Definition 6:

$$\alpha(a) \sqsubseteq_\mathbb{B} b_i$$

Therefore, we have that:

$$\alpha(a) \sqsubseteq_\mathbb{B} b_1 \sqcap_\mathbb{B} \ldots \sqcap_\mathbb{B} b_n$$

And again from Definition 6 follows:

$$a \sqsubseteq_\mathbb{A} \gamma(b_1 \sqcap_\mathbb{B} \ldots \sqcap_\mathbb{B} b_n)$$

$\square$

Lemma 11. *Let us regard two computations: π_1 and π_2. From $[\![\pi_1]\!]s_0 = s$, $[\![\pi_2]\!]t_0 = t$, $\begin{bmatrix}s_0\\t_0\end{bmatrix} \in \gamma(d_0)$ and $d \sqsupseteq \bigsqcap_{\omega \in A\begin{bmatrix}\pi_1\\\pi_2\end{bmatrix}} \mathcal{S}[\![\omega]\!]^\sharp d_0$ follows that $\begin{bmatrix}s\\t\end{bmatrix} \in \gamma(d)$.*

Proof. Let us regard a specific $\omega \in L\left(A\begin{bmatrix}\pi_1\\\pi_2\end{bmatrix}\right)$, where $\omega = \begin{bmatrix}f^\omega_{n_\omega}\\g^\omega_{n_\omega}\end{bmatrix}, \ldots, \begin{bmatrix}f^\omega_1\\g^\omega_1\end{bmatrix}$ and for all i it holds that $d^\omega_i = \mathcal{S}\begin{bmatrix}f^\omega_i\\g^\omega_i\end{bmatrix}^\sharp d^\omega_{i-1}$, so that $d^\omega_0 = d_0$. Furthermore, let us suppose that $s_i = [\![f^\omega_i, \ldots, f^\omega_1]\!]s_0$ and $t_i = [\![g^\omega_i, \ldots, g^\omega_1]\!]t_0$. We prove inductively on the length of ω that $\begin{bmatrix}s^\omega_i\\t^\omega_i\end{bmatrix} \in \gamma(d^\omega_i)$. The inductive assumption is that $\begin{bmatrix}s^\omega_i\\t^\omega_i\end{bmatrix} \in \gamma(d^\omega_i)$. The inductive assumption holds on d_0, s_0 and t_0, because of the assumptions of the lemma. According to the requirement in (3.1) we know now that:

$$\begin{bmatrix}s^\omega_{i+1}\\t^\omega_{i+1}\end{bmatrix} \in \gamma(\begin{bmatrix}f^\omega_{i+1}\\g^\omega_{i+1}\end{bmatrix}^\sharp d^\omega_i)$$

We know that $[\![f^\omega_{n_\omega} \ldots f^\omega_1]\!] = [\![\pi_1]\!]$ and $[\![g^\omega_{n_\omega} \ldots g^\omega_1]\!] = [\![\pi_2]\!]$, because according to the semantics in Figure 2.3 inserting skip operations in a sequence of instructions does not alter the result of a computation. It follows then that $\begin{bmatrix}s\\t\end{bmatrix} = \begin{bmatrix}s^\omega_n\\t^\omega_n\end{bmatrix} \in \gamma(\mathcal{S}[\![\omega]\!]^\sharp d_0)$. Therefore, for each $\omega \in L\left(A\begin{bmatrix}\pi_1\\\pi_2\end{bmatrix}\right)$ we know that $\begin{bmatrix}s\\t\end{bmatrix} \in \gamma(\mathcal{S}[\![\omega]\!]^\sharp d_0)$. It follows then that $\begin{bmatrix}s\\t\end{bmatrix} \in \bigcap_{\omega \in L\left(A\begin{bmatrix}\pi_1\\\pi_2\end{bmatrix}\right)} \gamma(\mathcal{S}[\![\omega]\!]^\sharp d_0)$. Otherwise put it we have $\{\begin{bmatrix}s\\t\end{bmatrix}\} \subseteq \bigcap_{\omega \in L\left(A\begin{bmatrix}\pi_1\\\pi_2\end{bmatrix}\right)} \gamma(\mathcal{S}[\![\omega]\!]^\sharp d_0)$. According to Lemma 10 we have $\{\begin{bmatrix}s\\t\end{bmatrix}\} \subseteq \gamma(\bigsqcap_{\omega \in L\left(A\begin{bmatrix}\pi_1\\\pi_2\end{bmatrix}\right)} \mathcal{S}[\![\omega]\!]^\sharp d_0)$.

6.2. PROOFS FOR CHAPTER 3

From Definition 6 of Galois connections follows that:

$$\alpha(\{\begin{bmatrix} s \\ t \end{bmatrix}\}) \sqsubseteq \bigsqcap_{\omega \in L\left(A\begin{bmatrix} \pi_1 \\ \pi_2 \end{bmatrix}\right)} \mathcal{S}[\![\omega]\!]^\sharp d_0$$

If for some d it holds that $\bigsqcap_{\omega \in L\left(A\begin{bmatrix} \pi_1 \\ \pi_2 \end{bmatrix}\right)} \mathcal{S}[\![\omega]\!]^\sharp d_0 \sqsubseteq d$ then $\alpha(\{\begin{bmatrix} s \\ t \end{bmatrix}\}) \sqsubseteq d$ too.
Therefore, from Definition 6 follows that $\{\begin{bmatrix} s \\ t \end{bmatrix}\} \subseteq \gamma(d)$. □

Theorem 3. *Consider a pair of sequences of labels $\pi_1, \pi_2 \in n_{in} \leadsto n_{fi}$ on the CFG $G = (N, E, n_{in}, n_{fi})$, and states $s_0, s, t_0, t \in S$, where $s = [\![\pi_1]\!]s_0$, $t = [\![\pi_2]\!]t_0$ and $\begin{bmatrix} s_0 \\ t_0 \end{bmatrix} \in \gamma(d_0)$. In this case $d \sqsupseteq MTC(G, d_0)$ implies $\begin{bmatrix} s \\ t \end{bmatrix} \in \gamma(d)$.*

Proof. We know that:

$$\text{MTC}(G, d_0) = \bigsqcup_{\substack{\pi_1 \in n_{in} \leadsto n_{fi} \\ \pi_2 \in n_{in} \leadsto n_{fi}}} \bigsqcap_{\omega \in L\left(A\begin{bmatrix} \pi_1 \\ \pi_2 \end{bmatrix}\right)} \mathcal{S}[\![\omega]\!]^\sharp d_0$$

From Lemma 11 follows that if $d' \sqsupseteq \bigsqcap_{\omega \in L\left(A\begin{bmatrix} \pi_1 \\ \pi_2 \end{bmatrix}\right)} \mathcal{S}[\![\omega]\!]^\sharp d_0$ then $\begin{bmatrix} s \\ t \end{bmatrix} \in \gamma(d')$.
Since $\pi_1 \in n_{in} \leadsto n_{fi}$ and $\pi_2 \in n_{in} \leadsto n_{fi}$, $\text{MTC}(G, d_0) \sqsupseteq d'$. □

Theorem 4. *Given the CFG $G = (N, E, n_{in}, n_{fi})$ and one of its self-compositions $GG = (N', E', n'_{in}, n'_{fi})$, the following holds for all d_0:*

$$\bigsqcup_{\omega \in n'_{in} \leadsto n'_{fi}} \mathcal{S}[\![\omega]\!]^\sharp d_0 \sqsupseteq MTC(G, d_0)$$

Proof. According to Definition 8 for all $\pi_1, \pi_2 \in n_{in} \leadsto n_{fi}$ there is an $\omega_{\pi_1,\pi_2} \in n'_{in} \leadsto n'_{fi}$ so that $\omega_{\pi_1,\pi_2} \in L\left(A\begin{bmatrix} \pi_1 \\ \pi_2 \end{bmatrix}\right)$. Therefore:

$$\text{MTC}(G, d_0) = \bigsqcup_{\substack{\pi_1 \in n_{in} \leadsto n_{fi} \\ \pi_2 \in n_{in} \leadsto n_{fi}}} \bigsqcap_{\omega \in L\left(A\begin{bmatrix} \pi_1 \\ \pi_2 \end{bmatrix}\right)} \mathcal{S}[\![\omega]\!]^\sharp d_0 \sqsubseteq$$
$$\bigsqcup_{\substack{\pi_1 \in n_{in} \leadsto n_{fi} \\ \pi_2 \in n_{in} \leadsto n_{fi}}} \mathcal{S}[\![\omega_{\pi_1,\pi_2}]\!]^\sharp d_0 =$$
$$\bigsqcup_{\omega_{\pi_1,\pi_2} \in n'_{in} \leadsto n'_{fi}} \mathcal{S}[\![\omega_{\pi_1,\pi_2}]\!]^\sharp d_0$$

□

Lemma 12. *The following holds for any pair of sequences of sequences $\pi_{1,1}...\pi_{1,n}$ and $\pi_{2,1}...\pi_{2,n}$:*

$$L\left(A\begin{bmatrix} \pi_{1,1}...\pi_{1,n} \\ \pi_{2,1}...\pi_{2,n} \end{bmatrix}\right) \supseteq L\left(A\begin{bmatrix} \pi_{1,1} \\ \pi_{2,1} \end{bmatrix}...A\begin{bmatrix} \pi_{1,n} \\ \pi_{2,n} \end{bmatrix}\right)$$

Note, that any $\pi_{i,j}$ above may equal to ε, which is the empty sequence.

Proof. Let us denote the configurations of the derivation starting with the series of nonterminals $A\begin{bmatrix}\pi_{1,1}\\\pi_{2,1}\end{bmatrix}...A\begin{bmatrix}\pi_{1,n}\\\pi_{2,n}\end{bmatrix}$ using $\langle\omega_1 A\begin{bmatrix}\pi_{1,i}^k\\\pi_{2,i}^l\end{bmatrix}...A\begin{bmatrix}\pi_{1,n}\\\pi_{1,n}\end{bmatrix}\rangle_1$, and similarly, denote the configurations of the derivation starting with $A\begin{bmatrix}\pi_{1,1}...\pi_{1,n}\\\pi_{2,1}...\pi_{2,n}\end{bmatrix}$ using $\langle\omega_2 A\begin{bmatrix}\pi_{1,i}^k...\pi_{1,n}\\\pi_{2,i}^l...\pi_{2,n}\end{bmatrix}\rangle_2$, where ω_1 and ω_2 are the sequences of pairs that have been generated, and $\pi_{1,i}^k$ and $\pi_{2,i}^l$ are the postfixes of $\pi_{1,i}$ and $\pi_{2,i}$ where k and l indicate the length of the prefixes of $\pi_{1,i}$ and $\pi_{2,i}$ that have been processed already.

Now we prove inductively on the length of the derivations that whenever there is an α and an ω such that

$$\langle A\begin{bmatrix}\pi_{1,1}\\\pi_{2,1}\end{bmatrix}...A\begin{bmatrix}\pi_{1,n}\\\pi_{1,n}\end{bmatrix}\rangle_1 \xrightarrow{\alpha}{}^* \langle\omega A\begin{bmatrix}\pi_{1,i}^k\\\pi_{2,i}^l\end{bmatrix}...A\begin{bmatrix}\pi_{1,n}\\\pi_{1,n}\end{bmatrix}\rangle_1,$$

then there is a β such that

$$\langle A\begin{bmatrix}\pi_{1,1}...\pi_{1,n}\\\pi_{2,1}...\pi_{2,n}\end{bmatrix}\rangle_2 \xrightarrow{\beta}{}^* \langle\omega A\begin{bmatrix}\pi_{1,i}^k...\pi_{1,n}\\\pi_{2,i}^l...\pi_{2,n}\end{bmatrix}\rangle_2$$

holds. Above, α and β denote sequences of numbers indicating the order of the application of the rules of the grammar in (3.2). The rules corresponding to α are always applied to the left-most nonterminal of the configuration cfg_1. The inductive assumption is that the configurations of the two derivations are in relation $cfg_1 \sim cfg_2$. $cfg_1 \sim cfg_2$ holds if cfg_1 and cfg_2 are of the form:

$$cfg_1 = \langle\omega A\begin{bmatrix}\pi_{1,i}^k\\\pi_{2,i}^l\end{bmatrix}...A\begin{bmatrix}\pi_{1,n}\\\pi_{1,n}\end{bmatrix}\rangle_1 \sim \langle\omega A\begin{bmatrix}\pi_{1,i}^k...\pi_{1,n}\\\pi_{2,i}^l...\pi_{2,n}\end{bmatrix}\rangle_2 = cfg_2$$

In each step we apply one rule on

$$cfg_1 = \langle\omega A\begin{bmatrix}\pi_{1,i}^k\\\pi_{2,i}^l\end{bmatrix}...A\begin{bmatrix}\pi_{1,n}\\\pi_{1,n}\end{bmatrix}\rangle_1$$

and show what to do with

$$cfg_2 = \langle\omega A\begin{bmatrix}\pi_{1,i}^k...\pi_{1,n}\\\pi_{2,i}^l...\pi_{2,n}\end{bmatrix}\rangle_2$$

in order to preserve the inductive assumption. During the application of the rules on cfg_1, we always expand the leftmost nonterminal. In the initial case when $\omega = \varepsilon$ and no rules have been applied yet, the statement trivially holds.

Now we make a case distinction, based on the form of cfg_1.

1) $\pi_{1,i}^k \neq \varepsilon$ and $\pi_{2,i}^l \neq \varepsilon$. In this case we apply the same rule x on both of the configurations cfg_1 and cfg_2:

$$\langle\omega A\begin{bmatrix}\pi_{1,i}^k\\\pi_{2,i}^l\end{bmatrix}...A\begin{bmatrix}\pi_{1,n}\\\pi_{1,n}\end{bmatrix}\rangle_1 \xrightarrow{x} \langle\omega\begin{bmatrix}f\\g\end{bmatrix}A\begin{bmatrix}\pi_{1,i}^{k'}\\\pi_{2,i}^{l'}\end{bmatrix}...A\begin{bmatrix}\pi_{1,n}\\\pi_{1,n}\end{bmatrix}\rangle_1$$

$$\langle\omega A\begin{bmatrix}\pi_{1,i}^k...\pi_{1,n}\\\pi_{2,i}^l...\pi_{2,n}\end{bmatrix}\rangle_2 \xrightarrow{x} \langle\omega\begin{bmatrix}f\\g\end{bmatrix}A\begin{bmatrix}\pi_{1,i}^{k'}...\pi_{1,n}\\\pi_{2,i}^{l'}...\pi_{2,n}\end{bmatrix}\rangle_2$$

The inductive assumption holds on the resulting configurations.

6.2. PROOFS FOR CHAPTER 3   93

2) $\pi_{1,i}^k = \varepsilon$ and $\pi_{2,i}^l \neq \varepsilon$, but $\pi_{1,i}^k...\pi_{1,n} \neq \varepsilon$. If rule 3 is applied on cfg_1 then rule 7 is applied on cfg_2:

$$\langle \omega A \begin{bmatrix} \varepsilon \\ \pi_{2,i}^l \end{bmatrix} A \begin{bmatrix} \pi_{1,i+1}^0 \\ \pi_{2,i+1}^0 \end{bmatrix} ...A \begin{bmatrix} \pi_{1,n} \\ \pi_{1,n} \end{bmatrix} \rangle_1 \xrightarrow{3}$$
$$\langle \omega \begin{bmatrix} \text{skip} \\ g \end{bmatrix} A \begin{bmatrix} \varepsilon \\ \pi_{2,i}^{l+1} \end{bmatrix} A \begin{bmatrix} \pi_{1,i+1}^0 \\ \pi_{2,i+1}^0 \end{bmatrix} ...A \begin{bmatrix} \pi_{1,n} \\ \pi_{1,n} \end{bmatrix} \rangle_1$$
$$\langle \omega A \begin{bmatrix} \pi_{1,i+1}^0...\pi_{1,n} \\ \pi_{2,i}^l...\pi_{2,n} \end{bmatrix} \rangle_2 \xrightarrow{7} \langle \omega \begin{bmatrix} \text{skip} \\ g \end{bmatrix} A \begin{bmatrix} \pi_{1,i+1}^0...\pi_{1,n} \\ \pi_{2,i}^{l+1}...\pi_{2,n} \end{bmatrix} \rangle_2$$

If rule 4 is applied on cfg_1, then rule 10 is applied on cfg_2:

$$\langle \omega A \begin{bmatrix} \varepsilon \\ \pi_{2,i}^l \end{bmatrix} A \begin{bmatrix} \pi_{1,i+1}^0 \\ \pi_{2,i+1}^0 \end{bmatrix} ...A \begin{bmatrix} \pi_{1,n} \\ \pi_{1,n} \end{bmatrix} \rangle_1 \xrightarrow{4}$$
$$\langle \omega \begin{bmatrix} \text{skip} \\ \text{skip} \end{bmatrix} A \begin{bmatrix} \varepsilon \\ \pi_{2,i}^l \end{bmatrix} A \begin{bmatrix} \pi_{1,i+1}^0 \\ \pi_{2,i+1}^0 \end{bmatrix} ...A \begin{bmatrix} \pi_{1,n} \\ \pi_{1,n} \end{bmatrix} \rangle_1$$
$$\langle \omega A \begin{bmatrix} \pi_{1,i+1}^0...\pi_{1,n} \\ \pi_{2,i}^l...\pi_{2,n} \end{bmatrix} \rangle_2 \xrightarrow{10} \langle \omega \begin{bmatrix} \text{skip} \\ \text{skip} \end{bmatrix} A \begin{bmatrix} \pi_{1,i+1}^0...\pi_{1,n} \\ \pi_{2,i}^l...\pi_{2,n} \end{bmatrix} \rangle_2$$

The application of these rules preserve the inductive assumption, furthermore, no other rules can be applied on the left-most nonterminal in cfg_1.

2a) The case when $\pi_{1,i}^k \neq \varepsilon$ and $\pi_{2,i}^l = \varepsilon$, but $\pi_{2,i}^k...\pi_{2,n} \neq \varepsilon$ can be proved analogously to case 2). If rule 5 is applied on cfg_1 then rule 8 is applied on cfg_2, and if rule 6 is applied on cfg_1 then rule 10 is applied on cfg_2. No other rules can be applied on the left-most nonterminal in cfg_1.

3) $\pi_{1,i}^k = \varepsilon$ and $\pi_{2,i}^l \neq \varepsilon$ and $\pi_{1,i}^k...\pi_{1,n} = \varepsilon$. Either rule 3 can be applied on cfg_1, and we apply the same rule on cfg_2:

$$\langle \omega A \begin{bmatrix} \varepsilon \\ \pi_{2,i}^l \end{bmatrix} A \begin{bmatrix} \varepsilon \\ \pi_{2,i+1}^0 \end{bmatrix} ...A \begin{bmatrix} \varepsilon \\ \pi_{1,n} \end{bmatrix} \rangle_1 \xrightarrow{3}$$
$$\langle \omega \begin{bmatrix} \text{skip} \\ g \end{bmatrix} A \begin{bmatrix} \varepsilon \\ \pi_{2,i}^{l+1} \end{bmatrix} A \begin{bmatrix} \varepsilon \\ \pi_{2,i+1}^0 \end{bmatrix} ...A \begin{bmatrix} \varepsilon \\ \pi_{1,n} \end{bmatrix} \rangle_1$$
$$\langle \omega A \begin{bmatrix} \varepsilon \\ \pi_{2,i}^l...\pi_{2,n} \end{bmatrix} \rangle_2 \xrightarrow{3} \langle \omega \begin{bmatrix} \text{skip} \\ g \end{bmatrix} A \begin{bmatrix} \varepsilon \\ \pi_{2,i}^{l+1}...\pi_{2,n} \end{bmatrix} \rangle_2$$

Or we can apply rule 4 on both of the configurations:

$$\langle \omega A \begin{bmatrix} \varepsilon \\ \pi_{2,i}^l \end{bmatrix} A \begin{bmatrix} \varepsilon \\ \pi_{2,i+1}^0 \end{bmatrix} ...A \begin{bmatrix} \varepsilon \\ \pi_{1,n} \end{bmatrix} \rangle_1 \xrightarrow{4}$$
$$\langle \omega \begin{bmatrix} \text{skip} \\ \text{skip} \end{bmatrix} A \begin{bmatrix} \varepsilon \\ \pi_{2,i}^l \end{bmatrix} A \begin{bmatrix} \varepsilon \\ \pi_{2,i+1}^0 \end{bmatrix} ...A \begin{bmatrix} \varepsilon \\ \pi_{1,n} \end{bmatrix} \rangle_1$$
$$\langle \omega A \begin{bmatrix} \varepsilon \\ \pi_{2,i}^l...\pi_{2,n} \end{bmatrix} \rangle_2 \xrightarrow{4} \langle \omega \begin{bmatrix} \text{skip} \\ \text{skip} \end{bmatrix} A \begin{bmatrix} \varepsilon \\ \pi_{2,i}^l...\pi_{2,n} \end{bmatrix} \rangle_2$$

There are no other rules that can be applied on the left-most nonterminal of configuration cfg_1, furthermore, the inductive assumption has been preserved by the application of the above rules.

3a) The case when $\pi_{1,i}^k \neq \varepsilon$ and $\pi_{2,i}^l = \varepsilon$ and $\pi_{2,i}^k...\pi_{2,n} = \varepsilon$ can be proved similarly. Either rule 5 or rule 6 is applied on the left-most nonterminal of the configurations, which preserves the inductive assumption.

4) $\pi_{1,i}^k = \varepsilon$, $\pi_{2,i}^l = \varepsilon$, $\pi_{1,i}^k...\pi_{1,n} = \varepsilon$, but $\pi_{2,i}^l...\pi_{2,n} \neq \varepsilon$. In this case one of the rules 1 and 2 may be applied on the left-most nonterminal of configuration cfg_1. If rule 1 is applied on cfg_1 then we do not apply anything on cfg_2:

$$\langle \omega A \begin{bmatrix} \varepsilon \\ \varepsilon \end{bmatrix} A \begin{bmatrix} \varepsilon \\ \pi_{2,i+1}^0 \end{bmatrix} ...A \begin{bmatrix} \varepsilon \\ \pi_{1,n} \end{bmatrix} \rangle_1 \xrightarrow{1} \langle \omega A \begin{bmatrix} \varepsilon \\ \pi_{2,i+1}^0 \end{bmatrix} ...A \begin{bmatrix} \varepsilon \\ \pi_{1,n} \end{bmatrix} \rangle_1$$
$$\langle \omega A \begin{bmatrix} \varepsilon \\ \pi_{2,i+1}^0...\pi_{2,n} \end{bmatrix} \rangle_2 \qquad \langle \omega A \begin{bmatrix} \varepsilon \\ \pi_{2,i+1}^0...\pi_{2,n} \end{bmatrix} \rangle_2$$

If rule 2 is applied on cfg_1 then rule 4 is applied on cfg_2:

$$\langle \omega A\begin{bmatrix}\varepsilon\\\varepsilon\end{bmatrix}A\begin{bmatrix}\varepsilon\\\pi^0_{2,i+1}\end{bmatrix}...A\begin{bmatrix}\varepsilon\\\pi_{1,n}\end{bmatrix}\rangle_1 \xrightarrow{2} \langle \omega\begin{bmatrix}\texttt{skip}\\\texttt{skip}\end{bmatrix}A\begin{bmatrix}\varepsilon\\\varepsilon\end{bmatrix}A\begin{bmatrix}\varepsilon\\\pi^0_{2,i+1}\end{bmatrix}...A\begin{bmatrix}\varepsilon\\\pi_{1,n}\end{bmatrix}\rangle_1$$

$$\langle \omega A\begin{bmatrix}\varepsilon\\\pi^0_{2,i+1}...\pi_{2,n}\end{bmatrix}\rangle_2 \xrightarrow{4} \langle \omega\begin{bmatrix}\texttt{skip}\\\texttt{skip}\end{bmatrix}A\begin{bmatrix}\varepsilon\\\pi^0_{2,i+1}...\pi_{2,n}\end{bmatrix}\rangle_2$$

The application of these rules preserves the inductive assumption, furthermore, no other rules can be applied on the left-most nonterminal of cfg_1.

4a) The case when $\pi^k_{1,i} = \varepsilon$, $\pi^l_{2,i} = \varepsilon$, $\pi^k_{1,i}...\pi_{1,n} \neq \varepsilon$, but $\pi^l_{2,i}...\pi_{2,n} = \varepsilon$ can be proved similarly to case 4). Whenever rule 1 is applied on cfg_1 then cfg_2 is not modified. And whenever rule 2 is applied on cfg_1, then rule 6 is applied on cfg_2.

5) $\pi^k_{1,i} = \varepsilon$, $\pi^l_{2,i} = \varepsilon$, $\pi^k_{1,i}...\pi_{1,n} = \varepsilon$, and $\pi^l_{2,i}...\pi_{2,n} = \varepsilon$. In this case one of the rules 1 and 2 may be applied on the configuration cfg_1. If rule 2 is applied on cfg_1 then this rule is also applied on cfg_2:

$$\langle \omega A\begin{bmatrix}\varepsilon\\\varepsilon\end{bmatrix}A\begin{bmatrix}\varepsilon\\\varepsilon\end{bmatrix}...A\begin{bmatrix}\varepsilon\\\varepsilon\end{bmatrix}\rangle_1 \xrightarrow{2} \langle \omega\begin{bmatrix}\texttt{skip}\\\texttt{skip}\end{bmatrix}A\begin{bmatrix}\varepsilon\\\varepsilon\end{bmatrix}A\begin{bmatrix}\varepsilon\\\varepsilon\end{bmatrix}...A\begin{bmatrix}\varepsilon\\\varepsilon\end{bmatrix}\rangle_1$$

$$\langle \omega A\begin{bmatrix}\varepsilon\\\varepsilon\end{bmatrix}\rangle_2 \xrightarrow{2} \langle \omega\begin{bmatrix}\texttt{skip}\\\texttt{skip}\end{bmatrix}A\begin{bmatrix}\varepsilon\\\varepsilon\end{bmatrix}\rangle_2$$

However, if rule 1 is applied on cfg_1 then this rule is only applied on cfg_2 if $cfg_1 = \langle \omega A\begin{bmatrix}\varepsilon\\\varepsilon\end{bmatrix}\rangle_1$:

$$\langle \omega A\begin{bmatrix}\varepsilon\\\varepsilon\end{bmatrix}\rangle_1 \xrightarrow{1} \langle \omega \rangle_1$$

$$\langle \omega A\begin{bmatrix}\varepsilon\\\varepsilon\end{bmatrix}\rangle_2 \xrightarrow{1} \langle \omega \rangle_2$$

Otherwise no rule is applied on cfg_2:

$$\langle \omega A\begin{bmatrix}\varepsilon\\\varepsilon\end{bmatrix}A\begin{bmatrix}\varepsilon\\\varepsilon\end{bmatrix}...A\begin{bmatrix}\varepsilon\\\varepsilon\end{bmatrix}\rangle_1 \xrightarrow{1} \langle \omega A\begin{bmatrix}\varepsilon\\\varepsilon\end{bmatrix}...A\begin{bmatrix}\varepsilon\\\varepsilon\end{bmatrix}\rangle_1$$

$$\langle \omega A\begin{bmatrix}\varepsilon\\\varepsilon\end{bmatrix}\rangle_2 \qquad \langle \omega A\begin{bmatrix}\varepsilon\\\varepsilon\end{bmatrix}\rangle_2$$

These rule applications preserve the inductive assumption. Furthermore, no other rules can be applied on the left-most nonterminal of cfg_1.

6) $\pi^k_{1,i} = \varepsilon$, $\pi^l_{2,i} = \varepsilon$, but $\pi^k_{1,i}...\pi_{1,n} \neq \varepsilon$ and $\pi^l_{2,i}...\pi_{2,n} \neq \varepsilon$. Now rules 1 and 2 can be applied on the left-most nonterminal of cfg_1. If rule 1 is applied, then we do not modify cfg_2:

$$\langle \omega A\begin{bmatrix}\varepsilon\\\varepsilon\end{bmatrix}A\begin{bmatrix}\pi^0_{1,i+1}\\\pi^0_{2,i+1}\end{bmatrix}...A\begin{bmatrix}\pi_{1,n}\\\pi_{1,n}\end{bmatrix}\rangle_1 \xrightarrow{1} \langle \omega A\begin{bmatrix}\pi^0_{1,i+1}\\\pi^0_{2,i+1}\end{bmatrix}...A\begin{bmatrix}\pi_{1,n}\\\pi_{1,n}\end{bmatrix}\rangle_1$$

$$\langle \omega A\begin{bmatrix}\pi^0_{1,i+1}...\pi_{1,n}\\\pi^0_{2,i+1}...\pi_{2,n}\end{bmatrix}\rangle_2 \qquad \langle \omega A\begin{bmatrix}\pi^0_{1,i+1}...\pi_{1,n}\\\pi^0_{2,i+1}...\pi_{2,n}\end{bmatrix}\rangle_2$$

If rule 2 is applied on cfg_1 then rule 10 is applied on cfg_2:

$$\langle \omega A\begin{bmatrix}\varepsilon\\\varepsilon\end{bmatrix}A\begin{bmatrix}\pi^0_{1,i+1}\\\pi^0_{2,i+1}\end{bmatrix}...A\begin{bmatrix}\pi_{1,n}\\\pi_{1,n}\end{bmatrix}\rangle_1 \xrightarrow{2} \langle \omega\begin{bmatrix}\texttt{skip}\\\texttt{skip}\end{bmatrix}A\begin{bmatrix}\varepsilon\\\varepsilon\end{bmatrix}A\begin{bmatrix}\pi^0_{1,i+1}\\\pi^0_{2,i+1}\end{bmatrix}...A\begin{bmatrix}\pi_{1,n}\\\pi_{1,n}\end{bmatrix}\rangle_1$$

$$\langle \omega A\begin{bmatrix}\pi^0_{1,i+1}...\pi_{1,n}\\\pi^0_{2,i+1}...\pi_{2,n}\end{bmatrix}\rangle_2 \xrightarrow{10} \langle \omega\begin{bmatrix}\texttt{skip}\\\texttt{skip}\end{bmatrix}A\begin{bmatrix}\pi^{k'}_{1,i}...\pi_{1,n}\\\pi^{l'}_{2,i}...\pi_{2,n}\end{bmatrix}\rangle_2$$

The application of these rules preserves the inductive assumption.

6.2. PROOFS FOR CHAPTER 3

Lemma 13. *The following holds for all sequences π:*

$$L\left(A\begin{bmatrix}\varepsilon\\\pi\end{bmatrix}\right) \supseteq L\left(A\begin{bmatrix}\text{skip}\\\pi\end{bmatrix}\right)$$

and

$$L\left(A\begin{bmatrix}\pi\\\varepsilon\end{bmatrix}\right) \supseteq L\left(A\begin{bmatrix}\pi\\\text{skip}\end{bmatrix}\right)$$

Proof. We prove now the first statement, the second can be proved analogously. We show that for all $\omega \in L\left(A\begin{bmatrix}\text{skip}\\\pi\end{bmatrix}\right)$, ω is an element of $L\left(A\begin{bmatrix}\varepsilon\\\pi\end{bmatrix}\right)$ too. We denote the configurations of the derivation of an arbitrary ω starting from $A\begin{bmatrix}\text{skip}\\\pi\end{bmatrix}$ with $\langle \omega^* A\begin{bmatrix}\pi_1\\\pi_2\end{bmatrix}\rangle_1$, where ω^* stands for a prefix of ω that has already been generated, and $A\begin{bmatrix}\pi_1\\\pi_2\end{bmatrix}$ is the nonterminal that has not been expanded yet. Similarly, tuples of the form $\langle \omega^* A\begin{bmatrix}\pi_1\\\pi_2\end{bmatrix}\rangle_2$ denote the configurations of the derivation starting from the nonterminal $A\begin{bmatrix}\varepsilon\\\pi\end{bmatrix}$.

The initial configurations of the derivations are $\langle \varepsilon A\begin{bmatrix}\text{skip}\\\pi\end{bmatrix}\rangle_1$ and $\langle \varepsilon A\begin{bmatrix}\varepsilon\\\pi\end{bmatrix}\rangle_2$ respectively. During the construction of $\omega \in L\left(A\begin{bmatrix}\text{skip}\\\pi\end{bmatrix}\right)$ there must be a step when the upper label of the nonterminal $A\begin{bmatrix}\text{skip}\\\pi\end{bmatrix}$, skip, is processed using one of the rules 5, 8 or 9. Therefore, we split ω into subsequences so that $\omega = \omega_1 \begin{bmatrix}\text{skip}\\g\end{bmatrix} \omega_2$. Accordingly, during the derivation of ω we need to have the following step:

$$\langle \omega_1 A\begin{bmatrix}\text{skip}\\\pi'\end{bmatrix}\rangle_1 \to \langle \omega_1 \begin{bmatrix}\text{skip}\\g\end{bmatrix} A\begin{bmatrix}\varepsilon\\\pi''\end{bmatrix}\rangle_1$$

The following production rules in (3.2) are used for the generation of ω_1 by the two derivations:

$$\langle \varepsilon A\begin{bmatrix}\text{skip}\\\pi\end{bmatrix}\rangle_1 \xrightarrow{\alpha,*} \langle \omega_1 A\begin{bmatrix}\text{skip}\\\pi'\end{bmatrix}\rangle_1$$
$$\langle \varepsilon A\begin{bmatrix}\varepsilon\\\pi\end{bmatrix}\rangle_2 \xrightarrow{\beta,*} \langle \omega_1 A\begin{bmatrix}\varepsilon\\\pi'\end{bmatrix}\rangle_2$$

Above $\alpha, \beta \in \{1, ..., 10\}$ are strings identifying the sequences of production rules in (3.2) that have been used for the generation of ω_1, where we assume that always the left-most nonterminals are expanded in the configurations. Below we give a function $\eta : \{1, ..., 10\} \to \{1, ..., 10\}$ to construct β from α by applying η on the members of α:

$$\eta(7) = 3$$
$$\eta(10) = 4$$

Other rules than 7 and 10 can not occur in α without consuming the upper skip of the nonterminal $A\begin{bmatrix}\text{skip}\\\pi\end{bmatrix}$. Now we make a case distinction based on the rule, which is applied on $\langle \omega_1 A\begin{bmatrix}\text{skip}\\\pi'\end{bmatrix}\rangle_1$ after the prefix ω_1 has been generated:

- If $\pi' = \varepsilon$, then rule 5 can be applied:

$$\langle \omega_1 A\begin{bmatrix}\text{skip}\\\pi'\end{bmatrix}\rangle_1 \xrightarrow{5} \langle \omega_1 \begin{bmatrix}\text{skip}\\\text{skip}\end{bmatrix} A\begin{bmatrix}\varepsilon\\\varepsilon\end{bmatrix}\rangle_1$$

In this case rule 2 must be applied on the other derivation:

$$\langle \omega_1 A \begin{bmatrix} \varepsilon \\ \pi' \end{bmatrix} \rangle_2 \xrightarrow{2} \langle \omega_1 \begin{bmatrix} \text{skip} \\ \text{skip} \end{bmatrix} A \begin{bmatrix} \varepsilon \\ \varepsilon \end{bmatrix} \rangle_2$$

After the steps above, rule 2 is applied on both of the configurations an equal number of times to construct ω_2 and then finally rule 1 is applied once.

- Rule 8 is applied:

$$\langle \omega_1 A \begin{bmatrix} \text{skip} \\ \pi' \end{bmatrix} \rangle_1 \xrightarrow{8} \langle \omega_1 \begin{bmatrix} \text{skip} \\ \text{skip} \end{bmatrix} A \begin{bmatrix} \varepsilon \\ \pi' \end{bmatrix} \rangle_1$$

Rule 4 is applied on the other derivation:

$$\langle \omega_1 A \begin{bmatrix} \varepsilon \\ \pi' \end{bmatrix} \rangle_2 \xrightarrow{4} \langle \omega_1 \begin{bmatrix} \text{skip} \\ \text{skip} \end{bmatrix} A \begin{bmatrix} \varepsilon \\ \pi' \end{bmatrix} \rangle_2$$

And then an identical sequence of production rules is applied on both of the configurations to produce ω_2.

- Rule 9 is applied:

$$\langle \omega_1 A \begin{bmatrix} \text{skip} \\ \pi' \end{bmatrix} \rangle_1 \xrightarrow{9} \langle \omega_1 \begin{bmatrix} \text{skip} \\ g \end{bmatrix} A \begin{bmatrix} \varepsilon \\ \pi'' \end{bmatrix} \rangle_1$$

Here we suppose that $\pi' = g\pi''$. Furthermore, rule 3 is applied on the other derivation:

$$\langle \omega_1 A \begin{bmatrix} \varepsilon \\ \pi' \end{bmatrix} \rangle_2 \xrightarrow{3} \langle \omega_1 \begin{bmatrix} \text{skip} \\ g \end{bmatrix} A \begin{bmatrix} \varepsilon \\ \pi'' \end{bmatrix} \rangle$$

Now an identical sequence or production rules is applied on both of the configurations in order to produce ω_2.

□

Lemma 14. *We consider the two CFGs:*

$$G_c = c2cfg(c, n_{in}^c, n_{fi}^c)$$
$$\text{and}$$
$$G_d = c2cfg(d, n_{in}^d, n_{fi}^d)$$

and their compositions: $G_{c,d} = pc2cfg(c, d, n_{in}, n_{fi})$. *The following holds:*

a) *If c and d are not composable, then $G_{c,d} = pc2cfg(c, d, n_{in}, n_{fi})$ satisfies the conditions of Definition 8 with respect to G_c and G_d without further conditions.*

b) *If $c = d = \text{skip}$ or $c = d = x := e$, then $G_{c,d} = pc2cfg(c, d, n_{in}, n_{fi})$ satisfies the conditions of Definition 8 with respect to G_c and G_d without further conditions.*

6.2. PROOFS FOR CHAPTER 3

c) We suppose that $G_{p_{tt},r_{tt}} = pp2cfg(p_{tt}, r_{tt}, n_{in}^{tt,tt}, n_{fi})$ is a composition of $G_{p_{tt}} = p2cfg(p_{tt}, n_{in}^{tt,c}, n_{fi}^c)$ and $G_{r_{tt}} = p2cfg(r_{tt}, n_{in}^{tt,d}, n_{fi}^d)$ according to Definition 8, $G_{p_{tt},r_{ff}} = pp2cfg(p_{tt}, r_{ff}, n_{in}^{tt,ff}, n_{fi})$ is a composition of $G_{p_{tt}} = p2cfg(p_{tt}, n_{in}^{tt,c}, n_{fi}^c)$ and $G_{r_{ff}} = p2cfg(r_{ff}, n_{in}^{ff,c}, n_{fi}^d)$ according to Definition 8, $G_{ff,tt} = pp2cfg(p_{ff}, r_{tt}, n_{in}^{ff,tt}, n_{fi})$ is a composition of $G_{p_{ff}} = p2cfg(p_{ff}, n_{in}^{ff,c}, n_{fi}^c)$ and $G_{r_{tt}} = p2cfg(r_{tt}, n_{in}^{tt,d}, n_{fi}^d)$ according to Definition 8 and $G_{ff,ff} = pp2cfg(p_{ff}, r_{ff}, n_{in}^{ff,ff}, n_{fi})$ is a composition of $G_{p_{ff}} = p2cfg(p_{ff}, n_{in}^{ff,c}, n_{fi}^c)$ and $G_{r_{ff}} = p2cfg(r_{ff}, n_{in}^{ff,d}, n_{fi}^d)$ according to Definition 8.

In this case, if $c =$ if b_1 then $\{p_{tt}\}$ else $\{p_{ff}\}$ and $d =$ if b_2 then $\{r_{tt}\}$ else $\{r_{ff}\}$ then $G_{c,d} = pc2cfg(c, d, n_{in}, n_{fi})$ satisfies the conditions of Definition 8 with respect to $G_c = (c, n_{in}^c, n_{fi}^c)$ and $G_d = (d, n_{in}^d, n_{fi}^d)$.

d) We suppose that $G_{p,r} = pp2cfg(p, r, n_{in}^{tt,tt}, n_{in})$ is a composition of $G_p = p2cfg(p, n_{in}^{tt,c}, n_{in}^c)$ and $G_r = p2cfg(r, n_{in}^{tt,d}, n_{in}^d)$ according to Definition 8.

In this case if $c =$ while b_1 do $\{p\}$ and $d =$ while b_2 do $\{r\}$ then $G_{c,d} = pc2cfg(c, d, n_{in}, n_{fi})$ satisfies the conditions of Definition 8 with respect to $G_c = c2cfg(c, n_{in}^c, n_{fi}^c)$ and $G_d = c2cfg(d, n_{in}^d, n_{fi}^d)$.

Proof. We assume that the nodes generated by the functions c2cfg, p2cfg, pc2cfg and pp2cfg are always fresh. Therefore, the generated subgraphs of the function calls are only connected by the initial and final nodes given in the arguments.

We prove according to the cases of the statement of the lemma.

a) In this case according to Section 3.2:

$$\text{pc2cfg}(c, d, n_{in}, n_{fi}) = \text{skip2}(\text{c2cfg}(c, n_{in}, n')) \cup \text{skip1}(\text{c2cfg}(d, n', n_{fi}))$$

According to the properties of the function c2cfg there is only one common node in $\text{skip2}(\text{c2cfg}(c, n_{in}, n'))$ and $\text{skip1}(\text{c2cfg}(d, n', n_{fi}))$, which is n'. Let us consider an arbitrary path $\pi_c = f_1, ..., f_k$ of the graph $G_c = \text{c2cfg}(c, n_{in}, n')$ from node n_{in} to n', and an arbitrary path $\pi_d = g_1, ..., g_l$ of the graph $G_d = \text{c2cfg}(d, n', n_{fi})$ from n' to n_{fi}. According to the definition of the functions skip1 and skip2, then $\text{skip2}(G_c)$ has a path $\pi_c' = \begin{bmatrix} f_1 \\ \text{skip} \end{bmatrix} ... \begin{bmatrix} f_k \\ \text{skip} \end{bmatrix}$ and $\text{skip1}(G_d)$ has a path $\pi_d' = \begin{bmatrix} \text{skip} \\ g_1 \end{bmatrix} ... \begin{bmatrix} \text{skip} \\ g_l \end{bmatrix}$ with the same initial and final nodes as π_c and π_d. Since the final node of π_c' on the subgraph $\text{skip2}(G_c)$ and the initial node of π_d' on the subgraph $\text{skip1}(G_d)$ is n' in $G_{c,d}$, $\omega = \begin{bmatrix} f_1 \\ \text{skip} \end{bmatrix} ... \begin{bmatrix} f_k \\ \text{skip} \end{bmatrix} \begin{bmatrix} \text{skip} \\ g_1 \end{bmatrix} ... \begin{bmatrix} \text{skip} \\ g_l \end{bmatrix}$ is a path of $G_{c,d}$ from n_{in} to n_{fi}. Furthermore we know that:

$$\omega = \begin{bmatrix} f_1 \\ \text{skip} \end{bmatrix} ... \begin{bmatrix} f_k \\ \text{skip} \end{bmatrix} \begin{bmatrix} \text{skip} \\ g_1 \end{bmatrix} ... \begin{bmatrix} \text{skip} \\ g_l \end{bmatrix} \in L\left(A \begin{bmatrix} \pi_c \\ \pi_d \end{bmatrix}\right)$$

Therefore, our statement is proved.

b) $c = x_1 := e_1$, $d = x_2 := e_2$ or $c = d =$ skip. Now, $\text{pc2cfg}(c, d, n_{in}, n_{fi}) = (n_{in}, \begin{bmatrix} c \\ d \end{bmatrix}, n_{fi})$, and this graph has only one path $\begin{bmatrix} c \\ d \end{bmatrix}$. $\text{c2cfg}(c, n_{in}^c, n_{fi}^c) = (n_{in}^c, c, n_{fi}^c)$ has the only path c and $\text{c2cfg}(d, n_{in}^d, n_{fi}^d) = (n_{in}^d, d, n_{fi}^d)$ has the only path d. Since $\begin{bmatrix} c \\ d \end{bmatrix} \in L\left(A \begin{bmatrix} c \\ d \end{bmatrix}\right)$, our statement trivially holds.

c) Now we investigate the case when $c =$ if b_1 then $\{p_{tt}\}$ else $\{p_{ff}\}$ and $d =$ if b_2 then $\{r_{tt}\}$ else $\{r_{ff}\}$.

Let us suppose that the graph $G_c = $ c2cfg(c, n_{in}^c, n_{fi}^c) has a path $\pi_c = f_0, f_1, ..., f_k$ from node n_{in}^c to node n_{fi}^c, and similarly, the graph $G_d =$ c2cfg(d, n_{in}^d, n_{fi}^d) has a path $\pi_d = g_0, g_1, ..., g_l$ from node n_{in}^d to node n_{fi}^d. According to the CFG corresponding to the if construct in Figure 3.1 each path of G_c begins with either a $f_0 = b_1$ or a $f_0 = \neg b_1$. Similarly, each path on G_d must start with either a $g_0 = b_2$ or a $g_0 = \neg b_2$. Therefore, we would need to examine four cases depending on the values of f_0 and g_0. We show the proof for the case when $f_0 = b_1$ and $g_0 = \neg b_2$, the other three cases can be shown analogously. In this case $\pi_{p_{tt}} = f_1, ..., f_k$ is a path on $G_{p_{tt}}$ from node $n_{in}^{tt,c}$ to node n_{fi}^c, and $\pi_{r_{ff}} = g_1, ..., g_l$ is a path on $G_{r_{ff}}$ from node $n_{in}^{ff,d}$ to node n_{fi}^d. According to the assumptions, there is an $\omega \in L\left(A\begin{bmatrix}f_1,...,f_k \\ g_1,...,g_l\end{bmatrix}\right)$ on $G_{p_{tt},r_{ff}}$ from node $n_{in}^{tt,ff}$ to node n_{fi}. Furthermore, $\begin{bmatrix}b_1 \\ \neg b_2\end{bmatrix}\omega$ is a path on $G_{c,d}$ from node n_{in} to node n_{fi}. Since $\begin{bmatrix}b_1 \\ \neg b_2\end{bmatrix}\omega \in L\left(A\begin{bmatrix}\pi_c \\ \pi_d\end{bmatrix}\right)$ and it is a path on $G_{c,d} = $ pc2cfg(c, d, n_{in}, n_{fi}) according to the graph in Figure 3.2 the statement is proved.

d) Now we consider the case when $c =$ while b_1 do $\{p\}$ and $d =$ while b_2 do $\{r\}$.

Let us suppose that the graph $G_c = $ c2cfg(c, n_{in}^c, n_{fi}^c) has a path π_c from node n_{in}^c to node n_{fi}^c, and similarly, the graph $G_d = $ c2cfg(d, n_{in}^d, n_{fi}^d) has a path π_d from node n_{in}^d to node n_{fi}^d. In general π_c starts with i number of loops $b_1\pi_p^k$ on G_c from node n_{in}^c to n_{in}^c so that π_p^k is a path from $n_{in}^{tt,c}$ to n_{in}^c on G_p during loop number k, and π_d starts with j number of loops $b_2\pi_r^l$ on G_d from node n_{in}^d to n_{in}^d so that π_r^l is a path from $n_{in}^{tt,d}$ to n_{in}^d on G_r during the loop number l. We prove here the statement for the case when $i \leq j$. For the case when $i > j$ the statement can be proved analogously. Therefore, we split π_d into two parts. In the first part the body of d is executed i times, in the second yet another $j - i$ times. Accordingly, π_c and π_d look the following:

$$\begin{aligned} \pi_c &= \overbrace{b_1\pi_p^1 b_1\pi_p^2...\pi_p^i}^{\pi_c'} \neg b_1 \\ \pi_d &= \underbrace{b_2\pi_r^1 b_2\pi_r^2...\pi_r^i b_2}_{\pi_d'} \overbrace{\pi_r^{i+1}...b_2\pi_r^j}^{\pi_d''} \neg b_2 \end{aligned} \quad (6.1)$$

According to our assumption, for all pairs of paths π_p^ξ and π_r^ξ of G_p and G_r where $1 \leq \xi \leq i$ there is a path ω^ξ on $G_{p,r} = $ pp2cfg$(p, r, n_{in}^{tt,tt}, n_{in})$ so that $\omega^\xi \in L\left(A\begin{bmatrix}\pi_p^\xi \\ \pi_r^\xi\end{bmatrix}\right)$. Therefore, we have a path

$$\omega' = \begin{bmatrix}b_1 \\ b_2\end{bmatrix}\omega^1...\begin{bmatrix}b_1 \\ b_2\end{bmatrix}\omega^i$$

on $G_{c,d} = $ pc2cfg(c, d, n_{in}, n_{fi}) from node n_{in} to n_{in} according to Figure 3.2. There are two cases now.

- If $i = j$ then $\pi_c = \pi'_c \neg b_1$ and $\pi_d = \pi'_d \neg b_2$. Now we have an ω on $G_{c,d}$:

$$\omega = \omega' \begin{bmatrix} \neg b_1 \\ \neg b_2 \end{bmatrix} = \begin{bmatrix} b_1 \\ b_2 \end{bmatrix} \omega^1 ... \begin{bmatrix} b_1 \\ b_2 \end{bmatrix} \omega^i \begin{bmatrix} \neg b_1 \\ \neg b_2 \end{bmatrix}$$

We know about ω the following:

$$\omega \in L\Big(\begin{bmatrix} b_1 \\ b_2 \end{bmatrix} A \begin{bmatrix} \pi_p^1 \\ \pi_r^1 \end{bmatrix} ... \begin{bmatrix} b_1 \\ b_2 \end{bmatrix} A \begin{bmatrix} \pi_p^i \\ \pi_r^i \end{bmatrix} \begin{bmatrix} \neg b_1 \\ \neg b_2 \end{bmatrix}\Big)$$

Because $\begin{bmatrix} f \\ g \end{bmatrix} \in L\Big(A \begin{bmatrix} f \\ g \end{bmatrix}\Big)$, it follows that:

$$\omega \in L\Big(A \begin{bmatrix} b_1 \\ b_2 \end{bmatrix} A \begin{bmatrix} \pi_p^1 \\ \pi_r^1 \end{bmatrix} ... A \begin{bmatrix} b_1 \\ b_2 \end{bmatrix} A \begin{bmatrix} \pi_p^i \\ \pi_r^i \end{bmatrix} A \begin{bmatrix} \neg b_1 \\ \neg b_2 \end{bmatrix}\Big)$$

From Lemma 12 follows:

$$\omega \in L\Big(A \begin{bmatrix} b_1 \pi_p^1 ... b_1 \pi_p^i \neg b_1 \\ b_2 \pi_r^1 ... b_2 \pi_r^i \neg b_2 \end{bmatrix}\Big) = L\Big(A \begin{bmatrix} \pi_c \\ \pi_d \end{bmatrix}\Big)$$

Furthermore, because ω is a path from n_{in} to n_{fi} on $G_{c,d}$, the statement is proved.

- In this case $i < j$. According to the graph $G_{c,d}$ in Figure 3.2 and the definition of skip1(p2cfg($r, n_{in}^{\mathrm{ff,tt}}, n''$)) there is a path ω'' beginning with $n_{in}^{\mathrm{ff,tt}}$ and ending with n_{fi} so that it trespasses the graph $G_{\mathrm{skip},2} = \mathrm{skip1}(\mathrm{p2cfg}(r, n_{in}^{\mathrm{ff,tt}}, n''))$ at least once. Now, it holds that $\omega'' \in L\Big(A \begin{bmatrix} \varepsilon \\ \pi''_d \end{bmatrix}\Big)$. Therefore, $\omega' \begin{bmatrix} \neg b_2 \\ b_1 \end{bmatrix} \omega''$ is a path on $G_{c,d}$ from n_{in} to n_{fi}. Furthermore, we know the following about $\omega = \omega' \begin{bmatrix} \neg b_2 \\ b_1 \end{bmatrix} \omega''$:

$$\omega = \omega' \begin{bmatrix} \neg b_1 \\ \neg b_2 \end{bmatrix} \omega'' = \begin{bmatrix} b_1 \\ b_2 \end{bmatrix} \omega^1 ... \begin{bmatrix} b_1 \\ b_2 \end{bmatrix} \omega^i \begin{bmatrix} \neg b_1 \\ \neg b_2 \end{bmatrix} \omega''$$

Therefore:

$$\omega \in L\Big(\begin{bmatrix} b_1 \\ b_2 \end{bmatrix} A \begin{bmatrix} \pi_p^1 \\ \pi_r^1 \end{bmatrix} ... \begin{bmatrix} b_1 \\ b_2 \end{bmatrix} A \begin{bmatrix} \pi_p^i \\ \pi_r^i \end{bmatrix} \begin{bmatrix} \neg b_1 \\ \neg b_2 \end{bmatrix} A \begin{bmatrix} \varepsilon \\ \pi''_d \end{bmatrix}\Big)$$

Because $\begin{bmatrix} f \\ g \end{bmatrix} \in L\Big(A \begin{bmatrix} f \\ g \end{bmatrix}\Big)$, it follows now that:

$$\omega \in L\Big(A \begin{bmatrix} b_1 \\ b_2 \end{bmatrix} A \begin{bmatrix} \pi_p^1 \\ \pi_r^1 \end{bmatrix} ... A \begin{bmatrix} b_1 \\ b_2 \end{bmatrix} A \begin{bmatrix} \pi_p^i \\ \pi_r^i \end{bmatrix} A \begin{bmatrix} \neg b_1 \\ \neg b_2 \end{bmatrix} A \begin{bmatrix} \varepsilon \\ \pi''_d \end{bmatrix}\Big)$$

From Lemma 12 follows:

$$\omega \in L\Big(A \begin{bmatrix} b_1 \pi_p^1 ... b_1 \pi_p^i \neg b_1 \\ b_2 \pi_r^1 ... b_2 \pi_r^i \neg b_2 \pi''_d \end{bmatrix}\Big) = L\Big(A \begin{bmatrix} \pi_c \\ \pi_d \end{bmatrix}\Big)$$

Therefore, the statement is proved.

□

Lemma 15. *We suppose for all commands $c, d \in C \cup \{\texttt{skip}\}$ that $G_{c,d} = \text{pc2cfg}(c, d, n_{in}^{c,d}, n_{fi}^{c,d})$ satisfies the conditions of Definition 8 with respect to the CFGs $G_c = \text{c2cfg}(c, n_{in}^c, n_{fi}^c)$ and $G_d = \text{c2cfg}(d, n_{in}^d, n_{fi}^d)$. In this case, if $p = c_1; \ldots; c_k$ and $r = d_1; \ldots; d_l$ are so that for each i and j, $c_i, d_j \in C \cup \{\texttt{skip}\}$ then $G_{p,r} = \text{pp2cfg}(p, r, n_{in}, n_{fi})$ satisfies the conditions of Definition 8 with respect to $G_p = \text{p2cfg}(p, n_{in}^p, n_{fi}^p)$ and $G_r = \text{p2cfg}(r, n_{in}^r, n_{fi}^r)$.*

Proof. We assume that the nodes generated by the functions c2cfg, p2cfg, pc2cfg and pp2cfg are always fresh. Therefore, the generated subgraphs of the function calls are only connected by the initial and final nodes given in the arguments.

Let us suppose that the function $\text{pp2cfg}(p, r, n_{in}, n_{fi})$ computes the alignment of commands: $\Omega = \begin{bmatrix} c'_1 \\ d'_1 \end{bmatrix}, \ldots, \begin{bmatrix} c'_m \\ d'_m \end{bmatrix} \in L\left(A\begin{bmatrix} p \\ r \end{bmatrix}\right) = L\left(A\begin{bmatrix} c_1;\ldots;c_k \\ d_1;\ldots;d_l \end{bmatrix}\right)$. The result of the function $\text{pp2cfg}(p, r, n_{in}, n_{fi})$ equals to the following:

$$\text{pc2cfg}(c'_1, d'_1, n_{in}, n_1) \cup \text{pc2cfg}(c'_2, d'_2, n_1, n_2) \cup \ldots \cup \text{pc2cfg}(c'_m, d'_m, n_{m-1}, n_{fi})$$

Therefore, any path from n_{in} to n_{fi} in $G_{p,r}$ crosses the nodes $n_{in}, n_1, \ldots, n_{fi}$. Therefore, we can split any path $\omega_{p,r}$ on $G_{p,r}$ into subpaths $\omega_{c'_i, d'_i}$, each corresponding to the actual pair of commands $\begin{bmatrix} c'_i \\ d'_i \end{bmatrix}$.

Now we construct a path ω on $G_{p,r}$ from node n_{in} to node n_{fi} for any pair of paths π_p and π_r so that it fulfills the requirements of this lemma, where π_p is a path on G_p from node n_{in}^p to node n_{fi}^p and π_r is a path on G_r from node n_{in}^r to n_{fi}^r. We follow the choices made by the function $\text{pp2cfg}(p, r, n_{in}, n_{fi})$ at the construction of the alignment of commands Ω, and we construct ω along these choices. We prove the statement inductively on the length of the prefix $\omega^{i,j}$ of ω which has already been constructed. Let us suppose that the prefix $\omega^{i,j}$ is already constructed so that it holds that $\omega^{i,j} \in L\left(A\begin{bmatrix} \pi_p^i \\ \pi_r^j \end{bmatrix}\right)$ where $\pi_p = \pi_p^i \pi_{c_{i+1}} \pi_p^{i+2,k}$ and $\pi_r = \pi_r^j \pi_{d_{j+1}} \pi_r^{j+2,l}$, so that the path π_p^i is on the CFG of the program $c_1;\ldots;c_i$ and π_r^j is on the CFG of the program $d_1;\ldots;d_j$ from the corresponding initial to the corresponding final nodes. $\pi_{c_{i+1}}$ and $\pi_{d_{j+1}}$ are fragments of the path on G_p and G_r corresponding to the commands c_{i+1} and d_{j+1}. Therefore, $\pi_{c_{i+1}}$ is a path on $G_{c_{i+1}} = \text{c2cfg}(c_{i+1}, n_{in}^{c_{i+1}}, n_{fi}^{c_{i+1}})$ from node $n_{in}^{c_{i+1}}$ to node $n_{fi}^{c_{i+1}}$, and $\pi_{d_{j+1}}$ is a path on $G_{d_{j+1}} = \text{c2cfg}(d_{j+1}, n_{in}^{d_{j+1}}, n_{fi}^{d_{j+1}})$. $\pi^{i+2,k}$ stands for a path on the CFG of the program $c_{i+2};\ldots;c_k$, and $\pi^{j+2,l}$ stands for a path on the CFG of the program $d_{j+2};\ldots;d_l$.

Initially, $i = j = 0$, and $\omega^{0,0} = \pi_p^0 = \pi_r^0 = \varepsilon$. In the initial case the statement holds because $\varepsilon \in L\left(A\begin{bmatrix} \varepsilon \\ \varepsilon \end{bmatrix}\right)$. In the next step of the construction of the alignment of commands Ω the following choices can be made:

- The next element of the alignment of commands Ω is $\begin{bmatrix} \texttt{skip} \\ d_{j+1} \end{bmatrix}$. We suppose that this twin command is number o in the sequence of twin commands that have already been processed. According to the assumptions of the lemma there is a path $\omega_{\texttt{skip},d_{j+1}}$ on $G_{\texttt{skip},d_{j+1}} = \text{pc2cfg}(\texttt{skip}, d_{j+1}, n_o, n_{o+1})$ so that $\omega_{\texttt{skip},d_{j+1}} \in L\left(A\begin{bmatrix} \pi_{\texttt{skip}} \\ \pi_{d_{j+1}} \end{bmatrix}\right)$, where $\pi_{\texttt{skip}} = \texttt{skip}$ is a path on the CFG $G_{\texttt{skip}} = \text{c2cfg}(\texttt{skip}, n_{in}^*, n_{fi}^*)$ and $\pi_{d_{j+1}}$ is a path on the CFG

6.2. PROOFS FOR CHAPTER 3   101

$G_{d_{j+1}} = \text{c2cfg}(d_{j+1}, n_{in}^{**}, n_{fi}^{**})$. From Lemma 12 follows that:

$$L\left(A\left[\begin{smallmatrix}\pi_p^i\\ \pi_r^j \pi_{d_{j+1}}\end{smallmatrix}\right]\right) \supseteq L\left(A\left[\begin{smallmatrix}\pi_p^i\\ \pi_r^j\end{smallmatrix}\right]A\left[\begin{smallmatrix}\varepsilon\\ \pi_{d_{j+1}}\end{smallmatrix}\right]\right)$$

From Lemma 13 follows that:

$$L\left(A\left[\begin{smallmatrix}\pi_p^i\\ \pi_r^j\end{smallmatrix}\right]A\left[\begin{smallmatrix}\varepsilon\\ \pi_{d_{j+1}}\end{smallmatrix}\right]\right) \supseteq L\left(A\left[\begin{smallmatrix}\pi_p^i\\ \pi_r^j\end{smallmatrix}\right]A\left[\begin{smallmatrix}\pi_{\text{skip}}\\ \pi_{d_{j+1}}\end{smallmatrix}\right]\right)$$

Therefore, $\omega_{p^i,r^i}\omega_{\text{skip},d_{j+1}} \in L\left(A\left[\begin{smallmatrix}\pi_p^i\\ \pi_r^j\end{smallmatrix}\right]A\left[\begin{smallmatrix}\pi_{\text{skip}}\\ \pi_{d_{j+1}}\end{smallmatrix}\right]\right)$ entails $\omega_{p^i,r^i}\omega_{\text{skip},d_{j+1}} \in L\left(A\left[\begin{smallmatrix}\pi_p^i\\ \pi_r^j \pi_{d_{j+1}}\end{smallmatrix}\right]\right)$. The rest postfix of the path π_p that needs to be processed in the next step is $\pi_{c_{i+1}}\pi_p^{i+2,k}$, and the rest postfix of the path π_r that needs to be processed in the next step is $\pi_r^{j+2,l}$.

- If the next element of the alignment of commands Ω is $\left[\begin{smallmatrix}c_{j+1}\\ \text{skip}\end{smallmatrix}\right]$ then the statement of the lemma can be proved symmetrically to the case above.

- The next element of the alignment of commands Ω to be processed is $\left[\begin{smallmatrix}c_{i+1}\\ d_{j+1}\end{smallmatrix}\right]$. We suppose that this is number o in the sequence of twin commands that have already been processed. According to the assumptions of the lemma there is a path $\omega_{c_{i+1},d_{j+1}}$ on $G_{c_{i+1},d_{j+1}} = \text{pc2cfg}(c_{i+1}, d_{j+1}, n_o, n_{o+1})$ from n_o to n_{o+1}, so that $\omega_{c_{i+1},d_{j+1}} \in L\left(A\left[\begin{smallmatrix}\pi_{c_{i+1}}\\ \pi_{d_{j+1}}\end{smallmatrix}\right]\right)$, where $\pi_{c_{i+1}}$ is a path on the CFG $G_{c_{i+1}} = \text{c2cfg}(c_{i+1}, n_{in}^*, n_{fi}^*)$ and $\pi_{d_{j+1}}$ is a path on the CFG $G_{d_{j+1}} = \text{c2cfg}(d_{j+1}, n_{in}^{**}, n_{fi}^{**})$ from the corresponding initial nodes to the corresponding final nodes. Therefore, $\omega_{p^i,r^j}\omega_{c_{i+1},d_{j+1}} \in L\left(A\left[\begin{smallmatrix}p^i\\ r^j\end{smallmatrix}\right]A\left[\begin{smallmatrix}c_{i+1}\\ d_{j+1}\end{smallmatrix}\right]\right)$. According to Lemma 12:

$$\omega_{p^i,r^j}\omega_{c_{i+1},d_{j+1}} \in L\left(A\left[\begin{smallmatrix}p^i\\ r^j\end{smallmatrix}\right]A\left[\begin{smallmatrix}c_{i+1}\\ d_{j+1}\end{smallmatrix}\right]\right) \text{ entails}$$
$$\omega_{p^i,r^j}\omega_{c_{i+1},d_{j+1}} \in L\left(A\left[\begin{smallmatrix}p^i c_{i+1}\\ r^j d_{j+1}\end{smallmatrix}\right]\right)$$

Therefore, the statement of the lemma holds. The rest postfix of the path π_p that needs to be processed in the next step is $\pi_p^{i+2,k}$, and the rest postfix of the path π_r that needs to be processed in the next step is $\pi_r^{j+2,l}$.

□

Lemma 16. *Given two programs p, r, and the corresponding CFGs $G_p = p2cfg(p, n_{in}^p, n_{fi}^p)$ and $G_r = p2cfg(r, n_{in}^r, n_{fi}^r)$, their composition $G_{p,r}$ constructed by the call $pp2cfg(p, r, n_{in}, n_{fi})$ satisfies the conditions of Definition 8.*

Proof. We prove the statement inductively on the maximal number of commands embedded into each other on the root-leaf paths of the abstract syntax trees corresponding to the subprograms of p and r. We collect the subprograms of p and r having m commands on their root-leaf paths at the maximum into the set P_m.

The initial case. In the initial case, the members $p', r' \in P_1$ consist of programs with no commands embedded into each other. Therefore, each member of P_1 is a sequence of commands of the form skip and $x\!:\!=\!e$. According to Lemma 14 for pairs of commands c and d of this form it always holds that $G_{c,d} = \text{pc2cfg}(c, d, n_{in}^*, n_{fi}^*)$ satisfies the conditions of Definition 8 with respect to $G_c = \text{c2cfg}(c, n_{in}^c, n_{fi}^c)$ and $G_d = \text{c2cfg}(d, n_{in}^d, n_{fi}^d)$. According to Lemma 15, $G_{p',r'} = \text{pp2cfg}(p', r', n_{in}, n_{fi})$ then satisfies the conditions of Definition 8 with respect to $G_{p'} = \text{p2cfg}(p', n_{in}^{p'}, n_{fi}^{p'})$ and $G_{r'} = \text{p2cfg}(r', n_{in}^{r'}, n_{fi}^{r'})$.

The inductive case. We suppose now that the members of the set P_m are programs having at most m commands on any root-leaf paths of the corresponding abstract syntax trees. We suppose that for each pair $p', r' \in P_m$ it holds that $G_{p',r'} = \text{pp2cfg}(p', r', n_{in}, n_{fi})$ satisfies the conditions of Definition 8 with respect to $G_{p'} = \text{p2cfg}(p', n_{in}^{p'}, n_{fi}^{p'})$ and $G_{r'} = \text{p2cfg}(r', n_{in}^{r'}, n_{fi}^{r'})$. In this case according to Lemma 14 for each pair of commands c and d that are composed of the members of P_m, $G_{c,d} = \text{pc2cfg}(c, d, n_{in}, n_{fi})$ satisfies the conditions of Definition 8 with respect to $G_c = \text{c2cfg}(c, n_{in}^c, n_{fi}^c)$ and $G_d = \text{c2cfg}(d, n_{in}^d, n_{fi}^d)$. Let us call the set of these commands C_{m+1}. Let us denote the set of programs composed from the set of commands in C_{m+1} by P_{m+1}. According to Lemma 15, for all pairs of programs $p'', r'' \in P_{m+1}$, $G_{p'',r''} = \text{pp2cfg}(p'', r'', n_{in}, n_{fi})$ satisfies the conditions of Definition 8 with respect to $G_{p''} = \text{p2cfg}(p'', n_{in}^{p''}, n_{fi}^{p''})$ and $G_{r''} = \text{p2cfg}(r'', n_{in}^{r''}, n_{fi}^{r''})$. Therefore, the statement of this lemma holds on each pair of programs that are members of P_{m+1}. □

Lemma 17. *We suppose that $G_{c,d}$ is the composition of the graphs G_c and G_d corresponding to the commands c and d. Given that the additional conditions below are met, we have that $N_{c,d} \leq M \cdot N_c \cdot N_d$ and $E_{c,d} \leq M \cdot E_c \cdot E_d$, where $M > 4$, N_c and E_c are the number of nodes and edges in $G_c = c2cfg(c, n_{in}^c, n_{fi}^c)$, N_d and E_d are the number of nodes and edges in $G_d = c2cfg(d, n_{in}^d, n_{fi}^d)$, and $N_{c,d}$ and $E_{c,d}$ are the number of nodes and edges in $G_{c,d} = pc2cfg(c, d, n_{in}^{c,d}, n_{fi}^{c,d})$ respectively. The additional conditions are:*

1) *If c and d are not composable then no additional conditions are imposed.*

2) *If $c = d =$ skip or $c = d = x\!:\!=\!e$ then no additional conditions are imposed.*

3) *If $c = $ if b_1 then $\{p_{tt}\}$ else $\{p_{ff}\}$ and $d = $ if b_2 then $\{r_{tt}\}$ else $\{r_{ff}\}$ then the additional conditions are the following:*

- $N_{p_{tt}, r_{tt}} \leq M \cdot N_{p_{tt}} \cdot N_{r_{tt}}$
- $N_{p_{ff}, r_{tt}} \leq M \cdot N_{p_{ff}} \cdot N_{r_{tt}}$
- $N_{p_{tt}, r_{ff}} \leq M \cdot N_{p_{tt}} \cdot N_{r_{ff}}$
- $N_{p_{ff}, r_{ff}} \leq M \cdot N_{p_{ff}} \cdot N_{r_{ff}}$
- $E_{p_{tt}, r_{tt}} \leq M \cdot E_{p_{tt}} \cdot E_{r_{tt}}$
- $E_{p_{ff}, r_{tt}} \leq M \cdot E_{p_{ff}} \cdot E_{r_{tt}}$
- $E_{p_{tt}, r_{ff}} \leq M \cdot E_{p_{tt}} \cdot E_{r_{ff}}$

6.2. PROOFS FOR CHAPTER 3

- $E_{p_{ff},r_{ff}} \leq M \cdot E_{p_{ff}} \cdot E_{r_{ff}}$

Above, N_x and E_x denote then number of edges of the graph G_x where we have that:

- $G_{p_{tt},r_{tt}} = pp2cfg(p_{tt}, r_{tt}, n_{in}^{tt,tt}, n_{fi})$
- $G_{p_{ff},r_{tt}} = pp2cfg(p_{ff}, r_{tt}, n_{in}^{ff,tt}, n_{fi})$
- $G_{p_{tt},r_{ff}} = pp2cfg(p_{tt}, r_{ff}, n_{in}^{tt,ff}, n_{fi})$
- $G_{p_{ff},r_{ff}} = pp2cfg(p_{ff}, r_{ff}, n_{in}^{ff,ff}, n_{fi})$
- $G_{p_{tt}} = p2cfg(p_{tt}, n_{in}^{tt,c}, n_{fi}^c)$
- $G_{p_{ff}} = p2cfg(p_{ff}, n_{in}^{ff,c}, n_{fi}^c)$
- $G_{r_{tt}} = p2cfg(r_{tt}, n_{in}^{tt,d}, n_{fi}^d)$
- $G_{r_{ff}} = p2cfg(r_{ff}, n_{in}^{ff,d}, n_{fi}^d)$

4) If $c =$ while b_1 do $\{p\}$ and $d =$ while b_2 do $\{r\}$ then the additional conditions are that:

- $N_{p,r} \leq M \cdot N_p \cdot N_r$
- $E_{p,r} \leq M \cdot E_p \cdot E_r$

Above, N_x and E_x denote then number of edges of the graph G_x where we have that:

- $G_{p,r} = pp2cfg(p, r, n_{in}^{tt,tt}, n_{in})$,
- $G_p = p2cfg(p, n_{in}^{tt,c}, n_{in}^c)$
- $G_r = p2cfg(r, n_{in}^{tt,d}, n_{fi}^d)$

Proof. We prove each case separately:

1) If c and d are not composable, then we have:

$$G_{c,d} = \text{skip2}(\text{c2cfg}(c, n_{in}, n')) \cup \text{skip1}(\text{c2cfg}(d, n', n_{fi}))$$

Accordingly:

$$\begin{array}{rcl} N_{c,d} & = & N_c + N_d - 1 \\ E_{c,d} & = & E_c + E_d \end{array} \qquad (6.2)$$

Considering the number of nodes in $N_{c,d}$, we need to subtract one from the sum of N_c and N_d because they have one node n' in common. Because $N_c, N_d \geq 2$ and $E_c, E_d \geq 1$ we have:

$$\begin{array}{rcl} N_{c,d} & = & N_c + N_d - 1 \leq 2 \cdot N_c \cdot N_d \leq M \cdot N_c \cdot N_d \\ E_{c,d} & = & E_c + E_d \leq 2 \cdot E_c \cdot E_d \leq M \cdot E_c \cdot E_d \end{array} \qquad (6.3)$$

(6.3) holds because $M > 4$.

2) In this case $G_c = (n_{in}^c, c, n_{fi}^d)$, $G_d = (n_{in}^d, d, n_{fi}^d)$ and $G_{c,d} = (n_{in}, \begin{bmatrix} c \\ d \end{bmatrix}, n_{fi})$. Therefore, we have:

$$N_{c,d} = 2 \leq M \cdot 2 \cdot 2 = M \cdot N_c \cdot N_d$$

Concerning the edges we have:

$$E_{c,d} = 1 \leq M \cdot 1 \cdot 1 = M \cdot E_c \cdot E_d$$

Since according to our assumptions $M > 4$, our statement holds.

3) First we prove the statement considering the number of nodes in the CFGs. In this case according to Figures 3.1 and 3.2 we have:

$$\begin{aligned} N_c &= N_{p_{tt}} + N_{p_{tt}} \\ N_d &= N_{r_{tt}} + N_{r_{tt}} \\ N_{c,d} &= N_{p_{tt},r_{tt}} + N_{p_{tt},r_{tt}} + N_{p_{tt},r_{tt}} + N_{p_{tt},r_{tt}} - 2 \end{aligned} \quad (6.4)$$

What we want to prove is:

$$N_{c,d} \leq M \cdot N_c \cdot N_d$$

Using (6.4) we can reformulate our goal above:

$$N_{p_{tt},r_{tt}} + N_{p_{tt},r_{tt}} + N_{p_{tt},r_{tt}} + N_{p_{tt},r_{tt}} - 2 \leq M \cdot (N_{p_{tt}} + N_{p_{tt}}) \cdot (N_{r_{tt}} + N_{r_{tt}})$$

Using the assumption of the lemma considering the number of nodes in $G_{p_{tt},r_{tt}}$, $G_{p_{tt},r_{tt}}$, $G_{p_{tt},r_{tt}}$ and $G_{p_{tt},r_{tt}}$, we have:

$$M \cdot N_{p_{tt}} \cdot N_{r_{tt}} + M \cdot N_{p_{tt}} \cdot N_{r_{tt}} + M \cdot N_{p_{tt}} \cdot N_{r_{tt}} + M \cdot N_{p_{tt}} \cdot N_{r_{tt}} - 2 \leq M \cdot (N_{p_{tt}} + N_{p_{tt}}) \cdot (N_{r_{tt}} + N_{r_{tt}})$$

Using algebraic reorganizations we obtain:

$$\frac{N_{p_{tt}} \cdot N_{r_{tt}} + N_{p_{tt}} \cdot N_{r_{tt}} + N_{p_{tt}} \cdot N_{r_{tt}} + N_{p_{tt}} \cdot N_{r_{tt}} - \frac{2}{M}}{N_{p_{tt}} \cdot N_{r_{tt}} + N_{p_{tt}} \cdot N_{r_{tt}} + N_{p_{tt}} \cdot N_{r_{tt}} + N_{p_{tt}} \cdot N_{r_{tt}}} \leq$$

The above statement reduces to:

$$-\frac{2}{M} \leq 0$$

Therefore, our statement holds.

Now we prove the statement for the number of edges. According to Figures 3.1 and 3.2 we have:

$$\begin{aligned} E_c &= E_{p_{tt}} + E_{p_{tt}} + 2 \\ E_d &= E_{r_{tt}} + E_{r_{tt}} + 2 \\ E_{c,d} &= E_{p_{tt},r_{tt}} + E_{p_{tt},r_{tt}} + E_{p_{tt},r_{tt}} + E_{p_{tt},r_{tt}} + 4 \end{aligned} \quad (6.5)$$

What we want to prove is:

$$E_{c,d} \leq M \cdot E_c \cdot E_d$$

6.2. PROOFS FOR CHAPTER 3

Using (6.5) we can reformulate our goal above:

$$E_{p_{tt},r_{tt}} + E_{p_{tt},r_{tt}} + E_{p_{tt},r_{tt}} + E_{p_{tt},r_{tt}} + 4 \leq M \cdot (E_{p_{tt}} + E_{p_{tt}} + 2) \cdot (E_{r_{tt}} + E_{r_{tt}} + 2)$$

Using the assumptions of the lemma considering the number of edges in $G_{p_{tt},r_{tt}}$, $G_{p_{tt},r_{tt}}$, $G_{p_{tt},r_{tt}}$ and $G_{p_{tt},r_{tt}}$, we can reformulate our goal again:

$$M \cdot E_{p_{tt}} \cdot E_{r_{tt}} + M \cdot E_{p_{tt}} \cdot E_{r_{tt}} + M \cdot E_{p_{tt}} \cdot E_{r_{tt}} + M \cdot E_{p_{tt}} \cdot E_{r_{tt}} + 4 \leq \\ M \cdot (E_{p_{tt}} + E_{p_{tt}} + 2) \cdot (E_{r_{tt}} + E_{r_{tt}} + 2)$$

Using algebraic reformulations we obtain:

$$\begin{array}{r} E_{p_{tt}} \cdot E_{r_{tt}} + E_{p_{tt}} \cdot E_{r_{tt}} + E_{p_{tt}} \cdot E_{r_{tt}} + E_{p_{tt}} \cdot E_{r_{tt}} + \frac{4}{M} \leq \\ E_{p_{tt}} \cdot E_{r_{tt}} + E_{p_{tt}} \cdot E_{r_{tt}} + E_{p_{tt}} \cdot 2 \\ + E_{p_{tt}} \cdot E_{r_{tt}} + E_{p_{tt}} \cdot E_{r_{tt}} + E_{p_{tt}} \cdot 2 \\ + 2 \cdot E_{r_{tt}} + 2 \cdot E_{r_{tt}} + 2 \cdot 2 \end{array}$$

After further algebraic reformulations we obtain:

$$+ \frac{4}{M} \leq E_{p_{tt}} \cdot 2 + E_{p_{tt}} \cdot 2 + 2 \cdot E_{r_{tt}} + 2 \cdot E_{r_{tt}} + 2 \cdot 2$$

Because the number of edges of a CFG is always a non-negative number, the above statement holds.

4) First we prove the statement considering the number of nodes in a CFG. Based on Figures 3.1 and 3.2 we know the following:

$$\begin{array}{rcl} N_c & = & N_p + 1 \\ N_d & = & N_r + 1 \\ N_{c,d} & = & N_{p,r} + N_p + N_r + 1 \end{array} \quad (6.6)$$

What we want to prove is:

$$N_{c,d} \leq M \cdot N_c \cdot N_d$$

Using (6.6) we can reformulate our goal above:

$$N_{p,r} + N_p + N_r + 1 \leq M \cdot (N_p + 1) \cdot (N_r + 1)$$

Using algebraic reorganizations we obtain:

$$N_{p,r} + N_p + N_r + 1 \leq M \cdot N_p \cdot N_r + M \cdot N_p + M \cdot N_r + M$$

Using the assumption of the lemma that $N_{p,r} \leq M \cdot N_p \cdot N_r$ we can reorganize the statement above:

$$M \cdot N_p \cdot N_r + N_p + N_r + 1 \leq M \cdot N_p \cdot N_r + M \cdot N_p + M \cdot N_r + M$$

Further algebraic reorganizations result:

$$N_p + N_r + 1 \leq M \cdot N_p + M \cdot N_r + M$$

The above statement trivially holds because the values of all variables are positive numbers, and $M > 4$.

Now we investigate the number of edges in $G_{c,d}$. What we know based on Figures 3.1 and 3.2 is:

$$\begin{aligned} E_c &= E_p + 2 \\ E_d &= E_p + 2 \\ E_{c,d} &= E_{p,r} + E_p + E_r + 8 \end{aligned} \qquad (6.7)$$

What we want to prove is:

$$E_{c,d} \leq M \cdot E_c \cdot E_d$$

By substituting (6.7) into the above statement we get:

$$E_{p,r} + E_p + E_r + 8 \leq M \cdot (E_p + 2) \cdot (E_r + 2)$$

Algebraic reorganizations result:

$$E_{p,r} + E_p + E_r + 8 \leq M \cdot E_p \cdot E_r + 2 \cdot M \cdot E_p + 2 \cdot M \cdot E_r + 4 \cdot M$$

Using the assumption of the lemma concerning the number of edges in $G_{p,r}$ that $E_{p,r} \leq M \cdot E_p \cdot E_r$ we obtain:

$$M \cdot E_p \cdot E_r + E_p + E_r + 8 \leq M \cdot E_p \cdot E_r + 2 \cdot M \cdot E_p + 2 \cdot M \cdot E_r + 4 \cdot M$$

Using algebraic reorganizations we obtain:

$$8 \leq (2 \cdot M - 1) \cdot E_p + (2 \cdot M - 1) \cdot E_r + 4 \cdot M$$

The above statement holds because according the assumptions $M > 4$ which entails that $(2 \cdot M - 1) > 7$, furthermore $E_p \geq 1$ and $E_r \geq 1$. $\square$

Lemma 18. *We consider the programs $p = c_1;...;c_k;$ and $r = d_1;...;d_l;$, where $G_p = p2cfg(p, n_{in}^p, n_{fi}^p)$, $G_r = p2cfg(p, n_{in}^r, n_{fi}^r)$, $G_{p,r} = pp2cfg(p, r, n_{in}, n_{fi})$ and N_x and E_x are the number of nodes and edges of the graph G_x respectively. Given that for all $M > 4$, c_i and d_j it holds that $N_{c_i, d_j} \leq M \cdot N_{c_i} \cdot N_{d_j}$ and $E_{c_i, d_j} \leq M \cdot E_{c_i} \cdot E_{d_j}$, where $G_{c_i} = c2cfg(c_i, n_{in}^{c_i}, n_{fi}^{c_i})$, $G_{d_j} = c2cfg(d_j, n_{in}^{d_j}, n_{fi}^{d_j})$ and $G_{c_i, d_j} = pc2cfg(c_i, d_j, n_{in}^{c_i, d_j}, n_{fi}^{c_i, d_j})$, the following holds:*

- $N_{p,r} \leq M \cdot N_p \cdot N_r$
- $E_{p,r} \leq M \cdot E_p \cdot E_r$

Proof. The function pp2cfg constructs an alignment $\Omega = \begin{bmatrix} c'_1 \\ d'_1 \end{bmatrix} ... \begin{bmatrix} c'_p \\ d'_p \end{bmatrix}$ of the two programs p and r, where each c'_i is either a c_j for some j or skip, and similarly, each d'_i is a d_j for some j or skip. We reorder Ω so that the first m members are matched, i.e., they are of the form $\begin{bmatrix} c_i \\ d_j \end{bmatrix}$, and the rest is of the form $\begin{bmatrix} c_i \\ \text{skip} \end{bmatrix}$ or $\begin{bmatrix} \text{skip} \\ d_j \end{bmatrix}$. The CFGs of sequences of pairs commands are the sequences of CFGs corresponding to the pairs of commands, so that the members are connected by their initial and final nodes. Therefore, the reordering of Ω does not change the number of nodes and edges occurring in $N_{p,r}$. This statement holds on the reordering of sequences of commands (i.e., programs) as well. Therefore from now on we assume that, $\Omega = \Omega' \Omega''$ so that:

6.2. PROOFS FOR CHAPTER 3

- $\Omega' = \begin{bmatrix} c_{\alpha_1} \\ d_{\beta_1} \end{bmatrix} ... \begin{bmatrix} c_{\alpha_m} \\ d_{\beta_m} \end{bmatrix}$

- $\Omega'' = \begin{bmatrix} c_{\alpha_{m+1}} \\ \texttt{skip} \end{bmatrix} ... \begin{bmatrix} c_{\alpha_k} \\ \texttt{skip} \end{bmatrix} \begin{bmatrix} \texttt{skip} \\ d_{\beta_{m+1}} \end{bmatrix} ... \begin{bmatrix} \texttt{skip} \\ d_{\beta_l} \end{bmatrix}$

We reorder p and r accordingly:

$$p = \overbrace{c_{\alpha_1};...;c_{\alpha_m}}^{p'}; \overbrace{c_{\alpha_{m+1}};...;c_{\alpha_k}}^{p''};$$

$$r = \overbrace{d_{\beta_1};...;d_{\beta_m}}^{r'}; \overbrace{d_{\beta_{m+1}};...;d_{\beta_l}}^{r''};$$

Above, $1 \leq \alpha_i \leq k$ and $1 \leq \beta_j \leq l$ are two sequences of integers identifying indexes of commands in p and r.

First we prove the statement of the lemma separately on Ω' and on Ω''.

The matched subsequence of Ω: Ω'. The subgraph $G_{\Omega'} = \bigcup_{j=1}^{m} G_{c_{\alpha_j}, d_{\beta_j}}$ corresponding to Ω' consists of graphs $G_{c_{\alpha_j}, d_{\beta_j}} = \text{pc2cfg}(c_{\alpha_j}, d_{\beta_j}, n_{j-1}, n_j)$ connected by their initial and final nodes. We prove inductively, therefore, in the rest we denote the i long subsequence of Ω' with Ω'_i, and we denote the number of nodes and edges of the subgraph $G_{\Omega'_i}$ by $N_{\Omega'_i}$ and $E_{\Omega'_i}$ respectively.

First we prove the statement concerning the number of nodes inductively on the length of Ω'_i. Our inductive assumption is that $N_{\Omega'_i} \leq M \cdot N_{p'_i} \cdot N_{r'_i}$, where $\Omega'_i = \begin{bmatrix} c_{\alpha_1} \\ d_{\beta_1} \end{bmatrix} ... \begin{bmatrix} c_{\alpha_i} \\ d_{\beta_i} \end{bmatrix}$, $p'_i = c_{\alpha_1};...;c_{\alpha_i}$ and $r'_i = d_{\beta_1};...;d_{\beta_i}$.

In the initial case $i = 1$. Therefore, $G_{\Omega'_1} = G_{c_{\alpha_1}, d_{\beta_1}}$, and the statement follows from the assumptions of the lemma.

We would like to prove now the following:

$$N_{\Omega'_{i+1}} \leq M \cdot N_{p'_{i+1}} \cdot N_{r'_{i+1}} \tag{6.8}$$

We know that:

$$N_{\Omega'_{i+1}} = N_{\Omega'_i} + N_{c_{\alpha_{i+1}}, d_{\beta_{i+1}}} - 1 \tag{6.9}$$

And:

$$\begin{aligned} N_{p'_{i+1}} &= N_{p'_i} + N_{c_{\alpha_{i+1}}} - 1 \\ N_{r'_{i+1}} &= N_{r'_i} + N_{d_{\beta_{i+1}}} - 1 \end{aligned} \tag{6.10}$$

In (6.9) and (6.10) there is 1 subtracted from the sum of nodes of the i long prefix and the member $i+1$ because their initial and final nodes are common. By substituting (6.9) and (6.10) into (6.8) we get:

$$N_{\Omega'_i} + N_{c_{\alpha_{i+1}}, d_{\beta_{i+1}}} - 1 \leq M \cdot (N_{p'_i} + N_{c_{\alpha_{i+1}}} - 1) \cdot (N_{r'_i} + N_{d_{\beta_{i+1}}} - 1)$$

Because of the inductive assumption concerning $N_{\Omega'_i}$ we can reformulate the statement that we want to prove:

$$M \cdot N_{p'_i} \cdot N_{r'_i} + N_{c_{\alpha_{i+1}}, d_{\beta_{i+1}}} - 1 \leq M \cdot (N_{p'_i} + N_{c_{\alpha_{i+1}}} - 1) \cdot (N_{r'_i} + N_{d_{\beta_{i+1}}} - 1)$$

Because of the assumption of the lemma concerning the number of nodes of $G_{c_{\alpha_{i+1}}, d_{\beta_{i+1}}}$ that $N_{c_{\alpha_{i+1}}, d_{\beta_{i+1}}} \leq M \cdot N_{c_{\alpha_{i+1}}} \cdot N_{d_{\beta_{i+1}}}$ we can rewrite the statement that we want to prove:

$$M \cdot N_{p'_i} \cdot N_{r'_i} + M \cdot N_{c_{\alpha_{i+1}}} \cdot N_{d_{\beta_{i+1}}} - 1 \leq M \cdot (N_{p'_i} + N_{c_{\alpha_{i+1}}} - 1) \cdot (N_{r'_i} + N_{d_{\beta_{i+1}}} - 1)$$

By reorganizing the right hand side of the above inequation we get:

$$M \cdot N_{p'_i} \cdot N_{r'_i} + M \cdot N_{c_{\alpha_{i+1}}} \cdot N_{d_{\beta_{i+1}}} - 1 \leq$$
$$M \cdot N_{p'_i} \cdot N_{r'_i} + M \cdot N_{c_{\alpha_{i+1}}} \cdot N_{r'_i} - M \cdot N_{r'_i}$$
$$+ M \cdot N_{p'_i} \cdot N_{d_{\beta_{i+1}}} + M \cdot N_{c_{\alpha_{i+1}}} \cdot N_{d_{\beta_{i+1}}} - M \cdot N_{d_{\beta_{i+1}}}$$
$$- M \cdot N_{p'_i} - M \cdot N_{c_{\alpha_{i+1}}} + M$$

By applying simplifications we get:

$$0 \leq N_{c_{\alpha_{i+1}}} \cdot N_{r'_i} - N_{c_{\alpha_{i+1}}} - N_{r'_i} + N_{p'_i} \cdot N_{d_{\beta_{i+1}}} - N_{d_{\beta_{i+1}}} - N_{p'_i} + 1 + \tfrac{1}{M} \quad (6.11)$$

Because the number of nodes of CFGs are at least two, we have:

$$N_{c_{\alpha_{i+1}}} \cdot N_{r'_i} \geq N_{c_{\alpha_{i+1}}} + N_{r'_i}$$
$$\text{and}$$
$$N_{p'_i} \cdot N_{d_{\beta_{i+1}}} \geq N_{d_{\beta_{i+1}}} + N_{p'_i}$$

The above observation implies (6.11), therefore, our statement is proved.

Now we prove the statement concerning the number of edges in CFGs. In the initial case we have that $G_{\Omega'_1} = G_{c_{\alpha_1}, d_{\beta_1}}$, therefore, the statement follows from the conditions of the lemma.

Our inductive assumption is that $E_{\Omega'_i} \leq M \cdot E_{p'_i} \cdot E_{r'_i}$. We would like to prove the following:

$$E_{\Omega'_{i+1}} \leq M \cdot E_{p'_{i+1}} \cdot E_{r'_{i+1}} \quad (6.12)$$

We know the following:

$$\begin{aligned} E_{\Omega'_{i+1}} &= E_{\Omega'_i} + E_{c_{\alpha_{i+1}}, d_{\beta_{i+1}}} \\ E_{p'_{i+1}} &= E_{p'_i} + E_{c_{\alpha_{i+1}}} \\ E_{r'_{i+1}} &= E_{r'_i} + E_{d_{\beta_{i+1}}} \end{aligned} \quad (6.13)$$

By substituting (6.13) into (6.12) we get:

$$E_{\Omega'_i} + E_{c_{\alpha_{i+1}}, d_{\beta_{i+1}}} \leq M \cdot (E_{p'_i} + E_{c_{\alpha_{i+1}}}) \cdot (E_{r'_i} + E_{d_{\beta_{i+1}}})$$

Because of the inductive assumption we can write:

$$M \cdot E_{p'_i} \cdot E_{r'_i} + E_{c_{\alpha_{i+1}}, d_{\beta_{i+1}}} \leq M \cdot (E_{p'_i} + E_{c_{\alpha_{i+1}}}) \cdot (E_{r'_i} + E_{d_{\beta_{i+1}}})$$

Because of the assumption of the lemma considering the number of edges in $G_{c_{\alpha_{i+1}}, d_{\beta_{i+1}}}$ that $E_{c_{\alpha_{i+1}}, d_{\beta_{i+1}}} \leq M \cdot E_{c_{\alpha_{i+1}}} \cdot E_{d_{\beta_{i+1}}}$ we can rewrite the statement that we want to prove:

$$M \cdot E_{p'_i} \cdot E_{r'_i} + M \cdot E_{c_{\alpha_{i+1}}} \cdot E_{d_{\beta_{i+1}}} \leq M \cdot (E_{p'_i} + E_{c_{\alpha_{i+1}}}) \cdot (E_{r'_i} + E_{d_{\beta_{i+1}}})$$

After simplifications we obtain:

$$E_{p'_i} \cdot E_{r'_i} + E_{c_{\alpha_{i+1}}} \cdot E_{d_{\beta_{i+1}}} \leq E_{p'_i} \cdot E_{r'_i} + E_{p'_i} \cdot E_{d_{\beta_{i+1}}} + E_{c_{\alpha_{i+1}}} \cdot E_{r'_i} + E_{c_{\alpha_{i+1}}} \cdot E_{d_{\beta_{i+1}}}$$

We can further reduce the above inequality and get:

$$0 \leq E_{p'_i} \cdot E_{d_{\beta_{i+1}}} + E_{c_{\alpha_{i+1}}} \cdot E_{r'_i}$$

The above inequality trivially holds, therefore our statement is proved for Ω'.

6.2. PROOFS FOR CHAPTER 3

The unmatched subsequence of Ω: Ω''. We know that:

$$\Omega'' = \begin{bmatrix} c_{\alpha_{m+1}} \\ \text{skip} \end{bmatrix} \cdots \begin{bmatrix} c_{\alpha_k} \\ \text{skip} \end{bmatrix} \begin{bmatrix} \text{skip} \\ d_{\beta_{m+1}} \end{bmatrix} \cdots \begin{bmatrix} \text{skip} \\ d_{\beta_l} \end{bmatrix}$$

There are two possibilities concerning the CFG of a pair of the form $\begin{bmatrix} c \\ \text{skip} \end{bmatrix}$ or $\begin{bmatrix} \text{skip} \\ d \end{bmatrix}$. If $c = d = \text{skip}$, then the components of the pairs are alignable. In this case $G_{c,\text{skip}} = G_{\text{skip},d} = (n_{in}^*, \begin{bmatrix} \text{skip} \\ \text{skip} \end{bmatrix}, n_{fi}^*)$. Accordingly, $N_{\text{skip}} = N_{\text{skip,skip}} = 2$ and $E_{\text{skip}} = E_{\text{skip,skip}} = 1$.

If $c \neq \text{skip}$ or $d \neq \text{skip}$ then the pairs are not alignable. In this case for $\begin{bmatrix} c \\ \text{skip} \end{bmatrix}$ we have:

$$G_{c,\text{skip}} = \text{skip2}(\text{c2cfg}(c, n_{in}^*, n')) \cup \text{skip1}(\text{c2cfg}(\text{skip}, n', n_{fi}^*))$$

And for $\begin{bmatrix} \text{skip} \\ d \end{bmatrix}$ we have:

$$G_{\text{skip},d} = \text{skip2}(\text{c2cfg}(\text{skip}, n_{in}^{**}, n')) \cup \text{skip1}(\text{c2cfg}(d, n', n_{fi}^{**}))$$

Because $G_{\text{skip}} = (n_{in}^{\text{skip}}, \text{skip}, n_{fi}^{\text{skip}})$ we can say that:

$$\begin{array}{ll} N_{c,\text{skip}} = N_c + 1 & E_{c,\text{skip}} = E_c + 1 \\ N_{\text{skip},d} = N_d + 1 & E_{\text{skip},d} = E_d + 1 \end{array}$$

Therefore, in the rest of the proof we will assume that for all c and d:

$$\begin{array}{ll} N_{c,\text{skip}} \leq N_c + 1 & E_{c,\text{skip}} \leq E_c + 1 \\ N_{\text{skip},d} \leq N_d + 1 & E_{\text{skip},d} \leq E_d + 1 \end{array} \quad (6.14)$$

We prove the statement now concerning the number of nodes in $G_{\Omega''}$. We have $p'' = c_{\alpha_{m+1}}; \ldots; c_{\alpha_k}$ and $r'' = d_{\beta_{m+1}}; \ldots; d_{\beta_l}$. Since the number of nodes of the CFG of a command is at least two, we can write the following:

$$\begin{aligned} N_{p''} &= \sum_{i=m+1}^{k}(N_{c_{\alpha_i}} - 1) + 1 = \sum_{i=m+1}^{k} N_{c_{\alpha_i}} - (k - m) + 1 = \\ & \quad 2 \cdot (k - m) - (k - m) + 1 + \theta_1 = (k - m) + 1 + \theta_1 \\ N_{r''} &= \sum_{j=m+1}^{l}(N_{d_{\beta_j}} - 1) + 1 = \sum_{j=m+1}^{l} N_{d_{\beta_j}} - (k - m) + 1 = \\ & \quad 2 \cdot (l - m) - (l - m) + 1 + \theta_2 = (l - m) + 1 + \theta_2 \end{aligned} \quad (6.15)$$

Above, $(k-m)$ and $(l-m)$ are the number of commands in the sequences p'' and r'' respectively, and θ_1 and θ_2 are non-negative numbers.

What we would like to prove is:

$$N_{\Omega''} \leq M \cdot N_{p''} \cdot N_{r''} \quad (6.16)$$

We can say the following about $N_{\Omega''}$:

$$N_{\Omega''} = \sum_{i=m+1}^{k} N_{c_{\alpha_i},\text{skip}} - (k-m) + 1 + \sum_{j=m+1}^{l} N_{\text{skip},d_{\beta_j}} - (l-m) + 1 - 1 \quad (6.17)$$

(6.17) holds because of the following. In Ω'' we have $k - m$ pieces of pairs of the form $\begin{bmatrix} c_i \\ \text{skip} \end{bmatrix}$. Since the initial node of each member is identical to the final node of the previous one, we need to subtract $k-m$. But this does not hold for the first piece of the form $\begin{bmatrix} c_i \\ \text{skip} \end{bmatrix}$, therefore we add one. Accordingly, we have $\sum_{i=m+1}^{k} N_{c_{\alpha_i},\text{skip}} - (k-m) + 1$ for the number of nodes for pairs of the form $\begin{bmatrix} c \\ \text{skip} \end{bmatrix}$. Similarly, we have $\sum_{j=m+1}^{l} N_{\text{skip},d_{\beta_j}} - (l-m) + 1$ for the sum of nodes for pairs of the form $\begin{bmatrix} \text{skip} \\ d_j \end{bmatrix}$. Since the final node of the sequence $\begin{bmatrix} c_{\alpha_{m+1}} \\ \text{skip} \end{bmatrix} \dots \begin{bmatrix} c_{\alpha_k} \\ \text{skip} \end{bmatrix}$ is identical to the initial node of the sequence $\begin{bmatrix} \text{skip} \\ d_{\beta_{m+1}} \end{bmatrix} \dots \begin{bmatrix} \text{skip} \\ d_{\beta_l} \end{bmatrix}$, therefore we finally subtract one.

In order to simplify the notation we have:

$$\begin{aligned} x &= (k-m) \\ y &= (l-m) \end{aligned} \quad (6.18)$$

Because of (6.14) we can reformulate (6.17):

$$N_{\Omega''} \leq \sum_{i=m+1}^{k} (N_{c_{\alpha_i}} + 1) - x + 1 + \sum_{j=m+1}^{l} (N_{d_{\beta_j}} + 1) - y + 1 - 1 \quad (6.19)$$

After reorganizing the above we have:

$$N_{\Omega''} \leq \sum_{i=m+1}^{k} (N_{c_{\alpha_i}}) + (k-m) - x + 1 + \sum_{j=m+1}^{l} (N_{d_{\beta_j}}) + (l-m) - y + 1 - 1 \quad (6.20)$$

After simplifications we have:

$$N_{\Omega''} \leq \sum_{i=m+1}^{k} (N_{c_{\alpha_i}}) + \sum_{j=m+1}^{l} (N_{d_{\beta_j}}) + 1 \quad (6.21)$$

Therefore, we can reformulate our goal that we would like to prove (6.16):

$$\sum_{i=m+1}^{k} (N_{c_{\alpha_i}}) + \sum_{j=m+1}^{l} (N_{d_{\beta_j}}) + 1 \leq M \cdot N_{p''} \cdot N_{r''} \quad (6.22)$$

Because of (6.21) (6.22) implies (6.16).

After substituting (6.15) into (6.22) we have:

$$\sum_{i=m+1}^{k} (N_{c_{\alpha_i}}) + \sum_{j=m+1}^{l} (N_{d_{\beta_j}}) + 1 \leq M \cdot (x + 1 + \theta_1) \cdot (y + 1 + \theta_2) \quad (6.23)$$

Because of (6.15) we know that:

$$\begin{aligned} N_{p''} &= \sum_{i=k-m}^{k} N_{c_{\alpha_i}} - x + 1 = x + 1 + \theta_1 \\ N_{r''} &= \sum_{j=k-m}^{k} N_{d_{\beta_j}} - y + 1 = y + 1 + \theta_2 \end{aligned}$$

6.2. PROOFS FOR CHAPTER 3

Therefore:
$$\sum_{i=k-m}^{k} N_{c_{\alpha_i}} = 2 \cdot x + \theta_1$$
$$\sum_{j=k-m}^{k} N_{d_{\beta_j}} = 2 \cdot y + \theta_2$$

After substituting the above into (6.23) we get:
$$2 \cdot x + \theta_1 + 2 \cdot y + \theta_2 + 1 \leq M \cdot (x + 1 + \theta_1) \cdot (y + 1 + \theta_2)$$

After simplifications we get:
$$\begin{aligned} 2 \cdot x + \theta_1 + 2 \cdot y + \theta_2 + 1 \leq\ & M \cdot x \cdot y + M \cdot x + M \cdot x \cdot \theta_2 \\ & + M \cdot y + M + M \cdot \theta_2 \\ & + M \cdot \theta_1 \cdot y + M \cdot \theta_1 + M \cdot \theta_1 \cdot \theta_2 \end{aligned}$$

After reorganizations we have:
$$\begin{aligned} 1 \leq\ & M \cdot x \cdot y + (M-2) \cdot x + M \cdot x \cdot \theta_2 \\ & + (M-2) \cdot y + M + (M-1) \cdot \theta_2 \\ & + M \cdot \theta_1 \cdot y + (M-1) \cdot \theta_1 + M \cdot \theta_1 \cdot \theta_2 \end{aligned}$$

Because M is a member of the summation on the right hand side of the inequality above and $M > 4$, furthermore, all the members of the summation are greater or equal to zero, the statement holds.

Now we prove that:
$$E_{\Omega''} \leq M \cdot E_{p''} \cdot E_{r''} \tag{6.24}$$

We know about Ω'' that:
$$E_{\Omega''} = \sum_{i=m+1}^{k} E_{c_{\alpha_i},\texttt{skip}} + \sum_{j=m+1}^{l} E_{\texttt{skip},d_{\beta_j}}$$

By substituting (6.14) into the above equation we get:
$$E_{\Omega''} \leq \sum_{i=m+1}^{k} E_{c_{\alpha_i}} + x + \sum_{j=m+1}^{l} E_{d_{\beta_j}} + y \tag{6.25}$$

Because the number of edges in a CFG is at least one, we know about p'' and r'' that:
$$\begin{aligned} E_{p''} &= \sum_{i=m+1}^{k} E_{c_{\alpha_i}} = (k-m) + \kappa_1 = x + \kappa_1 \\ E_{r''} &= \sum_{j=m+1}^{k} E_{d_{\beta_j}} = (l-m) + \kappa_2 = y + \kappa_2 \end{aligned} \tag{6.26}$$

Above, $\kappa_1 \geq 0$ and $\kappa_2 \geq 0$, and $k-m$ and $l-m$ are the number of commands in p'' and r'' respectively. Using (6.25) we reformulate the goal (6.24) to be proved:
$$E_{\Omega''} \leq_1 \sum_{i=k-m}^{k} E_{c_{\alpha_i}} + x + \sum_{j=l-m}^{l} E_{d_{\beta_j}} + y \leq_2 M \cdot E_{p''} \cdot E_{r''} \tag{6.27}$$

Now we prove $\leq^2$ in (6.27), which implies the validity of (6.24). We reorganize (6.27) using (6.26) and get:

$$x + \kappa_1 + x + y + \kappa_2 + y \leq_2 M \cdot (x + \kappa_1) \cdot (y + \kappa_2)$$

After further reorganizations we have:

$$2 \cdot x + \kappa_1 + 2 \cdot y + \kappa_2 \leq_2 M \cdot x \cdot y + M \cdot x \cdot \kappa_2 + M \cdot \kappa_1 \cdot y + M \cdot \kappa_1 \cdot \kappa_2$$

$\leq_2$ above follows from the validity of two inequalities where $M > 4$:

$$2 \cdot x + 2 \cdot y \leq_3 M \cdot x \cdot y$$
$$\kappa_1 + \kappa_2 \leq_4 M \cdot \kappa_1 \cdot \kappa_2$$

The entire sequence: $\Omega = \Omega'\Omega''$. Let us consider the sequences of pairs $\Omega' = \begin{bmatrix} c_{\alpha_1} \\ d_{\beta_1} \end{bmatrix} ... \begin{bmatrix} c_{\alpha_m} \\ d_{\beta_m} \end{bmatrix}$ and $\Omega'' = \begin{bmatrix} c_{\alpha_{m+1}} \\ \text{skip} \end{bmatrix} ... \begin{bmatrix} c_{\alpha_k} \\ \text{skip} \end{bmatrix} \begin{bmatrix} \text{skip} \\ d_{\beta_{m+1}} \end{bmatrix} ... \begin{bmatrix} \text{skip} \\ d_{\beta_l} \end{bmatrix}$ and the programs $p' = c_{\alpha_1}; ...; c_{\alpha_m}$, $r' = d_{\beta_1}; ...; d_{\beta_m}$, $p'' = c_{\alpha_{m+1}}; ...; c_{\alpha_k}$ and $r'' = d_{\beta_{m+1}}; ...; d_{\beta_l}$. Above we have proved that if $M > 4$ then:

$$\begin{aligned} N_{\Omega'} &\leq M \cdot N_{p'} \cdot N_{r'} \\ E_{\Omega'} &\leq M \cdot E_{p'} \cdot E_{r'} \\ N_{\Omega''} &\leq M \cdot N_{p''} \cdot N_{r''} \\ E_{\Omega''} &\leq M \cdot E_{p''} \cdot E_{r''} \end{aligned} \quad (6.28)$$

What we would like to prove is:

$$\begin{aligned} N_{p,r} = N_{\Omega} = &\leq M \cdot N_p \cdot N_r \\ E_{p,r} = E_{\Omega} = &\leq M \cdot E_p \cdot E_r \end{aligned} \quad (6.29)$$

We also know the following:

$$\begin{aligned} N_{p,r} = N_{\Omega} &= N_{\Omega'} + N_{\Omega''} - 1 \\ E_{p,r} = E_{\Omega} &= E_{\Omega'} + E_{\Omega''} \end{aligned} \quad (6.30)$$

In (6.30) there is one subtracted from the sum of nodes of $G_{\Omega'}$ and $G_{\Omega''}$ because they have one node in common in G_{Ω}. Furthermore:

$$\begin{aligned} N_p &= N_{p'} + N_{p''} - 1 \\ E_p &= E_{p'} + E_{p''} \\ N_r &= N_{r'} + N_{r''} - 1 \\ E_r &= E_{r'} + E_{r''} \end{aligned} \quad (6.31)$$

In (6.31) there is one subtracted from the number of nodes $N_{p'} + N_{p''}$ and $N_{r'} + N_{r''}$ because they have one node in common in N_p and N_r respectively. By substituting (6.28) into (6.30) we get:

$$\begin{aligned} N_{p,r} &\leq M \cdot N_{p'} \cdot N_{r'} + M \cdot N_{p''} \cdot N_{r''} - 1 \\ E_{p,r} &\leq M \cdot E_{p'} \cdot E_{r'} + M \cdot E_{p''} \cdot E_{r''} \end{aligned} \quad (6.32)$$

So in order to prove (6.29) it suffices to prove that:

$$\begin{aligned} M \cdot N_{p'} \cdot N_{r'} + M \cdot N_{p''} \cdot N_{r''} - 1 &\leq M \cdot N_p \cdot N_r \\ M \cdot E_{p'} \cdot E_{r'} + M \cdot E_{p''} \cdot E_{r''} &\leq M \cdot E_p \cdot E_r \end{aligned} \quad (6.33)$$

6.2. PROOFS FOR CHAPTER 3

By substituting (6.31) into (6.33) we get:

$$\begin{aligned}
M \cdot N_{p'} \cdot N_{r'} + M \cdot N_{p''} \cdot N_{r''} - 1 &\leq M \cdot (N_{p'} + N_{p''} - 1) \cdot (N_{r'} + N_{r''} - 1) \\
M \cdot E_{p'} \cdot E_{r'} + M \cdot E_{p''} \cdot E_{r''} &\leq M \cdot (E_{p'} + E_{p''}) \cdot (E_{r'} + E_{r''})
\end{aligned} \quad (6.34)$$

After reorganizing (6.34) we get:

$$\begin{aligned}
N_{p'} \cdot N_{r'} + N_{p''} \cdot N_{r''} - \tfrac{1}{M} &\leq N_{p'} \cdot N_{r'} + N_{p'} \cdot N_{r''} - N_{p'} \\
&\quad + N_{p''} \cdot N_{r'} + N_{p''} \cdot N_{r''} - N_{p''} \\
&\quad - N_{r'} - N_{r''} + 1 \\
E_{p'} \cdot E_{r'} + E_{p''} \cdot E_{r''} &\leq E_{p'} \cdot E_{r'} + E_{p'} \cdot E_{r''} + E_{p''} \cdot E_{r'} + E_{p''} \cdot E_{r''}
\end{aligned}$$

Further reorganizations lead us to:

$$\begin{aligned}
0 &\leq N_{p'} \cdot N_{r''} - N_{p'} - N_{r''} \\
&\quad + N_{p''} \cdot N_{r'} - N_{p''} - N_{r'} \\
&\quad + 1 + \tfrac{1}{M} \\
0 &\leq E_{p'} \cdot E_{r''} + E_{p''} \cdot E_{r'}
\end{aligned} \quad (6.35)$$

Because the number of nodes of a CFG is at least 2 and the number of edges is at least 1, (6.35) holds. □

Lemma 19. *We consider the two programs $p = c_1;...;c_k$ and $r = d_1;...;d_l$, and their CFGs $G_p = p2cfg(p, n_{in}^p, n_{fi}^p)$ and $G_r = p2cfg(r, n_{in}^r, n_{fi}^r)$. It holds on the number of nodes $N_{p,r}$ and edges $E_{p,r}$ of the composition of G_p and G_r, $G_{p,r} = pp2cfg(p, r, n_{in}, n_{fi})$ that $N_{p,r} \leq M \cdot N_p \cdot N_r$ and $E_{p,r} \leq M \cdot E_p \cdot E_r$ respectively, where $M > 4$, N_p and E_p are the number of nodes and edges in $G_p = p2cfg(p, n_{in}^p, n_{fi}^p)$ respectively, and N_r and E_r are the number of nodes and edges in $G_r = p2cfg(r, n_{in}^r, n_{fi}^r)$ respectively.*

Proof. We prove inductively on the maximal number of commands on the root-leaf paths of the abstract syntax trees of the subprograms of p and r inductively. Therefore, we organize the subprograms of p and r into sets P_m, where m is the maximal number of commands on the root-leaf paths of the abstract syntax trees of the members of P_m.

The initial case. In the initial case we consider the members p', r' of the set P_1. In this case each command c of p' and d of r' is either of the form `skip` or `x := e`. According to Lemma 17 in this case if N_c is the number of nodes and E_c is the number of edges of the graph $G_c = c2cfg(c, n_{in}^c, n_{fi}^c)$, N_d is the number of nodes and E_d is the number of edges of the graph $G_d = c2cfg(d, n_{in}^d, n_{fi}^d)$ and $N_{c,d}$ is the number of nodes and $E_{c,d}$ is the number of edges of the graph $G_{c,d} = pc2cfg(c, d, n_{in}^{c,d}, n_{fi}^{c,d})$ then $N_{c,d} \leq M \cdot N_c \cdot N_d$ and $E_{c,d} \leq M \cdot E_c \cdot E_d$. Therefore, according to Lemma 18, $N_{p',r'} \leq M \cdot N_{p'} \cdot N_{r'}$ and $E_{p',r'} \leq M \cdot E_{p'} \cdot E_{r'}$, where $N_{p'}$ is the number of nodes and $E_{p'}$ is the number of edges of the graph $G_{p'} = p2cfg(p', n_{in}^{p'}, n_{fi}^{p'})$, $N_{r'}$ is the number of nodes and $E_{r'}$ is the number of edges in $G_{r'} = p2cfg(r', n_{in}^{r'}, n_{fi}^{r'})$, and $N_{p',r'}$ is the number of nodes and $E_{p',r'}$ is the number of edges in the graph $G_{p',r'} = pp2cfg(p', r', n_{in}, n_{fi})$.

The inductive case. Let us consider the set of subprograms P_m, where it holds that for each $p^* \in P_m$ the number of commands on any root-leaf path of the corresponding abstract syntax tree is m at the maximum. We suppose now that for each $p^*, r^* \in P_m$ it holds that $N_{p^*,r^*} \leq M \cdot N_{p^*} \cdot N_{r^*}$ and $E_{p^*,r^*} \leq M \cdot E_{p^*} \cdot E_{r^*}$, where N_{p^*} is the number of nodes and E_{p^*} is the number of edges of the graph $G_{p^*} = \text{p2cfg}(p^*, n_{in}^{p^*}, n_{fi}^{p^*})$, N_{r^*} is the number of nodes and E_{r^*} is the number of edges in $G_{r^*} = \text{p2cfg}(r^*, n_{in}^{r^*}, n_{fi}^{r^*})$, and N_{p^*,r^*} is the number of nodes and E_{p^*,r^*} is the number of edges in the graph $G_{p^*,r^*} = \text{pp2cfg}(p^*, r^*, n_{in}, n_{fi})$.

Now we prove the statement for programs composed from the members of P_m having $m+1$ commands at the maximum on the root-leaf paths of the abstract syntax trees. According to Lemma 17, for each command c and d that are composed from the members of P_m it holds that $N_{c,d} \leq M \cdot N_c \cdot N_d$ and $E_{c,d} \leq M \cdot E_c \cdot E_d$, where N_c is the number of nodes and E_c is the number of edges of the graph $G_c = \text{c2cfg}(c, n_{in}^c, n_{fi}^c)$, N_d is the number of nodes and E_d is the number of edges of the graph $G_d = \text{c2cfg}(d, n_{in}^d, n_{fi}^d)$ and $N_{c,d}$ is the number of nodes and $E_{c,d}$ is the number of edges of the graph $G_{c,d} = \text{pc2cfg}(c, d, n_{in}^{c,d}, n_{fi}^{c,d})$. Let us call the set of these commands C_{m+1}. C_{m+1} may also contain commands composed of programs having less than m commands on the root-leaf paths on their abstract syntax trees, in particular, it can be zero. In the latter case, the commands are either of the form `skip` or $x := e$. According to Lemma 18, now it holds on all pairs of programs p'', r'' composed of the members of C_{m+1} that $N_{p'',r''} \leq M \cdot N_{p''} \cdot N_{r''}$ and $E_{p'',r''} \leq M \cdot E_{p''} \cdot E_{r''}$, where $N_{p''}$ is the number of nodes and $E_{p''}$ is the number of edges of the graph $G_{p''} = \text{p2cfg}(p'', n_{in}^{p''}, n_{fi}^{p''})$, $N_{r''}$ is the number of nodes and $E_{r''}$ is the number of edges in $G_{r''} = \text{p2cfg}(r'', n_{in}^{r''}, n_{fi}^{r''})$, and $N_{p'',r''}$ is the number of nodes and $E_{p'',r''}$ is the number of edges in the graph $G_{p'',r''} = \text{pp2cfg}(p'', r'', n_{in}, n_{fi})$.

Therefore, the statement of the lemma holds on any m, so the statement is proved.

□

6.3 Proofs for Chapter 4

Theorem 9. *Let us consider the state machine* $M = (\mathcal{X}_\mathcal{I}, \mathcal{X}_\mathcal{O}, \mathfrak{B}_{\Sigma_2, \Sigma_O}, S, s_0, \delta)$, *an arbitrary state of it* $s \in S$, *an arbitrary run* $\vec{a} = a_0, a_1, \ldots \in \mathsf{Runs}_{s,M}$ *and an arbitrary formula* φ *of the logic Restricted SecLTL having k hide operators. In this case,* $M, s, \vec{a} \models \mathsf{NNF}(\neg\varphi)$ *implies that for any* $\underline{s} = s^1, \ldots, s^k$ *there is a sequence* $\vartheta_0, \vartheta_1, \ldots$ *so that it holds for the run* $\vec{a}^* = (a_0, \vartheta_0), (a_1, \vartheta_1), \ldots$ *that* $\vec{a}^* \in \mathsf{Runs}_{(s,\underline{s}), M_k}$ *and* $M_k, (s, \underline{s}), \vec{a}^* \models \mathsf{tr}(\mathsf{NNF}(\neg\varphi))$, *where* $M_k = (\mathcal{X}_\mathcal{I}, \mathcal{X}_\mathcal{O}, \mathfrak{B}_{\Sigma_2, \Sigma_O}, k, S^*, s_0^*, \delta^*)$ *is the extended transition system corresponding to M.*

Proof. We prove the statement inductively on the height of the syntax tree of $\mathsf{NNF}(\neg\varphi)$, and the number of leak operators k occurring in $\mathsf{NNF}(\neg\varphi)$.

The initial case is the bottom of the abstract syntax tree, which is always of the form $x \triangle L$. If $\mathsf{NNF}(\neg\varphi) = x \triangle L$ then there is no $\mathcal{L}$ operator in $\mathsf{NNF}(\neg\varphi)$, therefore, $\mathsf{NNF}(\neg\varphi) = \mathsf{tr}(\mathsf{NNF}(\neg\varphi)) = x \triangle L$. The statement holds now trivially, because $M = M_0$, there is no extended machine needed in this case.

Now we investigate the inductive case. The inductive assumption is that if $M, s, \vec{a} \models \mathsf{NNF}(\neg\varphi)$ holds for the run $\vec{a} = a_0, a_1, \ldots$ then for any $\underline{s}$ there is a sequence $\vartheta_0, \vartheta_1, \ldots$ so that it holds for the run $\vec{a}^* = (a_0, \vartheta_0), (a_1, \vartheta_1), \ldots$ that $\vec{a}^* \in \mathsf{Runs}_{(s,\underline{s}), M_k}$ and $M_k, (s, \underline{s}), \vec{a}^* \models \mathsf{tr}(\mathsf{NNF}(\neg\varphi))$.

We make a case distinction based on the root of the syntax tree of $\mathsf{NNF}(\neg\varphi)$.

- $\mathsf{NNF}(\neg\varphi) = \mathcal{L}^1_{H,O} \psi$, where ψ is an LTL formula in negation normal form. Since in $\mathcal{L}^1_{H,O} \psi$ there is exactly one leak operator, the corresponding extended model is M_1. Here we suppose that $M, s, \vec{a} \models \mathcal{L}^1_{H,O} \psi$ holds for some $\vec{a} \in \mathsf{Runs}_{s,M}$ and some state s. From the assumptions above and the semantics of the leak operator according to Definition 15, we have that there is at least one $\vec{a}' \in \mathsf{AltRuns}_M(s, \vec{a}, H)$ and at least one $x_o \in O$ so that $\vec{a}[j](x_o) \neq \vec{a}'[j](x_o)$ for some j, meanwhile for all $0 \leq l \leq j$ it holds that $M, \vec{s}[l], \vec{a}[l, \infty) \models \psi$, where $\vec{s} = \mathsf{Exec}_M(s, \vec{a})$.

According to Section 4.3 in this case the corresponding $\mathsf{tr}(\mathsf{NNF}(\neg\varphi))$ is the following:

$$start^1 \wedge \psi \wedge \left[leak^1 \vee \bigcirc\left((\neg start^1 \wedge \psi) \mathcal{U} (\neg start^1 \wedge \psi \wedge leak^1) \right) \right] \tag{6.36}$$

A legal run $\vec{a}^*$ of M_1 satisfying (6.36) looks the following:

$$\begin{aligned} \vec{a}^* = a_0^*, a_1^*, \ldots &= (a_0, \{start^1\}), (a_1, \emptyset), \ldots \\ &\ldots, (a_j, \{leak^1\}), (a_{j+1}, \vartheta_{j+1}), \ldots \end{aligned} \tag{6.37}$$

In particular, it is possible that the first letter of the alternative run $\vec{a}'$ realizes the leakage, in this case $a_0^* = (a_0, \{start^1, leak^1\})$.

Now we examine the execution of M_1 on $\vec{a}^*$. Let us investigate the first transition of M_1 on the run $\vec{a}^*$. According to the construction of extended state machines described in Section 4.3 we have that:

$$\begin{aligned} \delta^*((s, s^1), (a_0, \{start^1\} \cup \vartheta_0^\dagger)) = \\ \{(s_1, s_1^1) \mid s_1 = \delta(s, a_0) \wedge \begin{bmatrix} a_0 \\ a_0' \end{bmatrix} \in \gamma_{\mathcal{X}_\mathcal{I}}(H) \wedge s_1^1 = \delta(s, a_0') \wedge \\ \exists x_o \in O : a_0(x_o) \neq a_0'(x_o) \Rightarrow leak^1 \in \vartheta_0^\dagger \wedge \\ \forall x_o \in O : a_0(x_o) = a_0'(x_o) \Rightarrow leak^1 \notin \vartheta_0^\dagger\} \end{aligned} \tag{6.38}$$

(6.38) shows that for each alternative run in $\text{AltRuns}_M(s, \vec{a}, H)$ there is a state (s_1, s_1^1) of M_1 where s_1^1 corresponds to the state of M on the alternative run. Note that because transition systems are input enabled according to Definition 9, for each a_0' there is an s_1^1 so that $s_1^1 = \delta(s_0, a_0')$. For each $l \geq 1$ the transition of an execution of M_1 on $\vec{a}^*$ is the following, where $start^1 \notin \vartheta_l$:

$$\delta^*((s_l, s_l^1), (a_l, \vartheta_l)) =$$
$$\{(s_{l+1}, s_{l+1}^1) \mid s_{l+1} = \delta(s_l, a_l) \wedge s_{l+1}^1 = \delta(s_l^1, a_l') \wedge a_l'|_{\mathcal{X}_\mathcal{I}} = a_l|_{\mathcal{X}_\mathcal{I}} \wedge$$
$$\exists x_o \in O : a_0(x_o) \neq a_0'(x_o) \Rightarrow leak^1 \in \vartheta_l \wedge$$
$$\forall x_o \in O : a_0(x_o) = a_0'(x_o) \Rightarrow leak^1 \notin \vartheta_l\}$$
(6.39)

According to Definition 9, state machines are input enabled. Therefore, there is always an a_l' and an s_{l+1}^1 so that $a_l'|_{\mathcal{X}_\mathcal{I}} = a_l|_{\mathcal{X}_\mathcal{I}}$ and $s_{l+1}^1 = \delta(s_l^1, a_l')$. Now we see, that there is a sequence of states $s_0^*, ..., s_{j+1}^*$ so that $s_{l+1}^* \in \delta^*(s_l^*, a_l^*)$ for each $0 \leq l \leq j$. Furthermore, the projection of the sequence of states of M_1 on the member s_l^1 is an execution of M on the alternative run $\vec{a}'$. Therefore, if there is a j where $s_{j+1} = \delta(s_j, a_j)$ and $s_{j+1}^1 = \delta(s_j^1, a_j')$ so that $a_j'|_{\mathcal{X}_\mathcal{I}} = a_j|_{\mathcal{X}_\mathcal{I}}$ and $a_j(x_o) \neq a_j'(x_o)$, then the runs $\vec{a}'$ and $\vec{a}$ satisfy the leak operator, and therefore, a_j^* is going to be of the form $(a_j, \{leak^1\})$. This enforces that 6.36 holds on $\vec{a}^*$ if ψ holds on $\vec{a}^*[l, \infty)$ for each $0 \leq l \leq j$. Because the projection of $\vec{a}^*$ on the first member equals to $\vec{a}$, according to the semantics in Definition 12 if there is an l so that $M, \vec{s}[l], \vec{a}[l, \infty) \models \psi$ then $M_1, \vec{s}^*[l], \vec{a}^*[l, \infty) \models \psi$. We have furthermore that $\text{tr}(\psi) = \psi$ because it is an LTL formula without leak operators.

We still need to determine the sequence $\vartheta_{j+1}, \vartheta_{j+2}, ...$ so that $\vec{a}^*[j+1, \infty) \in \text{Runs}_{s_{j+1}^*, M_1}$ where $\vec{a}^*[j+1, \infty) = (a_{j+1}, \vartheta_{j+1}), (a_{j+2}, \vartheta_{j+2}), ...$ Because of the fact that state machines are input enabled, the only thing that needs to be made sure is that whenever there is a variable $x_o \in O$ for which the values in the real run and the alternative run are different, then $leak^1 \in \vartheta_n$, otherwise $leak^1 \notin \vartheta_n$ for each $n \geq j + 1$.

Accordingly, we have found a run $\vec{a}^* \in \text{Runs}_{(s, s^1), M_1}$ corresponding to $\vec{a} \in \text{Runs}_{s, M}$ so that it satisfies our conditions.

- $\text{NNF}(\neg \varphi) = \bigcirc \varphi_1$. We suppose now that $M, s, \vec{a} \models \bigcirc \varphi_1$ for some run $\vec{a}$ and state s. According to the semantics of the $\bigcirc$ operator we have that $M, s_1, \vec{a}[1, \infty) \models \varphi_1$ where $s_1 = \delta(s, \vec{a}[0])$. Therefore, we need to show that there is a ϑ_0 and an $\underline{s}_1$ so that $(s_1, \underline{s}_1) \in \delta^*((s, \underline{s}), (a_0, \vartheta_0))$ for any $\underline{s}$. We choose ϑ_0 so that $start^\xi \notin \vartheta_0$ for any ξ. According to the definition of M_k in Section 4.3 we have:

$$\delta^*((s, ..., s^\xi, ...), (a_0, \vartheta_0)) = \{(s_1, ..., s_1^\xi, ...) \mid$$
$$s_1 = \delta(s, a_0) \wedge s_1^\xi = \delta(s^\xi, a_0') \wedge a_0'|_{\mathcal{X}_\mathcal{I}} = a_0|_{\mathcal{X}_\mathcal{I}}\}$$
(6.40)

Since transition systems according to Definition 9 are input enabled, there is always a possible transition $s_1^\xi = \delta(s_0^\xi, a_0')$, where $a_0'|_{\mathcal{X}_\mathcal{I}} = a_0|_{\mathcal{X}_\mathcal{I}}$. Considering the output values of a_0' we have the following options. If $s_1^\xi = \delta(s_0^\xi, a_0')$ so that there is an $x_o \in \mathcal{X}_\mathcal{O}$ where $a(x_o) \neq a_0'(x_o)$ then $leak^\xi \in \vartheta_0$, if $x_o \in O^\xi$ for the leak operator $\mathcal{L}_{H^\xi, O^\xi}^\xi$ in the formula φ_1. Otherwise $leak^\xi \notin \vartheta_0$.

6.3. PROOFS FOR CHAPTER 4

On the other hand from the inductive assumption follows that there is a $\vec{b}^* = (a_1, \vartheta_1), (a_2, \vartheta_2), ...$ so that $M_k, (s_1, \underline{s}_1), \vec{b}^* \models \text{tr}(\varphi_1)$ for any $\underline{s}_1$. Furthermore, we have seen above that for all $\underline{s}$ there is an $\underline{s}_1$ and a ϑ_0 so that $(s_1, \underline{s}_1) \in \delta^*((s, \underline{s}), (a_0, \vartheta_0))$. Accordingly, if $\vec{a}^* = (a_0, \vartheta), \vec{b}^*$ then $M_k, (s, \underline{s}), \vec{a}^* \models \bigcirc \text{tr}(\varphi_1)$. Since $\bigcirc(\text{tr}(\varphi_1)) = \text{tr}(\bigcirc \varphi_1)$ we have that for any $\underline{s}$ there is an $\vec{a}^*$ so that $M_k, (s, \underline{s}), \vec{a}^* \models \text{tr}(\bigcirc \varphi_1)$.

- $\text{NNF}(\neg \varphi) = \varphi_1 \mathcal{U} \varphi_2$ for some LTL formula φ_1 and some negated Restricted SecLTL formula φ_2 in negation normal form. Note that $\varphi_1 \mathcal{U} \varphi_2$ is a derivative of a negated Restricted SecLTL formula $\neg(\varphi_1' \mathcal{R} \varphi_2')$. According to the grammar (4.1), in a formula $\varphi_1' \mathcal{R} \varphi_2'$ of the logic Restricted SecLTL φ_1' needs to be an LTL formula.

  We assume now that $M, s, \vec{a} \models \text{NNF}(\neg \varphi)$ for some machine M, its arbitrary state s, and run $\vec{a}$. From the semantics according to Definition 12 it follows that for some $i \geq 0$ we have $M, \vec{s}[i], \vec{a}[i, \infty) \models \varphi_2$ and for all j with $0 \leq j < i$ we have $M, \vec{s}[j], \vec{a}[j, \infty) \models \varphi_1$, where $\vec{s} = \text{Exec}_M(s, \vec{a})$. Now we need to select a run $\vec{a}^* = (a_0, \vartheta_0), (a_1, \vartheta_1), ...$ for which it holds that $M_k, (s, \underline{s}), \vec{a}^* \models \text{tr}(\text{NNF}(\neg \varphi))$ and $\vec{a}^* \in \text{Runs}_{(s,\underline{s}), M_k}$ for any $\underline{s}$. Therefore, we select a finite sequence $\vartheta_0, ..., \vartheta_{i-1}$ by examining the transition rules of M_k. We select ϑ_j so that $start^\zeta \notin \vartheta_j$ for any $0 \leq j < i$ and for any $1 \leq \zeta \leq k$. Let us examine a transition of M_k on $\vec{a}^*[j]$ for any $0 \leq j < i$ if there is no $start^\zeta \in \vartheta_j$. According to the definition of M_k in Section 4.3 we have:

$$\delta^*((s_j, ..., s_j^\xi, ...), (a_j, \vartheta_j)) = \{(s_{j+1}, ..., s_{j+1}^\xi, ...) \mid \\ s_{j+1} = \delta(s_j, a_j) \land s_{j+1}^\xi = \delta(s_j^\xi, a_j') \land a_j'|_{\mathcal{X}_\mathcal{I}} = a_j|_{\mathcal{X}_\mathcal{I}}\} \quad (6.41)$$

Since transition systems according to Definition 9 are input enabled, there is always a possible transition $s_{j+1}^\xi = \delta(s_j^\xi, a_j')$, where $a_j'|_{\mathcal{X}_\mathcal{I}} = a_j|_{\mathcal{X}_\mathcal{I}}$. Considering the output values of a_j' we have the following options. If $s_{j+1}^\xi = \delta(s_j^\xi, a')$ so that there is an $x_o \in \mathcal{X}_\mathcal{O}$ where $a(x_o) \neq a'(x_o)$ then $leak^\xi \in \vartheta_j$ if $x_o \in O^\xi$ for the leak operator $\mathcal{L}_{H^\xi, O^\xi}^\xi$ in the formula φ_2. Otherwise $leak^\xi \notin \vartheta_j$. This way we have constructed a sequence of states $(s_0, \underline{s}_0), ..., (s_i, \underline{s}_i)$ so that $(s_{j+1}, \underline{s}_{j+1}) = \delta^*((s_j, \underline{s}_j), (a_j, \vartheta_j))$ for each $0 \leq j < i$.

Our assumption is that $M, \vec{s}[i], \vec{a}[i, \infty) \models \varphi_2$ holds. According to the inductive assumption, then there is a $\vec{b}^* = (a_i, \vartheta_0^b), (a_{i+1}, \vartheta_1^b), ...$ so that $M_k, (s_i, \underline{s}_i), \vec{b}^* \models \text{tr}(\varphi_2)$. Accordingly, there is a sequence of states $\vec{t}^* = (s_i, \underline{s}_i), (s_{i+1}, \underline{s}_{i+1}), ...$ so that $\vec{t}^* \in \text{Exec}_{M_k}((s_i, \underline{s}_i), \vec{b}^*)$.

Accordingly, the run we select is of the following form:

$$\vec{a}^* = (a_0, \vartheta_0), ..., (a_{i-1}, \vartheta_{i-1}), (a_i, \vartheta_0^b), (a_{i+1}, \vartheta_1^b), ...$$

From the arguments above follows that $\vec{a}^* \in \text{Runs}_{(s,\underline{s}), M_k}$.

  – Because the values of variables on $\vec{a}$ and on $\vec{a}^*$ are equal, it follows for all $0 \leq j < i$ that:

$$M_k, \vec{s}^*[j], \vec{a}^*[j, \infty) \models \text{tr}(\varphi_1) \quad (6.42)$$

In (6.42) $\vec{s}^* = (s_0, \underline{s}_0), ..., (s_{i+1}, \underline{s}_{i+1}), \vec{t}^*$. Note, that because φ_1 is an LTL formula, $\text{tr}(\varphi_1) = \varphi_1$.

– We have that $M, \vec{s}[i], \vec{a}[i, \infty) \models \varphi_2$. Therefore, from the inductive assumption follows that:

$$M_k, (s_i, \underline{s}_i), \vec{a}^*[i, \infty) \models \text{tr}(\varphi_2)$$

The above two statements entail that $M_k, (s, \underline{s}), \vec{a}^* \models \text{tr}(\varphi_1)\mathcal{U}\text{tr}(\varphi_2)$. Since $\text{tr}(\varphi_1)\mathcal{U}\text{tr}(\varphi_2) = \text{tr}(\varphi_1 \mathcal{U} \varphi_2)$, the statement is proved.

- $\text{NNF}(\neg \varphi) = \varphi_1 \mathcal{R} \varphi_2$ for some LTL formula φ_2 and negated Restricted SecLTL formula φ_1 in negation normal form. Note that $\varphi_1 \mathcal{R} \varphi_2$ is a negated Restricted SecLTL formula. According to the grammar (4.1), in a formula $\varphi_1' \mathcal{U} \varphi_2'$ of the logic Restricted SecLTL φ_2' needs to be an LTL formula. Here, $\varphi_1 \mathcal{R} \varphi_2$ is a derivation of $\neg(\varphi_1' \mathcal{U} \varphi_2')$.

We assume now that $M, s, \vec{a} \models \text{NNF}(\neg \varphi)$ for some machine M, its arbitrary state s, and run $\vec{a}$. From the semantics according to Definition 12 it follows that either

a) $M, \vec{s}[j], \vec{a}[j, \infty) \models \varphi_2$ holds for all $j \geq 0$

b) or there is a $i \geq 0$ such that $M, \vec{s}[i], \vec{a}[i, \infty) \models \varphi_1$ and for all $0 \leq j \leq i$ we have $M, \vec{s}[j], \vec{a}[j, \infty) \models \varphi_2$, where $\vec{s} = \text{Exec}_M(s, \vec{a})$

Now we need to select a run $\vec{a}^* = (a_0, \vartheta_0), (a_1, \vartheta_1), ...$ for which it holds that $M_k, (s, \underline{s}), \vec{a}^* \models \text{tr}(\text{NNF}(\neg \varphi))$ and $\vec{a}^* \in \text{Runs}_{(s,\underline{s}), M_k}$ for any $\underline{s}$. Therefore, we select a sequence $\vartheta_0, ..., \vartheta_{i-1}$ by examining the transition rules of M_k. We select ϑ_j so that $start^\zeta \notin \vartheta_j$ for any $0 \leq j < i$ and for any $1 \leq \zeta \leq k$. Let us examine a transition of M_k on $\vec{a}^*[j]$ for any $0 \leq j < i$ if there is no $start^\zeta \in \vartheta_j$. According to the definition of M_k in Section 4.3 we have:

$$\begin{aligned}\delta^*((s_j, ..., s_j^\xi, ...), (a_j, \vartheta_j)) = \{(s_{j+1}, ..., s_{j+1}^\xi, ...) \mid \\ s_{j+1} = \delta(s_j, a_j) \wedge s_{j+1}^\xi = \delta(s_j^\xi, a_j') \wedge a_j'|_{\mathcal{X}_\mathcal{I}} = a_j|_{\mathcal{X}_\mathcal{I}}\}\end{aligned} \quad (6.43)$$

Since transition systems according to Definition 9 are input enabled, there is always a possible transition $s_{j+1}^\xi = \delta(s_j^\xi, a')$, where $a_j'|_{\mathcal{X}_\mathcal{I}} = a_j|_{\mathcal{X}_\mathcal{I}}$. Considering the output values of a_j' we have the following options. If $s_{j+1}^\xi = \delta(s_j^\xi, a')$ so that there is an $x_o \in \mathcal{X}_\mathcal{O}$ where $a(x_o) \neq a'(x_o)$ then $leak^\xi \in \vartheta_j$ if $x_o \in O^\xi$ for the leak operator $\mathcal{L}_{H^\xi, O^\xi}^\xi$ in the formula φ_1. Otherwise $leak^\xi \notin \vartheta_j$. This way we have constructed a sequence of states $\vec{s}^* = (s, \underline{s}), ..., (s_i, \underline{s}_i)$ so that $(s_{j+1}, \underline{s}_{j+1}) = \delta^*((s_j, \underline{s}_j)(a_j, \vartheta_j))$ for each $0 \leq j < i$.

– If case a) holds above, then we continue the above described selection so that i goes to infinity. Therefore, we have found a run $\vec{a}^* = (a_0, \vartheta_0), (a_1, \vartheta_1), ...$ so that $\vec{a}^* \in \text{Runs}_{(s,\underline{s}), M_k}$. Furthermore, because the values of variables in $\vec{a}$ and $\vec{a}^*$ coincide and $M, \vec{s}[j], \vec{a}[j, \infty) \models \varphi_2$ holds for all $j \geq 0$, we have that $M_k, \vec{s}^*[j], \vec{a}^*[j, \infty) \models \text{tr}(\varphi_2)$. Note that φ_2 is an LTL formula, therefore, $\text{tr}(\varphi_2) = \varphi_2$.

6.3. PROOFS FOR CHAPTER 4

- Now we assume that case b) holds above. Our assumption is that $M, \vec{s}[i], \vec{a}[i, \infty) \models \varphi_1$ holds for some i. According to the inductive assumption, then there is a $\vec{b}^* = (a_i, \vartheta_0^b), (a_{i+1}, \vartheta_1^b), ...$ where it holds that $M_k, (s_i, \underline{s}_i), \vec{b}^* \models \text{tr}(\varphi_1)$ for any $\underline{s}_i$. Accordingly, there is a sequence $\vec{t}^* = (s_i, \underline{s}_i), (s_{i+1}, \underline{s}_{i+1}), ...$ so that $\vec{t}^* \in \text{Exec}_{M_k}((s_i, \underline{s}_i), \vec{b}^*)$. Accordingly, the run we select is of the following form:

$$\vec{a}^* = (a_0, \vartheta_0), ..., (a_{i-1}, \vartheta_{i-1}), (a_i, \vartheta_0^b), (a_{i+1}, \vartheta_1^b), ...$$

From the arguments above follows that $\vec{a}^* \in \text{Runs}_{(s,\underline{s}), M_k}$.

  * Because the values of variables on $\vec{a}$ and on $\vec{a}^*$ are equal, it follows for all $0 \leq j \leq i$ that:

  $$M_k, \vec{s}^*[j], \vec{a}^*[j, \infty) \models \text{tr}(\varphi_2) \tag{6.44}$$

  In (6.44) $\vec{s}^* = (s_0, \underline{s}_0), ..., (s_{i-1}, \underline{s}_{i-1}), \vec{t}^*$. Note, that because φ_2 is an LTL formula, $\text{tr}(\varphi_2) = \varphi_2$.

  * We have that $M, \vec{s}[i], \vec{a}[i, \infty) \models \varphi_1$. Therefore, from the inductive assumption follows that:

  $$M_k, (s_i, \underline{s}_i), \vec{a}^*[i, \infty) \models \text{tr}(\varphi_1)$$

  The above two statements entail that $M_k, (s, \underline{s}), \vec{a}^* \models \text{tr}(\varphi_1)\mathcal{R}\text{tr}(\varphi_2)$. Since $\text{tr}(\varphi_1)\mathcal{R}\text{tr}(\varphi_2) = \text{tr}(\varphi_1 \mathcal{R} \varphi_2)$, the statement is proved.

- $\text{NNF}(\neg \varphi) = \varphi_1 \wedge \varphi_2$. Let us suppose that the number of $\mathcal{L}$ operators in φ_1 is k_1 and the number of $\mathcal{L}$ operators in φ_2 is k_2. We define the function g so that it renames all occurrences of an index ξ in the object in its argument by $\xi + k_1$. Therefore, $g(\varphi_2)$ is an equivalent formula to φ_2 but each occurrence of an operator $\mathcal{L}_{H^\xi, O^\xi}^{\xi}$ is renamed to $\mathcal{L}_{H^{\xi+k_1}, O^{\xi+k_1}}^{\xi+k_1}$. Now we construct the corresponding extended machine $M_{k_1+k_2} = (\mathcal{X}_\mathcal{I}, \mathcal{X}_\mathcal{O}, \mathfrak{B}_{\Sigma_2, \Sigma_0}, k_1 + k_2, S^*, s_0^*, \delta^*)$ according to its description in Section 4.3.

  We consider now an arbitrary run $\vec{a} = a_0, a_1, ...$ for which the following holds:

  $$M, s, \vec{a} \models \varphi_1 \wedge \varphi_2$$

  Now according to the semantics of Restricted SecLTL in Definition 12 we have that:

  $$(M, s, \vec{a} \models \varphi_1) \text{ and } (M, s, \vec{a} \models \varphi_2)$$

  The inductive assumptions are now that for all $\underline{s}$ there is a $\vec{a}^*$ so that $M_{k_1}, (s, \underline{s}), \vec{a}^* \models \text{tr}(\varphi_1)$, and for all $\underline{t}$ there is a $\vec{b}^*$ so that $M_{k_2}, (s, \underline{t}), \vec{b}^* \models \text{tr}(\varphi_2)$, where:

  $$\begin{aligned} \vec{a}^* &= (a_0, \vartheta_0), (a_1, \vartheta_1), ... \text{ for some } \vartheta_0, \vartheta_2, ... \\ \vec{b}^* &= (a_0, \kappa_0), (a_1, \kappa_1), ... \text{ for some } \kappa_0, \kappa_2, ... \end{aligned}$$

  Let us define $\vec{c}^*$ the following way:

  $$\vec{c}^* = (a_0, \vartheta_0 \cup g(\kappa_0)), (a_1, \vartheta_1 \cup g(\kappa_1)), ...$$

Based on the construction of $M_{k_1+k_2}$ and the inductive assumption we have that:
$$M_{k_1+k_2}, (s, \underline{s}, \underline{t}), \vec{c}^* \models \mathsf{tr}(\varphi_1)$$
And:
$$M_{k_1+k_2}, (s, \underline{s}, \underline{t}), \vec{c}^* \models g(\mathsf{tr}(\varphi_2))$$
From this it follows that:
$$M_{k_1+k_2}, (s, \underline{s}, \underline{t}), \vec{c}^* \models \mathsf{tr}(\varphi_1) \wedge g(\mathsf{tr}(\varphi_2))$$
Because $\mathsf{tr}(\varphi_1) \wedge g(\mathsf{tr}(\varphi_2)) = \mathsf{tr}(\varphi_1 \wedge g(\varphi_2))$ our statement holds.

- NNF$(\neg \varphi) = \varphi_1 \vee \varphi_2$. Let us suppose that the number of $\mathcal{L}$ operators in φ_1 is k_1 and the number of $\mathcal{L}$ operators in φ_2 is k_2. We define the function g so that it renames all occurrences of an index ξ in the object in its argument by $\xi + k_1$. Therefore, $g(\varphi_2)$ is an equivalent formula to φ_2 but each occurrence of an operator $\mathcal{L}^\xi_{H^\xi, O^\xi}$ is renamed to $\mathcal{L}^{\xi+k_1}_{H^{\xi+k_1}, O^{\xi+k_1}}$. Now we construct the corresponding extended machine $M_{k_1+k_2} = (\mathcal{X}_\mathcal{I}, \mathcal{X}_\mathcal{O}, \mathfrak{B}_{\Sigma_2, \Sigma_0}, k_1 + k_2, S^*, s_0^*, \delta^*)$ according to its description in Section 4.3.

We consider now an arbitrary run $\vec{a} = a_0, a_1, \dots$ for which the following holds:
$$M, s, \vec{a} \models \varphi_1 \vee \varphi_2$$

Now according to the semantics of Restricted SecLTL in Definition 12 we have that:
$$(M, s, \vec{a} \models \varphi_1) \text{ or } (M, s, \vec{a} \models \varphi_2)$$

The inductive assumptions are now that if $M, s, \vec{a} \models \varphi_1$ then for all $\underline{s}$ there is a $\vec{a}^*$ so that $M_{k_1}, (s, \underline{s}), \vec{a}^* \models \mathsf{tr}(\varphi_1)$, and if $M, s, \vec{a} \models \varphi_2$ then for all $\underline{t}$ there is a $\vec{b}^*$ so that $M_{k_2}, (s, \underline{t}), \vec{b}^* \models \mathsf{tr}(\varphi_2)$, where:
$$\vec{a}^* = (a_0, \vartheta_0), (a_1, \vartheta_1), \dots \text{ for some } \vartheta_0, \vartheta_2, \dots$$
$$\vec{b}^* = (a_0, \kappa_0), (a_1, \kappa_1), \dots \text{ for some } \kappa_0, \kappa_2, \dots$$

Let us define $\vec{c}^*$ the following way:
$$\vec{c}^* = (a_0, \vartheta_0 \cup g(\kappa_0)), (a_1, \vartheta_1 \cup g(\kappa_1)), \dots$$

Based on the construction of $M_{k_1+k_2}$ and the inductive assumption we have that:
$$M_{k_1+k_2}, (s, \underline{s}, \underline{t}), \vec{c}^* \models \mathsf{tr}(\varphi_1)$$
Or:
$$M_{k_1+k_2}, (s, \underline{s}, \underline{t}), \vec{c}^* \models g(\mathsf{tr}(\varphi_2))$$
From this it follows that:
$$M_{k_1+k_2}, (s, \underline{s}, \underline{t}), \vec{c}^* \models \mathsf{tr}(\varphi_1) \vee g(\mathsf{tr}(\varphi_2))$$

Because $\mathsf{tr}(\varphi_1) \vee g(\mathsf{tr}(\varphi_2)) = \mathsf{tr}(\varphi_1 \vee g(\varphi_2))$ our statement follows.

□

6.3. PROOFS FOR CHAPTER 4

Theorem 10. *Let us consider the product $N_{M_k, N_{\text{tr}(\text{NNF}(\neg\varphi))}}$ of the extended state machine M_k and the Büchi automaton $N_{\text{tr}(\text{NNF}(\neg\varphi))}$ corresponding to the LTL formula $\text{tr}(\text{NNF}(\neg\varphi))$. Furthermore, let us consider the product $N_{\widehat{M}_k, N_{\text{tr}(\text{NNF}(\neg\varphi))}}$ of the abstract state machine $\widehat{M}_k$ and $N_{\text{tr}(\text{NNF}(\neg\varphi))}$. In this case the fact that $L(N_{\widehat{M}_k, N_{\text{tr}(\text{NNF}(\neg\varphi))}}) = \emptyset$ entails that $L(N_{M_k, N_{\text{tr}(\text{NNF}(\neg\varphi))}}) = \emptyset$.*

Proof. We prove the contrapositive of the statement. In other words, we prove that if there is a concrete run $\vec{a}^* = (a_0, \vartheta_0), (a_1, \vartheta_1), \ldots \in L(N_{M_k, N_{\text{tr}(\text{NNF}(\neg\varphi))}})$ then there is an abstract run $\vec{\hat{a}} = (\hat{a}_0, \vartheta_0), (\hat{a}_1, \vartheta_1), \ldots \in L(N_{\widehat{M}_k, N_{\text{tr}(\text{NNF}(\neg\varphi))}})$ so that for each i and each $x \in \mathcal{X}$ it holds that $a_i(x) \bigtriangleup \hat{a}_i(x)$.

Therefore, let us regard the run $\vec{a}^* = (a_0, \vartheta_0), (a_1, \vartheta_1), \ldots$ and the accepting execution $\vec{s}^\times = (s_0^*, s_0^N), (s_1^*, s_1^N), \ldots$ of $L(N_{M_k, N_{\text{tr}(\text{NNF}(\neg\varphi))}})$ on $\vec{a}^*$. The initial state of $N_{\widehat{M}_k, N_{\text{tr}(\text{NNF}(\neg\varphi))}}$ is $(\hat{\underline{s}}_0, s_0^N)$, where according to Definition 17 $s_0^* \in \gamma^S(\hat{\underline{s}}_0)$. Now we prove inductively, that there is a run $\vec{\hat{a}} = (\hat{a}_0, \vartheta_0), (\hat{a}_1, \vartheta_1), \ldots$ of $N_{\widehat{M}_k, N_{\text{tr}(\text{NNF}(\neg\varphi))}}$ and a corresponding execution $\vec{\hat{s}}^\times = (\hat{\underline{s}}_0, s_0^N), (\hat{\underline{s}}_1, s_1^N), \ldots$ on $\vec{\hat{a}}$ so that for each i and $x \in \mathcal{X}$ it holds that $a_i(x) \bigtriangleup \hat{a}_i(x)$ and $s_i^* \in \gamma^S(\hat{\underline{s}}^i)$. The inductive assumption is that if the member number i in $\vec{s}^\times$ is (s_i^*, s_i^N), then member number i in the abstract execution $\vec{\hat{s}}^\times$ is $(\hat{\underline{s}}_i, s_i^N)$, so that $s_i^* \in \gamma^S(\hat{\underline{s}}_i)$. Let us consider the next transition of $N_{M_k, N_{\text{tr}(\text{NNF}(\neg\varphi))}}$:

$$(s_{i+1}^*, s_{i+1}^N) \in \delta^\times((s_i^*, s_i^N), (a_i, \vartheta_i)) \quad (6.45)$$

According to the definition of $N_{M_k, N_{\text{tr}(\text{NNF}(\neg\varphi))}}$ in this case there is a transition $s_{i+1}^* \in \delta^*(s_i^*, (a_i, \vartheta_i))$ of M_k. From Definition 17 it follows now that there is a transition $\hat{\underline{s}}_{i+1} \in \hat{\delta}(\hat{\underline{s}}_i, (\hat{a}_i, \vartheta_i))$ for any $\hat{\underline{s}}_i$ where $s_i^* \in \gamma^S(\hat{\underline{s}}_i)$, and for any $(\hat{a}_i, \vartheta_i)$ where $(a_i, \vartheta_i) \in \gamma^A((\hat{a}_i, \vartheta_i))$ so that $s_{i+1}^* \in \gamma^S(\hat{\underline{s}}_{i+1})$.

Now we show that there is a corresponding successor state of $N_{\text{tr}(\text{NNF}(\neg\varphi))}$, too. Let us choose $\hat{a}_i$ so that for each $x \in \mathcal{X}$, $\hat{a}_i(x) = \{\tau_x\}$ is a singleton tree where $\tau_x \in \mathfrak{B}_{\Sigma, \{\#, bv\}}$. We construct τ_x by exchanging each leaf in $a_i(x)$ labeled with a basic value with the symbol bv. From (6.45) follows that $N_{\text{tr}(\text{NNF}(\neg\varphi))}$ has a transition $s_{i+1}^N \in \rho(s_i^N, \Psi_i)$. Now because we have that $s_{i+1}^N \in \rho(s_i^N, \Psi_i)$, it follows that $(a_i, \vartheta_i) \models \bigwedge_{P \in \Psi_i} P$. This entails that $a_i(x) \bigtriangleup L$, for each member of Ψ of the form $x \bigtriangleup L$. It follows that $\tau_x \in L$ for each member of Ψ of the form $x \bigtriangleup L$. Accordingly, if $\hat{a}_i(x) = \{\tau_x\}$ for each x, then we have for each x that $\hat{a}_i(x) \subseteq L$, where $(x \bigtriangleup L) \in \Psi_i$. According to the definition of $N_{\widehat{M}_k, N_{\text{tr}(\text{NNF}(\neg\varphi))}}$ now it follows that $(\hat{\underline{s}}_{i+1}, s_{i+1}^N) \in \hat{\delta}^\times((\hat{\underline{s}}_i, s_i^N), (\hat{a}_i, \vartheta_i))$. □

Theorem 11. *The abstract machine $\widehat{M}_k = (\mathcal{X}_\mathcal{I}, \mathcal{X}_\mathcal{O}, \mathcal{P}(\mathfrak{B}_{\Sigma_2, \{\#, bv\}}), k, \widehat{S}, \hat{\underline{s}}_0, \hat{\delta})$ constructed based on $M_k = (\mathcal{X}_\mathcal{I}, \mathcal{X}_\mathcal{O}, \mathfrak{B}_{\Sigma_2, \Sigma_0}, k, S^*, s_0^*, \delta^*)$ using the abstract interpretation techniques of Section 3.3, is indeed an abstraction of M_k according to Definition 17.*

Proof. Let us now investigate the relation between the initial state $s_0^* = (s_0^0, s_0^1, \ldots, s_0^k)$ of M_k and the initial state $\hat{\underline{s}}_0 = (\hat{s}^0{}_0, \hat{s}^1_0, \ldots, \hat{s}^k_0)$ of $\widehat{M}_k$. The initial state of M_k is $s_0^* = (\#, \ldots, \#)$, and the initial state of $\widehat{M}_k$ is $\hat{\underline{s}}_0 = (\{\#\}, \ldots, \{\#\})$. Therefore, it holds trivially that $s_0^* \in \gamma^S(\hat{\underline{s}}_0)$.

Let us now investigate the abstract transition function $\widehat{\delta}$ together with the concretization functions γ^S and γ^A. We suppose now that M_k is in the state $s^* = (s^0, s^1, ..., s^k)$ and $\widehat{M}_k$ is in the state $\widehat{\underline{s}} = (\widehat{s}^0, \widehat{s}^1, ..., \widehat{s}^k)$. Our assumption is that $s^* \in \gamma^S(\widehat{\underline{s}})$. Furthermore, we assume that the next letter a^* of M_k and the next letter $\widehat{\underline{a}}$ of $\widehat{M}_k$ are so that $a^* \in \gamma^A(\widehat{\underline{a}})$. Now we suppose that there is an $s^{*\prime} \in \delta^*(s^*, (a, \vartheta))$, where $a^* = (a, \vartheta)$. Let us suppose that M_k and $\widehat{M}_k$ have been constructed in connection with the Restricted SecLTL formula φ. If there is a $leak^i \in \vartheta$ it means that there is a subformula $\mathcal{H}^i_{H^i, O^i} \psi$ in φ so that there is an $x_o \in O^i$ where $s^0(x_o) \neq s^i(x_o)$. According to our assumption we have that $\begin{bmatrix} s^0(x_o) \\ s^i(x_o) \end{bmatrix} \in \gamma(\widehat{s}^i)$. Because $s^0(x_o) \neq s^i(x_o)$, there is at least one $\star$ in their public view which is contained in $\widehat{s}^i(x_o)$. Because the predicate secret in (3.7) will hold on the value of $\widehat{s}^i(x_o)$, the transition of $\widehat{M}_k$ is not going to be in conflict with the existence of any $leak^i \in \vartheta$ for any i.

There is still the constraint on the abstract transition that $a(o) \cap s^0(o) \neq \emptyset$ needs to hold for each $o \in \mathcal{X}_\mathcal{O}$. From the assumption that $s^{*\prime} \in \delta^*(s^*, (a, \vartheta))$ follows that for each $o \in \mathcal{X}_\mathcal{O}$, $a(o) = s^0(o) = \tau_o$ for some τ_o. Our assumptions entail that $\tau_o \triangle \widehat{s}^0(o)$ and $\tau_o \triangle \widehat{a}(o)$. Therefore, by exchanging all leaves of τ_o labeled with basic values with bv we get an abstract tree $\widehat{\tau}_o$, for which it holds that $\widehat{\tau}_o \in \widehat{a}(o) \cap \widehat{s}^0(o)$. Therefore, the corresponding condition holds on the abstract transition, and therefore, it can take place.

Now we will investigate the initial analysis information corresponding to the main run and each alternative run $(d_0^0, d_0^1, ..., d_0^k)$, and the state $s^{*\prime} = (s^{0\prime}, s^{1\prime}, ..., s^{k\prime})$ after the assignment of the input values in a^* to the input variables of the state took place. For each $x_i \in \mathcal{X}_\mathcal{I}$ we have that $s^{0\prime}(x_i) = a(x_i)$, and accordingly, we have that $d_0^0(x_i) = \widehat{a}(x_i)$. Therefore, we have that $s^{0\prime}(x_i) \triangle d_0^0(x_i)$. According to our assumptions we had for each $x_o \in \mathcal{X}_\mathcal{O}$ that $s^0(x_o) \triangle \widehat{s}^0(x_o)$. Since output variables of states on the main run are simply copied to the initial states of the computation, we have now that $s^{0\prime}(x_o) \triangle d_0^0(x_o)$. Therefore, we have for each $x \in \mathcal{X}$ that $s^{0\prime}(x) \triangle d_0^0(x)$. Considering states $s^{j\prime}$ where $j > 0$ we have two options.

- $start^j \notin \vartheta$. In this case $s^{j\prime}(x_i) = a(x_i)$ for each $x_i \in \mathcal{X}_\mathcal{I}$. Therefore, $s^{j\prime}(x_i) = s^{0\prime}(x_i)$ for each $x_i \in \mathcal{X}_\mathcal{I}$. In the abstract case we have that $d_0^j(x_i) = \widehat{a}(x_i)$. Furthermore, we supposed that $a(x_i) \triangle \widehat{a}(x_i)$. Therefore, there are no leaves labeled $\star$ in the members of $d_0^j(x_i)$. Accordingly, $\begin{bmatrix} s^{0\prime}(x_i) \\ s^{j\prime}(x_i) \end{bmatrix} \in \gamma(d_0^j(x_i))$.

  Furthermore, according to our assumptions, we have for each $x_o \in \mathcal{X}_\mathcal{O}$ that $\begin{bmatrix} s^0(x_o) \\ s^j(x_o) \end{bmatrix} \in \gamma(\widehat{s}^j(x_o))$. Because $s^{0\prime}(x_o) = s^0(x_o)$, $s^{j\prime}(x_o) = s^j(x_o)$ and $d_0^j(x_o) = \widehat{s}^j(x_o)$, it holds that $\begin{bmatrix} s^{0\prime}(x_o) \\ s^{j\prime}(x_o) \end{bmatrix} \in \gamma^S(d_0^j(x_o))$.

- $start^j \in \vartheta$. Now there is a letter $b \in \mathcal{A}$ which is the first letter on an alternative run of the original machine M. We suppose now that there is a subformula $\mathcal{H}^j_{H^j, O^j} \psi$ in the formula that corresponds to M_k and $\widehat{M}_k$. In this case it holds that $\begin{bmatrix} a \\ b \end{bmatrix} \in \gamma_{\mathcal{X}_\mathcal{I}}(H^j)$. This means according to Section 4.2 that for each $x \in \mathrm{dom}(H^j)$ it holds that $\begin{bmatrix} a(x) \\ b(x) \end{bmatrix} \in \gamma(H^j(x) \cup \mathfrak{B}_{\Sigma_2, \{\#, bv\}})$. This means that there is a public view τ in $H^j(x) \cup \mathfrak{B}_{\Sigma_2, \{\#, bv\}}$ which can

6.3. PROOFS FOR CHAPTER 4

be constructed from $a(x)$ and $b(x)$ by replacing the different subtrees by $\star$ and by replacing leaves having basic values with bv. There are two cases regarding τ:

- There is no leaf labeled $\star$ in τ. In this case $a(x)$ and $b(x)$ are equal so that $a(x), b(x) \triangle \tau$, and their common public view is of course in $\mathfrak{B}_{\Sigma_2, \{\#, bv\}}$, and therefore also in $\widehat{a}(x)$.
- There is at least one leaf labeled $\star$ in τ. In this case τ must be in $H^j(x)$, and in addition, there is a corresponding abstract document in $\widehat{a}(x)$, namely $a(x)$. According to the definition of $\widehat{M_k}$, $d_0^j(x) = \widehat{a}(x) \cup h$, where h is the subset of public views in $H^j(x)$ to which there is a corresponding document in $\widehat{a}(x)$. There is now at least one, namely $a(x)$, therefore, $\tau \in h$. τ cannot be an element either of $\mathfrak{B}_{\Sigma_2, \{\#, bv\}}$ or $\widehat{a}(x)$ because they do not contain trees having leaves labeled $\star$.

Therefore, we have that $\tau \in \widehat{a}(x) \cup h$. According to the definition of $\widehat{M_k}$, we have now that $d_0^j(x) = \widehat{a}(x) \cup h$, which entails that $\begin{bmatrix} a(x) \\ b(x) \end{bmatrix} \in \gamma(d_0^j(x))$. This in turn entails that $\begin{bmatrix} s^0(x)' \\ s^j(x)' \end{bmatrix} \in \gamma(d_0^j(x))$, because $s^0(x)' = a(x)$ and $s^j(x)' = b(x)$ in the concrete machine.

Regarding those variables $y \in \mathcal{X}_\mathcal{I}$ where $y \notin \text{dom}(H^j)$ we have the requirement that $a(y) = b(y)$. Therefore, $s^j(y) = a(y)$. According to the definition of $\widehat{M_k}$, $d_0^j(y) = \widehat{a}(y)$ in this case. $\widehat{a}(y)$ does not contain trees with nodes having labels $\star$, therefore, we have that $\begin{bmatrix} s^0(y)' \\ s^j(y)' \end{bmatrix} \in \gamma(d_0^j(y))$.

We consider now output variables $x_o \in \mathcal{X}_\mathcal{O}$. According to the definitions of M_k and $\widehat{M_k}$ we have in this case that $s^{0'}(x_o) = s^0(x_o)$, $s^{j'}(x_o) = s^0(x_o)$ and $d_0^j(x_o) = \widehat{s}^0(x_o)$. Furthermore, we had that $s^0(x_o) \triangle \widehat{s}^0(x_o)$. It follows now that $s^{0'}(x_o) = s^{j'}(x_o)$ for all $x_o \in \mathcal{X}_\mathcal{O}$, which entails that $\begin{bmatrix} s^{0'}(x_o) \\ s^{j'}(x_o) \end{bmatrix} \in \gamma(d_0^j(x_o))$.

From the above reasoning follows that for all $j > 0$ and for all $x \in \mathcal{X}$ we have that $\begin{bmatrix} s^0(x)' \\ s^j(x)' \end{bmatrix} \in \gamma(d_0^j(x))$. Furthermore, for all $x \in \mathcal{X}$ we have that $s^{0'}(x) \triangle d_0^0(x)$. Accordingly, we have that $(s^{0'}, s^{1'}, ..., s^{k'}) \in \gamma^S(d_0^0, d_0^1, ..., d_0^k)$.

Let us suppose now that $(s^{0''}, ..., s^{k''}) \in \delta^*(s^*, (a, \vartheta))$ and $(\widehat{s}^{0''}, ..., \widehat{s}^{k''}) = \widehat{\delta}(\widehat{s}, (\widehat{a}, \vartheta))$. Now based on the correctness of the static analysis described in Section 3.3 and the above reasoning, we have for each $j > 0$ and for all $x \in \mathcal{X}$ that $\begin{bmatrix} s^{0''}(x) \\ s^{j''}(x) \end{bmatrix} \in \gamma(\widehat{s}^{j''}(x))$, where $\widehat{s}^{j''}$ is the result of the analysis of Section 3.3 with initial abstract value d_0^j on the program p based on which M has been constructed. Furthermore, $s^{0''}$ is the result of the execution of the program p on the initial state $s^{0'}$ and $s^{j''}$ is the result of the execution of the program p with the initial state $s^{j'}$.

Furthermore, we have that d_0^0 does not contain trees with nodes labeled $\star$ in any variables. In this case the preconditions of implications generated for edges with labels $\begin{bmatrix} \neg b \\ b \end{bmatrix}$ do not hold, and therefore, all assignments are going to be carried out on the abstract values in synchrony. Therefore, no nodes labeled $\star$ will be introduced during the analysis based on the initial values in

d_0^0. Accordingly, the members of the concretization of $\widehat{s}^{0\prime\prime}(x)$ are pairs of equal trees for each variable x. Therefore, we have for all x that $s^{0\prime\prime}(x) \triangle \widehat{s}^{0\prime\prime}(x)$.

According to the above reasoning we have that:

$$(s^{0\prime\prime}, s^{1\prime\prime}, ..., s^{k\prime\prime}) \in \gamma^S(\widehat{s}^{0\prime\prime}, \widehat{s}^{1\prime\prime}, ..., \widehat{s}^{k\prime\prime})$$

□

Lemma 20. *Let us consider an arbitrary hide operator $\mathcal{H}^i_{H^i, O^i}\varphi$ and two regular tree grammars G_1 and G_2, where $L(G_1) \subseteq L(G_2)$. Let us suppose that the sets of public views h_1 and h_2 have been constructed using the algorithm of Section 4.4.1 based on the grammars G_1 and G_2, and the set of public views $H^i(x)$. In this case $L(h_1) \subseteq L(h_2)$.*

Proof. Let us suppose that the grammar G_1 consist of rules of the following form:

$$\begin{aligned} A_1 &\rightarrow \sigma(B_1, C_1) \\ D_1 &\rightarrow \# \\ E_1 &\rightarrow bv \end{aligned}$$

We suppose furthermore, that the initial nonterminal of G_1 is F_1.

Let us suppose furthermore, that G_2 consists of rules of the following form:

$$\begin{aligned} A_2 &\rightarrow \sigma(B_2, C_2) \\ D_2 &\rightarrow \# \\ E_2 &\rightarrow bv \end{aligned}$$

We suppose furthermore, that the initial nonterminal of G_2 is F_2.

Finally, let us suppose that $H^i(x)$ consists of rules of the following form:

$$\begin{aligned} U &\rightarrow \zeta(V, Z) \\ X &\rightarrow \# \\ Y &\rightarrow bv \\ W &\rightarrow \star \end{aligned}$$

We suppose that the initial nonterminal of $H^i(x)$ is Z.

We suppose that h_1 and h_2 have been constructed using the algorithm in Section 4.4.1. Now we suppose that h_1 consists of rules of the form:

$$\begin{aligned} [A_1, U] &\rightarrow \sigma([B_1, V], [C_1, Z]) \\ [D_1, X] &\rightarrow \# \\ [E_1, Y] &\rightarrow bv \\ [I_1, W] &\rightarrow \star \end{aligned}$$

We suppose that the initial nonterminal of h_1 is $[F_1, Z]$.

Now we suppose that h_2 consists of rules of the form:

$$\begin{aligned} [A_2, U] &\rightarrow \sigma([B_2, V], [C_2, Z]) \\ [D_2, X] &\rightarrow \# \\ [E_2, Y] &\rightarrow bv \\ [I_2, W] &\rightarrow \star \end{aligned}$$

We suppose that the initial nonterminal of h_2 is $[F_2, Z]$.

6.3. PROOFS FOR CHAPTER 4

Let us suppose that there is a tree τ in $L(h_1)$. This means that there is a corresponding document $\tau_0 \in L(G_1)$. The difference between τ and τ_0 is that τ_0 can be constructed from τ by replacing its leaves labeled $\star$ with some subtrees. Let us denote the upper prefix of τ where its leaves labeled $\star$ are replaced with some nonterminals of G_1 by τ_1. Since τ has been generated by the grammar resulting from the algorithm of Section 4.4.1, there exists a τ_1 that can be generated by the rules of G_1 too. Let us denote a tree, where the nonterminals of G_1 in τ_1 are replaced with nonterminals of G_2 by τ_2. Since $L(G_1) \subseteq L(G_2)$, there is a τ_2 that can be generated using the rules of G_2 too. But since h_2 has been constructed from G_2 and $H^i(x)$, τ_2 can now be generated from the rules of h_2 too. Here the components of rules corresponding to $H^i(x)$ are the same as by the generation τ_1. Therefore, whenever we could generate a leaf labeled $\star$ using the rules of h_1, then we can generate a $\star$ using the rules of h_2 too. By applying rules of the form $[I_2, W] \to \star$ on the nonterminals in τ_2 we obtain τ. From this, our statement follows. $\square$

Theorem 12. $L(N_{\widehat{\widetilde{M_k}, N_{\text{tr(NNF}(\neg\varphi))}}}) = \emptyset$ entails that $L(N_{\widehat{M_k, N_{\text{tr(NNF}(\neg\varphi))}}}) = \emptyset$.

Proof. We prove now the contrapositive. We prove that $\vec{\widehat{a}} \in L(N_{\widehat{M_k, N_{\text{tr(NNF}(\neg\varphi))}}})$ entails the existence of a run $\vec{\widetilde{\widehat{a}}}$ so that $\vec{\widetilde{\widehat{a}}} \in L(N_{\widehat{\widetilde{M_k}, N_{\text{tr(NNF}(\neg\varphi))}}})$. Let us suppose that $N_{\widehat{M_k, N_{\text{tr(NNF}(\neg\varphi))}}} = (\widehat{S}^\times, \widehat{A}, \widehat{\underline{s}}_0^\times, \widehat{\delta}^\times, \widehat{F}^\times)$ and $N_{\widehat{\widetilde{M_k}, N_{\text{tr(NNF}(\neg\varphi))}}} = (\widehat{\widetilde{S}}^\times, \widehat{A}, \widehat{\widetilde{\underline{s}}}_0^\times, \widehat{\widetilde{\delta}}^\times, \widehat{\widetilde{F}}^\times)$. We consider an accepting execution $\widehat{\underline{s}}_0^\times, \widehat{\underline{s}}_1^\times, \ldots$ of $N_{\widehat{M_k, N_{\text{tr(NNF}(\neg\varphi))}}}$ on $\vec{\widehat{a}} = (\widehat{a}_0, \vartheta_0), (\widehat{a}_1, \vartheta_1), \ldots$. We have now for each i that $\widehat{\underline{s}}_{i+1}^\times \in \widehat{\delta}^\times(\widehat{\underline{s}}_i^\times, (\widehat{a}_i, \vartheta_i))$. Given that $\widehat{\underline{s}}_i^\times = (\widehat{\underline{s}}_i, s_i^N)$ and $\widehat{\underline{s}}_{i+1}^\times = (\widehat{\underline{s}}_{i+1}, s_{i+1}^N)$, we have that $\widehat{\underline{s}}_{i+1} = \widehat{\delta}(\widehat{\underline{s}}_i, (\widehat{a}_i, \vartheta_i))$, $s_{i+1}^N \in \rho(s_i^N, \Psi_i)$, and that $(\widehat{a}_i, \vartheta_i) \models \bigwedge_{P \in \Psi_i} P$. The latter entails, that for all variables $x \in \mathcal{X}$ we have that $\widehat{a}_i(x) \subseteq \bigcap_{(x \Delta L) \in \Psi_i} L$. Let us now define the run $\vec{\widetilde{\widehat{a}}} = (\widetilde{\widehat{a}}_0, \vartheta_0), (\widetilde{\widehat{a}}_1, \vartheta_1), \ldots$ so that for each i and $x \in \mathcal{X}$ we have that $\widetilde{\widehat{a}}_i(x) = \bigcap_{(x \Delta L) \in \Psi_i} L$. This is how the letters of the transitions of $N_{\widehat{\widetilde{M_k}, N_{\text{tr(NNF}(\neg\varphi))}}}$ are defined by implications (4.9) and (4.8).

Now we prove inductively on the length of the execution $\widehat{\underline{s}}_0^\times, \widehat{\underline{s}}_1^\times, \ldots$ that there is an execution $\widehat{\widetilde{\underline{s}}}_0^\times, \widehat{\widetilde{\underline{s}}}_1^\times, \ldots$ of $N_{\widehat{\widetilde{M_k}, N_{\text{tr(NNF}(\neg\varphi))}}}$ on $\vec{\widetilde{\widehat{a}}}$ so that for each i whenever $\widehat{\underline{s}}_i^\times = ((\widehat{s}_i^0, \widehat{s}_i^1, \ldots, \widehat{s}_i^k), s_i^N)$ then $\widehat{\widetilde{\underline{s}}}_i^\times = ((\widehat{\widetilde{s}}_i^0, \widehat{\widetilde{s}}_i^1, \ldots, \widehat{\widetilde{s}}_i^k), s_i^N)$ so that for each $x \in \mathcal{X}$ and $0 \leq j \leq k$ we have that:

$$\widehat{\widetilde{s}}_i^j(x) \supseteq \widehat{s}_i^j(x)$$

We can say the following about the initial state. According to the definition of $N_{\widehat{M_k, N_{\text{tr(NNF}(\neg\varphi))}}}$ we have for each x and j that $\widehat{s}_0^j(x) = \{\#\}$. According to the definition of $N_{\widehat{\widetilde{M_k}, N_{\text{tr(NNF}(\neg\varphi))}}}$ we have that $\text{init}_x(\#)$ for each $x \in \mathcal{X}$. Furthermore, the following is defined for each variable x and execution j:

$$\text{state}_{x,j,s_0^N}(X) \Leftarrow \text{init}_x(X).$$

Based on the above statements, it follows that $\widehat{\underline{s}}_0^\times = \widehat{\widetilde{\underline{s}}}_0^\times$.

Now we treat the inductive case. We suppose about the states number i in the executions, $\widehat{\underline{s}}_i^\times = ((\widehat{s}_i^0, \widehat{s}_i^1, ..., \widehat{s}_i^k), s_i^N)$ and $\widehat{\widetilde{\underline{s}}}_i^\times = ((\widehat{\widetilde{s}}_i^0, \widehat{\widetilde{s}}_i^1, ..., \widehat{\widetilde{s}}_i^k), s_i^N)$, that for each $x \in \mathcal{X}$ and $0 \leq j \leq k$ it holds that:

$$\widehat{\widetilde{s}}_i^j(x) \supseteq \widehat{s}_i^j(x)$$

We also suppose about the letters $(\widehat{a}_i, \vartheta_i)$ and $(\widehat{\widetilde{a}}_i, \vartheta_i)$ that for each $x \in \mathcal{X}$ it holds that $\widehat{\widetilde{a}}_i(x) \supseteq \widehat{a}_i$. We suppose here that for each x and j, $\widehat{\widetilde{s}}_i^j(x) = \{\tau \mid \text{state}_{x,j,s^N}(\tau)\}$. We furthermore suppose that $((\widehat{s}_{i+1}^0, \widehat{s}_{i+1}^1, ..., \widehat{s}_{i+1}^k), s_{i+1}^N) \in \widehat{\delta}^\times((\widehat{\underline{s}}_i^\times), \widehat{a}_i)$. Let us suppose that the initial values of the analyses corresponding to $\widehat{\delta}$ are defined by d_0^j. Furthermore, let us suppose that the initial values of the analyses corresponding to $\widehat{\widetilde{\delta}}^\times$ are defined by $\widetilde{d}_0^j$.

Because of the above assumptions and Lemma 20, we can say that for each j and x, it holds on the initial abstract states of the analysis that:

$$\widetilde{\widehat{d}}_0^j(x) \supseteq d_0^j(x)$$

Let us denote the results of the analyses of Section 3.3 on initial states $d_0^j(x)$ and $\widetilde{\widehat{d}}_0^j(x)$ by $d^j(x)$ and $\widetilde{\widehat{d}}^j(x)$ respectively. The analysis of Section 3.3 consists exclusively of monotonous implications. Therefore, it holds that

$$\widetilde{\widehat{d}}^j(x) \supseteq d^j(x)$$

This guaranties that $\text{trans}_{(s_i^N, \Psi, s^N_{i+1})}$ holds, because the transition $\widehat{\delta}$ could take place, and therefore, the values of variables have been defined there. Furthermore, because of implication (4.7) we have for all variables $x \in \mathcal{X}$, executions j, and trees τ that:

$$\text{state}_{x,j,s^N_{i+1}}(\tau) \Leftarrow \widetilde{\widehat{d}}^j(\tau)$$

Therefore, we have that $((\widehat{\widetilde{s}}_{i+1}^0, \widehat{\widetilde{s}}_{i+1}^1, ..., \widehat{\widetilde{s}}_{i+1}^k), s_{i+1}^N) \in \widehat{\widetilde{\delta}}^\times((\widehat{\widetilde{\underline{s}}}_i^\times), \widehat{\widetilde{a}}_i)$ so that the resulting state satisfies the desired property. Since the projection of this resulting state on the component of $N_{\text{tr}(\text{NNF}(\neg\varphi))}$ is the same as by $((\widehat{s}_{i+1}^0, \widehat{s}_{i+1}^1, ..., \widehat{s}_{i+1}^k), s_{i+1}^N)$, it follows that the run $\widehat{\widetilde{\underline{s}}}_0^\times, \widehat{\widetilde{\underline{s}}}_1^\times, ...$ is accepting if and only if $\widehat{\underline{s}}_0^\times, \widehat{\underline{s}}_1^\times, ...$ is accepting. $\square$

Theorem 13. *Let us consider the transition system M and the formula φ of the logic Restricted SecLTL. We suppose that $N^*_{\text{tr}(\text{NNF}(\neg\varphi))}$ is the corresponding "distilled" automaton. In this case $L(N^*_{\text{tr}(\text{NNF}(\neg\varphi))}) = \emptyset$ entails that $M \models \varphi$.*

Proof. From the fact that $L(N^*_{\text{tr}(\text{NNF}(\neg\varphi))}) = \emptyset$ follows that:

$$L(N_{\widehat{M_k, N_{\text{tr}(\text{NNF}(\neg\varphi))}}}) = \emptyset$$

The above implication is true, because there is a corresponding transition of the form $(\widehat{\widetilde{\underline{s}}}', s^{N'}) \in \widehat{\widetilde{\delta}}^\times((\widehat{\widetilde{\underline{s}}}, s^N), \widehat{\widetilde{a}})$ of $N_{\widehat{M_k, N_{\text{tr}(\text{NNF}(\neg\varphi))}}}$ to each transition of the form

$s^{N'} \in \rho^*(s^N, \widehat{\underline{a}})$ of $N^*_{\text{tr}(\text{NNF}(\neg\varphi))}$ with additional constraints. Furthermore, there is no transition in $N_{\widehat{M_k}, N_{\text{tr}(\text{NNF}(\neg\varphi))}}$ for which there would not be a corresponding transition in $N^*_{\text{tr}(\text{NNF}(\neg\varphi))}$.

Based on Theorem 12 follows that $L(\widehat{N_{\widehat{M_k}, N_{\text{tr}(\text{NNF}(\neg\varphi))}}}) = \emptyset$ entails the fact that $L(N_{\widehat{M_k}, N_{\text{tr}(\text{NNF}(\neg\varphi))}}) = \emptyset$.

Theorem 11 together with Theorem 10 entail that $L(N_{\widehat{M_k}, N_{\text{tr}(\text{NNF}(\neg\varphi))}}) = \emptyset$ implies $L(N_{M_k, N_{\text{tr}(\text{NNF}(\neg\varphi))}}) = \emptyset$.

$L(N_{M_k, N_{\text{tr}(\text{NNF}(\neg\varphi))}}) = \emptyset$ implies that there is no run $\vec{a}^* \in \text{Runs}_{(s_0, \underline{s}_0) M_k}$ for which it would hold that $M_k, (s_0, \underline{s}_0), \vec{a}^* \models \text{tr}(\text{NNF}(\neg\varphi))$. Here, s_0 is the initial state of M, and $(s_0, \underline{s}_0) = (s_0, s_0, ..., s_0)$ is the initial state of M_k, a $k+1$ long tuple, where each member is s_0. It follows now from Theorem 9 that there is no such $\vec{a}$ either, for which it would hold that $M, s_0, \vec{a} \models \text{NNF}(\neg\varphi)$. This entails in turn that $M, s_0, \vec{a} \models \varphi$ holds for all $\vec{a}$, which implies that $M \models \varphi$. □

Lemma 21. *The set of runs satisfying the formulae $(\neg\varphi_1 \wedge \varphi_2)\mathcal{U}(\varphi_1 \wedge \varphi_2)$ and $\varphi_2 \mathcal{U}(\varphi_1 \wedge \varphi_2)$ are the same for any arbitrary formulae φ_1 and φ_2 of the logic LTL.*

Proof. Now we prove that $(\neg\varphi_1 \wedge \varphi_2)\mathcal{U}(\varphi_1 \wedge \varphi_2) \Rightarrow \varphi_2 \mathcal{U}(\varphi_1 \wedge \varphi_2)$. Let us consider an arbitrary extended machine M_k, an arbitrary state of it s^*, and a run $\vec{a}^* \in \text{Runs}_{s^*, M_k}$, where we have that $M_k, \vec{s}^*, \vec{a}^* \models (\neg\varphi_1 \wedge \varphi_2)\mathcal{U}(\varphi_1 \wedge \varphi_2)$. In this case there is at least one $i \geq 0$ for which it holds that $M_k, \vec{s}^*[i], \vec{a}^*[i, \infty) \models (\varphi_1 \wedge \varphi_2)$. Furthermore, for all $0 \leq j < i$ we have that $M_k, \vec{s}^*[j], \vec{a}^*[j, \infty) \models (\neg\varphi_1 \wedge \varphi_2)$. $(\neg\varphi_1 \wedge \varphi_2)$ entails φ_2. Accordingly, we have now that there is one $i \geq 0$ for which it holds that $M_k, \vec{s}^*[i], \vec{a}^*[i, \infty) \models (\varphi_1 \wedge \varphi_2)$, and for all $0 \leq j < i$ we have that $M_k, \vec{s}^*[j], \vec{a}^*[j, \infty) \models \varphi_2$. This satisfies the conditions of $M_k, \vec{s}^*, \vec{a}^* \models \varphi_2 \mathcal{U}(\varphi_1 \wedge \varphi_2)$.

Now we prove that $\varphi_2 \mathcal{U}(\varphi_1 \wedge \varphi_2) \Rightarrow (\neg\varphi_1 \wedge \varphi_2)\mathcal{U}(\varphi_1 \wedge \varphi_2)$. Let us consider an arbitrary extended machine M_k, an arbitrary state of it s^*, and a run $\vec{a}^* \in \text{Runs}_{s^*, M_k}$, where we have that $M_k, \vec{s}^*, \vec{a}^* \models \varphi_2 \mathcal{U}(\varphi_1 \wedge \varphi_2)$. According to the semantics in Definition 12 there is at least one $i \geq 0$ for which it holds that $M_k, \vec{s}^*[i], \vec{a}^*[i, \infty) \models (\varphi_1 \wedge \varphi_2)$, and for all $0 \leq j < i$ we have that $M_k, \vec{s}^*[j], \vec{a}^*[j, \infty) \models \varphi_2$. Let us consider the smallest such i for which the previous statement holds. Now we have for all $0 \leq j < i$ that $M_k, \vec{s}^*[j], \vec{a}^*[j, \infty) \not\models (\varphi_1 \wedge \varphi_2)$, and $M_k, \vec{s}^*[j], \vec{a}^*[j, \infty) \models \varphi_2$. This entails that for these j we have that $M_k, \vec{s}^*[j], \vec{a}^*[j, \infty) \models (\neg\varphi_1 \wedge \varphi_2)$. But this satisfies the conditions of $M_k, \vec{s}^*, \vec{a}^* \models (\neg\varphi_1 \wedge \varphi_2)\mathcal{U}(\varphi_1 \wedge \varphi_2)$. □

Theorem 14. $L(N'_{M_k, N_{\text{tr}'(\text{NNF}(\neg\varphi))}}) = \emptyset$ entails that $L(N_{M_k, N_{\text{tr}(\text{NNF}(\neg\varphi))}}) = \emptyset$.

Proof. We repeat now the formula replacing leak operators of the form $\mathcal{L}^i_{H^i, O^i}\psi$ in the theoretical elaboration of Section 4.3:

$$start^i \wedge \psi \wedge \left[leak^i \vee \bigcirc\left((\neg start^i \wedge \psi)\mathcal{U}(\neg start^i \wedge \psi \wedge leak^i) \right) \right] \quad (4.3)$$

We rewrite now (4.3) to the equivalent formula:

$$\xi = \left[start^i \wedge \psi \wedge leak^i \right] \vee \\ \left[start^i \wedge \psi \wedge \bigcirc\left((\neg start^i \wedge \psi)\mathcal{U}(\neg start^i \wedge \psi \wedge leak^i) \right) \right] \quad (6.46)$$

We rewrite now (4.14):

$$start^i \wedge \left(\psi \mathcal{U}(leak^i \wedge \psi)\right) \tag{6.47}$$

(6.47) equals to (4.14) because of Lemma 21. The expansion rule [75] of the until operator is:

$$\alpha \mathcal{U} \beta = \beta \vee \alpha \wedge \bigcirc(\alpha \mathcal{U} \beta) \tag{6.48}$$

We also rewrite (6.47) to an equivalent formula using the expansion rule:

$$start^i \wedge \left((leak^i \wedge \psi) \vee \psi \wedge \bigcirc \psi \mathcal{U}(leak^i \wedge \psi)\right) \tag{6.49}$$

Now by reformulating the above we obtain:

$$\left(start^i \wedge leak^i \wedge \psi\right) \vee \left(start^i \wedge \psi \wedge \bigcirc \psi \mathcal{U}(leak^i \wedge \psi)\right) \tag{6.50}$$

Another reformulation results in:

$$\begin{aligned}\xi' = &\left[start^i \wedge \psi \wedge leak^i\right] \vee \\ &\left[start^i \wedge \psi \wedge \bigcirc\left((\mathtt{tt} \wedge \psi)\mathcal{U}(\mathtt{tt} \wedge \psi \wedge leak^i)\right)\right]\end{aligned} \tag{6.51}$$

We see now that (4.3) equals to (6.46), and that (4.14) equals to (6.51). We therefore define the function $\mathsf{tr2}(\cdot)$ that replaces leak operators $\mathcal{L}^i_{H^i,O^i}\psi$ with (6.46), and we define the function $\mathsf{tr2}'(\cdot)$ that replaces leak operators $\mathcal{L}^i_{H^i,O^i}\psi$ with (6.51). Accordingly, we modify our statement. We are going to prove the following: $L(N'_{M_k, N_{\mathsf{tr2}'(\mathsf{NNF}(\neg\varphi))}}) = \emptyset$ entails that $L(N_{M_k, N_{\mathsf{tr2}(\mathsf{NNF}(\neg\varphi))}}) = \emptyset$.

Statement 1. We see now that by replacing all occurrences of $\neg start^i$ in (6.46) with $\mathtt{tt}$ we obtain (6.51). According to Section 4.3 the Büchi automata are constructed the following way. First they are transformed to alternating Büchi automata based on the proof of Theorem 22 in [75] and then into nondeterministic Büchi automata according to Proposition 2 in [28]. Since $N_{\mathsf{tr2}(\mathsf{NNF}(\neg\varphi))}$ and $N_{\mathsf{tr2}'(\mathsf{NNF}(\neg\varphi))}$ are generated based on the syntax trees of $\mathsf{tr2}(\mathsf{NNF}(\neg\varphi))$, and $\mathsf{tr2}'(\mathsf{NNF}(\neg\varphi))$ whenever there is a run $\vec{\Psi} = \Psi_0, \Psi_1, \ldots \in L(N_{\mathsf{tr2}(\mathsf{NNF}(\neg\varphi))})$ then there is a run $\vec{\Psi}' = \Psi'_0, \Psi'_1, \ldots \in L(N_{\mathsf{tr2}'(\mathsf{NNF}(\neg\varphi))})$ so that for each j we have that:

$$\Psi'_j = \Psi_j \setminus \{\neg start^i \mid 1 \leq i \leq k\} \tag{6.52}$$

Statement 2. We suppose now that $N_{\mathsf{tr2}(\mathsf{NNF}(\neg\varphi))} = (S^N, \mathcal{P}(Prop), s_0^N, \rho, F)$ and furthermore that $N_{\mathsf{tr2}'(\mathsf{NNF}(\neg\varphi))} = (S^{N'}, \mathcal{P}(Prop), s_0^{N'}, \rho', F')$. Let us consider now a run $\vec{\Psi} = \Psi_0, \Psi_1, \ldots \in \mathsf{Runs}_{s_0^N, N_{\mathsf{tr2}(\mathsf{NNF}(\neg\varphi))}}$ and a corresponding run $\vec{\Psi}' = \Psi'_0, \Psi'_1, \ldots \in \mathsf{Runs}_{s_0^{N'}, N_{\mathsf{tr2}'(\mathsf{NNF}(\neg\varphi))}}$, where for each j (6.52) holds. We can say the following based on the subformulae (6.46) and (6.51), and the automata construction [75]:

- If $start^i \in \Psi_j$ then the subsequence $\vec{\Psi}[j, \infty)$ has been generated based on ξ in (6.46) among other subformulae, and the subsequence $\vec{\Psi}'[j, \infty)$ has been generated based on ξ' in (6.51) among other subformulae. Therefore, there must be an $l \geq j$ so that $leak^i \in \Psi_l$ and $leak^i \in \Psi'_l$, and in the meanwhile for all $j < m \leq l$ we have $\neg start^i \in \Psi_m$ and $start^i \notin \Psi_m'$.

6.3. PROOFS FOR CHAPTER 4

- If there is an $\neg start^i \in \Psi_m$, then there is a $j < m$ so that $start^i \in \Psi_j$ and $start^i \in \Psi_j{}'$. Furthermore, for all $j < n \leq m$ we have that $\neg start^i \in \Psi_n$. In this case we have $start^i \notin \Psi_m{}'$, and for all $j < n \leq m$ we have that $start^i \notin \Psi_n{}'$ too.

- If $leak^i \in \Psi_l$ then there is a $j \leq l$ so that $start^i \in \Psi_j$, furthermore, for all $j < m \leq l$ we have that $\neg start^i \in \Psi_m$. In this case we have that $leak^i \in \Psi_l'$, $start^i \in \Psi_j{}'$ and for all $j < m \leq l$ we have that $start^i \notin \Psi_m{}'$.

Proof of the theorem. We prove now inductively that if there is a run $\vec{a}^* \in L(N_{M_k, N_{\text{tr2}(\text{NNF}(\neg \varphi))}})$ then there is a corresponding run $\vec{a}^{*\prime} \in L(N'_{M_k, N_{\text{tr2}'(\text{NNF}(\neg \varphi))}})$. This is the contrapositive of the statement of the theorem. Therefore, its validity entails the statement of the theorem.

We define now the relation $s^N \succeq s^{N\prime}$ between a state s^N of $N_{\text{tr2}(\text{NNF}(\neg \varphi))}$ and a state $s^{N\prime}$ of $N_{\text{tr2}'(\text{NNF}(\neg \varphi))}$. $s^N \succeq s^{N\prime}$ holds if and only if for all runs $\vec{\Psi} = \Psi_0, \Psi_1, ...$ accepted by $N_{\text{tr2}(\text{NNF}(\neg \varphi))}$ from the state s^N, there is a run $\vec{\Psi}' = \Psi_0', \Psi_1', ...$ accepted by $N_{\text{tr2}'(\text{NNF}(\neg \varphi))}$ from state $s^{N\prime}$ so that for all n we have that Ψ_n and Ψ_n' satisfy (6.52).

Let us consider now an arbitrary run $\vec{a}^* = (a_0, \vartheta_0), (a_1, \vartheta_1), ...$ for which it holds that $\vec{a}^* \in L(N_{M_k, N_{\text{tr2}(\text{NNF}(\neg \varphi))}})$. Because $\vec{a}^*$ is accepted, there must be an accepting execution $\vec{s}^\times \in \text{Exec}_{N_{M_k, N_{\text{tr2}(\text{NNF}(\neg \varphi))}}}(s_0^\times, \vec{a}^*)$ so that:

$$\vec{s}^\times = s_0^\times, s_1^\times, ... = ((s_0^0, s_0^1, ..., s_0^k), s_0^N), ((s_1^0, s_1^1, ..., s_1^k), s_1^N), ...$$

Accordingly, for each $n \geq 0$ we have that:

$$((s_{n+1}^0, s_{n+1}^1, ..., s_{n+1}^k), s_{n+1}^N) \in \delta^\times(((s_n^0, s_n^1, ..., s_n^k), s_n^N), (a_n, \vartheta_n))$$

where it holds that $s_{n+1}^N \in \rho(s_n^N, \Psi_n)$ so that $(a_n, \vartheta_n) \models \bigwedge_{P \in \Psi_n} P$, and furthermore $(s_{n+1}^0, s_{n+1}^1, ..., s_{n+1}^k) \in \delta^*((s_n^0, s_n^1, ..., s_n^k), (a_n, \vartheta_n))$.

Now we construct $\vec{a}^{*\prime} = (a_0, \vartheta_0'), (a_0, \vartheta_1'), ...$ from $\vec{a}^* = (a_0, \vartheta_0), (a_0, \vartheta_1), ...$. In the first step, for each n and i we remove $start^i$ from ϑ_n if $start^i \notin \Psi_n$. In the second step we add or remove $leak^i$ for each ϑ_n so that for the resulting run $\vec{a}^{*\prime}$ it holds that $\vec{a}^{*\prime} \in \text{Runs}_{M_k, ((s_0^0, s_0^1, ..., s_0^k), s_0^N)}$. There must be an $\vec{a}^{*\prime}$ like that, because the base transition system M is input enabled, so there is always a run if there are no constraints on the output variables of the states $s_n^1, ..., s_n^k$. The constraints on states s_n^0 remain the same. Now we prove inductively that there is an execution $\vec{s}^{\times\prime} \in \text{Exec}_{N'_{M_k, N_{\text{tr2}'(\text{NNF}(\neg \varphi))}}}(s_0^\times, \vec{a}^{*\prime})$ so that:

$$\vec{s}^{\times\prime} = s_0^{\times\prime}, s_1^{\times\prime}, ... = ((s_0^{0\prime}, s_0^{1\prime}, ..., s_0^{k\prime}), s_0^{N\prime}), ((s_1^{0\prime}, s_1^{1\prime}, ..., s_1^{k\prime}), s_1^{N\prime}), ...$$

where for each n it holds that $s_n^0 = s_n^{0\prime}$ and $s_n^N \succeq s_n^{N\prime}$. For $n = 0$ the statement holds because of Statement 1. Now we inductively assume that the statement holds on an arbitrary n, and prove that it holds on $n+1$ too.

According to the inductive assumption we have a state $((s_n^0, s_n^1, ..., s_n^k), s_n^N)$ of $N_{M_k, N_{\text{tr2}(\text{NNF}(\neg \varphi))}}$, and a state $((s_n^{0\prime}, s_n^{1\prime}, ..., s_n^{k\prime}), s_n^{N\prime})$ of $N'_{M_k, N_{\text{tr2}'(\text{NNF}(\neg \varphi))}}$, where $s_n^0 = s_n^{0\prime}$ and $s_n^N \succeq s_n^{N\prime}$. Let us consider the next transition of $N_{M_k, N_{\text{tr2}(\text{NNF}(\neg \varphi))}}$:

$$((s_{n+1}^0, s_{n+1}^1, ..., s_{n+1}^k), s_{n+1}^N) \in \delta^\times(((s_n^0, s_n^1, ..., s_n^k), s_n^N), (a_n, \vartheta_n))$$

where we have that $s_{n+1}^N \in \rho(s_n^N, \Psi_n)$ so that $(a_n, \vartheta_n) \models \bigwedge_{P \in \Psi_n} P$, and

$$(s_{n+1}^0, s_{n+1}^1, ..., s_{n+1}^k) \in \delta^*((s_n^0, s_n^1, ..., s_n^k), (a_n, \vartheta_n))$$

We prove now that there is a transition of $N'_{M_k, N_{tr2'(\text{NNF}(\neg\varphi))}}$:

$$((s_{n+1}^{0}{}', s_{n+1}^{1}{}', ..., s_{n+1}^{k}{}'), s_{n+1}^{N}{}') \in \delta^\times(((s_n^{0}{}', s_n^{1}{}', ..., s_n^{k}{}'), s_n^{N}{}'), (a_n, \vartheta_n'))$$

where we have that $s_{n+1}^{N}{}' \in \rho(s_n^{N}{}', \Psi_n')$ so that $(a_n, \vartheta_n') \models \bigwedge_{P \in \Psi_n'} P$, Ψ_n and Ψ_n' satisfy, (6.52), and in addition the following holds:

$$(s_{n+1}^{0}{}', s_{n+1}^{1}{}', ..., s_{n+1}^{k}{}') \in \delta^*((s_n^{0}{}', s_n^{1}{}', ..., s_n^{k}{}'), (a_n, \vartheta_n'))$$

We observe the following:

- The member a_n of $a_n^* = (a_n, \vartheta_n)$ and $a_n^{*\prime} = (a_n, \vartheta_n')$ is the same. Because Ψ_n and Ψ_n' satisfy (6.52), whenever there is an $x \vartriangle L \in \Psi_n$ for some language L, then we have that $x \vartriangle L \in \Psi_n'$. Therefore, if $(a_n, \vartheta_n) \models \bigwedge_{x \vartriangle L \in \Psi_n} x \vartriangle L$ then $(a_n, \vartheta_n') \models \bigwedge_{x \vartriangle L \in \Psi_n'} x \vartriangle L$. Accordingly, if a_n satisfies Ψ_n, then it satisfies Ψ_n' too.

- In the case when $start^i, leak^i \notin \vartheta_n$ for some i, then $(a_n, \vartheta_n) \models \Psi_n$ for example when $start^i, leak^i \notin \Psi_n$. But it is possible that $\neg start^i \in \Psi_n$. We have now that $start^i \notin \vartheta_n'$ according to the construction of $\vec{a}^{*\prime}$. On the other hand, it is not possible that $\neg leak^i \in \Psi_n$. According to the automata construction of Theorem 22 in [75], no transition having label $\neg leak^i$ can be generated based on ξ and ξ' in (6.46) and (6.51). On the other hand, the removal of any $start^i$ from any ϑ_m where $m \leq n$ might have introduced a $leak^i$ into ϑ_n'. According to above, the presence of $leak^i$ does not violate Ψ_n'. Furthermore, according to the input enabled property of M, the transition can always take place. The conditions of Ψ_n and Ψ_n' are now satisfied.

- Now, $start^i \in \vartheta_n$. There are two cases:
  - $start^i \notin \Psi_n$: In this case, according to the construction of $\vec{a}^{*\prime}$, we have that $start^i \notin \vartheta_n'$. Furthermore, we have that $start^i \notin \Psi_n'$, therefore, the conditions posed by Ψ_n and Ψ_n' are satisfied.
  - $start^i \in \Psi_n$: Now we have that $start^i \in \Psi_n'$ and $start^i \in \vartheta_n'$ too, and the conditions are satisfied.

- $leak^i \in \vartheta_n$. Again, there are two cases:
  - $leak^i \notin \Psi_n$. In this case $leak^i \notin \Psi_n'$ either. There is no constraint whether $leak^i \in \vartheta_n'$ or not, the conditions are satisfied.
  - $leak^i \in \Psi_n$. In this case there is a leakage observed on the alternative run corresponding to s_n^i. According to Statement 2 above, now we had a $0 \leq j \leq n$ so that $start^i \in \Psi_j$, and therefore $start^i \in \Psi_j'$. Furthermore, for all $j < m \leq n$ we had that $\neg start^i \in \Psi_m$ and $start^i \notin \Psi_m'$. According to the definition of M_k in Section 4.3, when $start^i \in \Psi_j$ the next state of an alternative run is chosen nondeterministically. Because the possible set of successor states depends

6.3. PROOFS FOR CHAPTER 4

only on s_j^0 and a_j, the value of s_j^i does not matter. Since we have that $s_j^{0\prime} = s_j^0$, it is possible to chose the same successor state for s_{j+1}^i and $s_{j+1}^i{}'$. Furthermore, we have that $start^i \notin \vartheta_m$ and $start^i \notin \vartheta_m'$ for any $j < m \leq n$, no additional alternative runs have been initialized between j and n. Therefore, we have for each $j < m \leq n$ that $s_m^i = s_m^i{}'$. Accordingly, there is also a leakage observed in $N'_{M_k, N_{\text{tr2}'(\text{NNF}(\neg\varphi))}}$, and therefore, the conditions are satisfied.

According to our inductive assumption, we had that $N_{M_k, N_{\text{tr2}(\text{NNF}(\neg\varphi))}}$ accepts $\Psi_n, \Psi_{n+1}, ...$ from state s^N. Furthermore, we had that $s_n^N \succeq s_n^{N\prime}$, which entails that $N'_{M_k, N_{\text{tr2}'(\text{NNF}(\neg\varphi))}}$ accepts $\Psi'_n, \Psi'_{n+1}, ...$ from $s_n^{N\prime}$, where for each j, Ψ_j and Ψ'_j satisfy (6.52). Accordingly, if $s_{n+1}^N \in \rho(s_n^N, \Psi_n)$ then there is a corresponding $s_{n+1}^N{}' \in \rho(s_n^{N\prime}, \Psi'_n)$ for which $s_{n+1}^N \succeq s_{n+1}^N{}'$ holds. We choose $s_{n+1}^N{}'$ for the component of $N_{\text{tr2}'(\text{NNF}(\neg\varphi))}$ in the state of $N'_{M_k, N_{\text{tr2}'(\text{NNF}(\neg\varphi))}}$, and our statement is proved. □

Bibliography

[1] Ryma Abassi, Florent Jacquemard, Michael Rusinowitch, and Sihem Guemara El Fatmi. XML access control: from XACML to annotated schemas. In *Second International Conference on Communications and Networking (ComNet)*, pages 1–8, Tozeur, Tunisie, 2010. IEEE Computer Society Press.

[2] Rafael Accorsi and Andreas Lehmann. Automatic information flow analysis of business process models. In Alistair P. Barros, Avigdor Gal, and Ekkart Kindler, editors, *Business Process Management - 10th International Conference, BPM 2012*, volume 7481 of *Lecture Notes in Computer Science*, pages 172–187. Springer, 2012.

[3] Rafael Accorsi and Claus Wonnemann. Static information flow analysis of workflow models. In Witold Abramowicz, Rainer Alt, Klaus-Peter Fähnrich, Bogdan Franczyk, and Leszek A. Maciaszek, editors, *INFORMATIK 2010 - Business Process and Service Science - Proceedings of ISSS and BPSC*, volume 177 of *LNI*, pages 194–205. GI, 2010.

[4] A.C.Myers, L.Zheng, S.Zdancewic, S.Chong, and N.Nystrom. Jif:Java + information flow, July 2001–2011. Software release. Located at http://www.cs.cornell.edu/jif.

[5] Rajeev Alur, Pavol Cerný, and Steve Zdancewic. Preserving secrecy under refinement. In Michele Bugliesi, Bart Preneel, Vladimiro Sassone, and Ingo Wegener, editors, *Automata, Languages and Programming, 33rd International Colloquium, ICALP 2006*, volume 4052 of *Lecture Notes in Computer Science*, pages 107–118. Springer, 2006.

[6] A. Alves, A. Arkin, S. Askary, C. Barreto, B. Bloch, F. Curbera, M. Ford, Y. Goland, A. Guízar, N. Kartha, C. K. Liu, R. Khalaf, Dieter Koenig, M. Marin, V. Mehta, S. Thatte, D. Rijn, P. Yendluri, and A. Yiu. Web Services Business Process Execution Language Version 2.0 (OASIS standard). WS-BPEL TC OASIS, http://docs.oasis-open.org/wsbpel/2.0/wsbpel-v2.0.html, 2007.

[7] Aslan Askarov, Sebastian Hunt, Andrei Sabelfeld, and David Sands. Termination-insensitive noninterference leaks more than just a bit. In Sushil Jajodia and Javier López, editors, *Computer Security - ESORICS 2008, 13th European Symposium on Research in Computer Security*, volume 5283 of *Lecture Notes in Computer Science*, pages 333–348. Springer, 2008.

[8] Michael Backes, Boris Köpf, and Andrey Rybalchenko. Automatic discovery and quantification of information leaks. In *30th IEEE Symposium on Security and Privacy (S&P 2009)*, pages 141–153. IEEE Computer Society, 2009.

[9] Musard Balliu, Mads Dam, and Gurvan Le Guernic. Epistemic temporal logic for information flow security. In *Proceedings of the ACM SIGPLAN 6th Workshop on Programming Languages and Analysis for Security*, PLAS '11, pages 6:1–6:12, New York, NY, USA, 2011. ACM.

[10] Roberto Barbuti, Cinzia Bernardeschi, and Nicoletta De Francesco. Checking security of Java bytecode by abstract interpretation. In *Proceedings of the 2002 ACM Symposium on Applied Computing (SAC)*, pages 229–236. ACM, 2002.

[11] Gilles Barthe, Juan Manuel Crespo, and César Kunz. Relational verification using product programs. In Michael Butler and Wolfram Schulte, editors, *FM 2011: Formal Methods - 17th International Symposium on Formal Methods*, volume 6664 of *Lecture Notes in Computer Science*, pages 200–214. Springer, 2011.

[12] Gilles Barthe, Juan Manuel Crespo, and César Kunz. Beyond 2-safety: asymmetric product programs for relational program verification. In Sergei N. Artëmov and Anil Nerode, editors, *Logical Foundations of Computer Science, International Symposium, LFCS 2013*, volume 7734 of *Lecture Notes in Computer Science*, pages 29–43. Springer, 2013.

[13] Gilles Barthe, Pedro R. D'Argenio, and Tamara Rezk. Secure information flow by self-composition. In *17th IEEE Computer Security Foundations Workshop, (CSFW-17 2004)*, pages 100–114. IEEE Computer Society, 2004.

[14] Anders Berglund, Scott Boag, Don Chamberlin, Mary F. Fernández, Michael Kay, Jonathan Robie, and Jérôme Siméon. XML path language (XPath) 2.0 (second edition). http://www.w3.org/TR/2010/REC-xpath20-20101214/, 14 December 2010.

[15] Bruno Blanchet, Patrick Cousot, Radhia Cousot, Jérôme Feret, Laurent Mauborgne, Antoine Miné, David Monniaux, and Xavier Rival. A static analyzer for large safety-critical software. *CoRR*, abs/cs/0701193, 2007.

[16] Tim Bray, Jean Paoli, C. M. Sperberg-McQueen, Eve Maler, and François Yergeau. Extensible Markup Language (XML) 1.0. Available on: http://www.w3.org/TR/2008/REC-xml-20081126/, 26 November 2008.

[17] Niklas Broberg and David Sands. Paralocks – role-based information flow control and beyond. In Manuel V. Hermenegildo and Jens Palsberg, editors, *Proceedings of the 37th ACM SIGPLAN-SIGACT Symposium on Principles of Programming Languages, POPL 2010*, pages 431–444. ACM, 2010.

[18] Roberto Bruni, Hernán C. Melgratti, and Ugo Montanari. Theoretical foundations for compensations in flow composition languages. In Jens Palsberg and Martín Abadi, editors, *Proceedings of the 32nd ACM SIGPLAN-SIGACT Symposium on Principles of Programming Languages, POPL 2005*, pages 209–220. ACM, 2005.

[19] Stephen Chong, K. Vikram, and Andrew C. Myers. SIF: enforcing confidentiality and integrity in web applications. In *Proceedings of 16th USENIX Security Symposium on USENIX Security Symposium*, pages 1:1–1:16, Berkeley, CA, USA, 2007. USENIX Association.

[20] E. Christensen, F. Curbera, G. Meredith, and S. Weerawarana. Web Services Description Language (WSDL) 1.1. W3c note, World Wide Web Consortium, March 2001.

[21] Michael R. Clarkson and Fred B. Schneider. Hyperproperties. *Journal of Computer Security*, 18(6):1157–1210, 2010.

[22] H. Comon, M. Dauchet, R. Gilleron, C. Löding, F. Jacquemard, D. Lugiez, S. Tison, and M. Tommasi. *Tree Automata Techniques and Applications*. Available on: http://www.grappa.univ-lille3.fr/tata, 2007. release October, 12th 2007.

[23] Patrick Cousot and Radhia Cousot. Abstract interpretation: A unified lattice model for static analysis of programs by construction or approximation of fixpoints. In Robert M. Graham, Michael A. Harrison, and Ravi Sethi, editors, *Conference Record of the Fourth ACM Symposium on Principles of Programming Languages*, pages 238–252. ACM, 1977.

[24] Ernesto Damiani, Sabrina De Capitani di Vimercati, Stefano Paraboschi, and Pierangela Samarati. A fine-grained access control system for XML documents. *ACM Trans. Inf. Syst. Secur.*, 5(2):169–202, 2002.

[25] Ádám Darvas, Reiner Hähnle, and David Sands. A theorem proving approach to analysis of secure information flow. In Dieter Hutter and Markus Ullmann, editors, *Security in Pervasive Computing, Second International Conference, SPC 2005*, volume 3450 of *Lecture Notes in Computer Science*, pages 193–209. Springer, 2005.

[26] Dorothy E. Denning. A lattice model of secure information flow. *Commun. ACM*, 19(5):236–243, 1976.

[27] Dorothy E. Denning and Peter J. Denning. Certification of programs for secure information flow. *Commun. ACM*, 20(7):504–513, 1977.

[28] Rayna Dimitrova, Bernd Finkbeiner, Máté Kovács, Markus N. Rabe, and Helmut Seidl. Model checking information flow in reactive systems. In Viktor Kuncak and Andrey Rybalchenko, editors, *Verification, Model Checking, and Abstract Interpretation - 13th International Conference, VMCAI 2012*, volume 7148 of *Lecture Notes in Computer Science*, pages 169–185. Springer, 2012.

[29] Guillaume Dufay, Amy P. Felty, and Stan Matwin. Privacy-sensitive information flow with JML. In Robert Nieuwenhuis, editor, *Automated Deduction - CADE-20, 20th International Conference on Automated Deduction*, volume 3632 of *Lecture Notes in Computer Science*, pages 116–130. Springer, 2005.

[30] Matthew B. Dwyer, John Hatcliff, Roby Joehanes, Shawn Laubach, Corina S. Pasareanu, Robby, Hongjun Zheng, and Willem Visser. Tool-supported program abstraction for finite-state verification. In Hausi A. Müller, Mary Jean Harrold, and Wilhelm Schäfer, editors, *Proceedings of the 23rd International Conference on Software Engineering, ICSE 2001*, pages 177–187, Washington, DC, USA, 2001. IEEE Computer Society.

[31] Kai Engelhardt, Peter Gammie, and Ron Meyden. Model checking knowledge and linear time: PSPACE cases. In Sergei N. Artëmov and Anil Nerode, editors, *Logical Foundations of Computer Science, International Symposium, LFCS 2007*, volume 4514 of *Lecture Notes in Computer Science*, pages 195–211. Springer-Verlag, 2007.

[32] Emmanuel Filiot. Binary tree automata library. Available on: http://www.grappa.univ-lille3.fr/~filiot/tata/.

[33] Irini Fundulaki and Maarten Marx. Specifying access control policies for XML documents with XPath. In Trent Jaeger and Elena Ferrari, editors, *SACMAT 2004, 9th ACM Symposium on Access Control Models and Technologies*, pages 61–69, New York, NY, USA, 2004. ACM.

[34] Roberto Giacobazzi and Isabella Mastroeni. Abstract non-interference: parameterizing non-interference by abstract interpretation. In Neil D. Jones and Xavier Leroy, editors, *Proceedings of the 31st ACM SIGPLAN-SIGACT Symposium on Principles of Programming Languages, POPL 2004*, pages 186–197. ACM, 2004.

[35] Dimitra Giannakopoulou and Jeff Magee. Fluent model checking for event-based systems. In *Proceedings of the 11th ACM SIGSOFT Symposium on Foundations of Software Engineering 2003 held jointly with 9th European Software Engineering Conference, ESEC/FSE 2003*, pages 257–266. ACM, 2003.

[36] Joseph A. Goguen and José Meseguer. Security policies and security models. In *IEEE Symposium on Security and Privacy*, pages 11–20, 1982.

[37] Martin Gudgin, Marc Hadley, Noah Mendelsohn, Yves Lafon, Jean-Jacques Moreau, Anish Karmarkar, and Henrik Frystyk Nielsen. SOAP version 1.2 part 1: Messaging framework (second edition). W3C recommendation, W3C, April 2007. http://www.w3.org/TR/2007/REC-soap12-part1-20070427/.

[38] Gurvan Le Guernic. Automaton-based confidentiality monitoring of concurrent programs. In *20th IEEE Computer Security Foundations Symposium, CSF 2007*, pages 218–232. IEEE Computer Society, 2007.

[39] Claudio Guidi, Roberto Lucchi, Roberto Gorrieri, Nadia Busi, and Gianluigi Zavattaro. SOCK: A calculus for service oriented computing. In Asit Dan and Winfried Lamersdorf, editors, *Service-Oriented Computing - ICSOC 2006, 4th International Conference*, volume 4294 of *Lecture Notes in Computer Science*, pages 327–338. Springer, 2006.

[40] HotCRP Conference Management Software. Available on: http://read.seas.harvard.edu/~kohler/hotcrp/.

[41] Christian Hammer and Gregor Snelting. Flow-sensitive, context-sensitive, and object-sensitive information flow control based on program dependence graphs. *International Journal of Information Security*, 8(6):399–422, December 2009.

[42] Sebastian Hinz, Karsten Schmidt, and Christian Stahl. Transforming BPEL to Petri nets. In Wil M. P. van der Aalst, B. Benatallah, F. Casati, and F. Curbera, editors, *Proceedings of the Third International Conference on Business Process Management (BPM 2005)*, volume 3649 of *Lecture Notes in Computer Science*, pages 220–235, Nancy, France, September 2005. Springer-Verlag.

[43] S. Horwitz, J. Prins, and T. Reps. On the adequacy of program dependence graphs for representing programs. In Jeanne Ferrante and P. Mager, editors, *Conference Record of the Fifteenth Annual ACM Symposium on Principles of Programming Languages*, pages 146–157, New York, NY, USA, 1988. ACM.

[44] Marieke Huisman, Pratik Worah, and Kim Sunesen. A temporal logic characterisation of observational determinism. In *19th IEEE Computer Security Foundations Workshop, (CSFW-19 2006)*, page 3. IEEE Computer Society, 2006.

[45] John B. Kam and Jeffrey D. Ullman. Monotone data flow analysis frameworks. *Acta Informatica*, 7(3):305–317, September 1977.

[46] Michael Kay. XSL transformations (XSLT) version 2.0. http://www.w3.org/TR/xslt20/, 23 January 2007.

[47] Boris Köpf and Heiko Mantel. Transformational typing and unification for automatically correcting insecure programs. *Int. J. Inf. Sec.*, 6(2-3):107–131, 2007.

[48] Máté Kovács and Helmut Seidl. Runtime enforcement of information flow security in tree manipulating processes. In Gilles Barthe, Benjamin Livshits, and Riccardo Scandariato, editors, *Engineering Secure Software and Systems - 4th International Symposium, ESSoS 2012*, volume 7159 of *Lecture Notes in Computer Science*, pages 46–59. Springer, 2012.

[49] Máté Kovács, Helmut Seidl, and Bernd Finkbeiner. Relational abstract interpretation for the verification of 2-hypersafety properties. In *ACM Conference on Computer and Communications Security (CCS)*, 2013. (To appear.).

[50] Roberto Lucchi and Manuel Mazzara. A pi-calculus based semantics for WS-BPEL. *J. Log. Algebr. Program.*, 70(1):96–118, 2007.

[51] Heiko Mantel and David Sands. Controlled declassification based on intransitive noninterference. In Wei-Ngan Chin, editor, *Programming Languages and Systems: Second Asian Symposium, APLAS 2004*, volume 3302 of *Lecture Notes in Computer Science*, pages 129–145. Springer, 2004.

[52] Robin Milner. *Communicating and Mobile Systems: the Π-calculus*. Cambridge University Press, 1999.

[53] Anders Møller and Michael I. Schwartzbach. XML graphs in program analysis. *Sci. Comput. Program.*, 76(6):492–515, 2011.

[54] Makoto Murata, Akihiko Tozawa, Michiharu Kudo, and Satoshi Hada. XML access control using static analysis. *ACM Trans. Inf. Syst. Secur.*, 9(3):292–324, 2006.

[55] Tadao Murata. Petri nets: Properties, analysis and applications. *Proceedings of the IEEE*, 77(4):541 – 580, April 1989.

[56] Andrew C. Myers. JFlow: Practical mostly-static information flow control. In Andrew W. Appel and Alex Aiken, editors, *POPL '99, Proceedings of the 26th ACM SIGPLAN-SIGACT Symposium on Principles of Programming Languages*, pages 228–241. ACM, 1999.

[57] Andrew C. Myers and Barbara Liskov. A decentralized model for information flow control. In *In Proc. 17th ACM Symp. on Operating System Principles (SOSP)*, pages 129–142. ACM, 1997.

[58] Aleksandar Nanevski, Anindya Banerjee, and Deepak Garg. Verification of information flow and access control policies with dependent types. In *32nd IEEE Symposium on Security and Privacy, S&P 2011*, pages 165–179. IEEE Computer Society, 2011.

[59] David A. Naumann. From coupling relations to mated invariants for checking information flow. In Dieter Gollmann, Jan Meier, and Andrei Sabelfeld, editors, *Computer Security - ESORICS 2006, 11th European Symposium on Research in Computer Security*, volume 4189 of *Lecture Notes in Computer Science*, pages 279–296. Springer, 2006.

[60] Flemming Nielson, Hanne Riis Nielson, and Helmut Seidl. Normalizable horn clauses, strongly recognizable relations, and Spi. In Manuel V. Hermenegildo and Germán Puebla, editors, *Static Analysis, 9th International Symposium, SAS 2002*, volume 2477 of *Lecture Notes in Computer Science*, pages 20–35. Springer, 2002.

[61] Chun Ouyang, Eric Verbeek, Wil M. P. van der Aalst, Stephan Breutel, Marlon Dumas, and Arthur H. M. ter Hofstede. WofBPEL: A tool for automated analysis of BPEL processes. In Boualem Benatallah, Fabio Casati, and Paolo Traverso, editors, *Service-Oriented Computing - ICSOC 2005, Third International Conference*, volume 3826 of *Lecture Notes in Computer Science*, pages 484–489. Springer, 2005.

[62] Mateusz Pawlik and Nikolaus Augsten. RTED: A robust algorithm for the tree edit distance. *Proceedings of the VLDB Endowment (PVLDB)*, 5(4):334–345, 2011.

[63] Mohsen Rouached and Claude Godart. Requirements-driven verification of WSBPEL processes. In *2007 IEEE International Conference on Web Services (ICWS 2007)*, pages 354–363. IEEE Computer Society, 2007.

[64] Alejandro Russo, Andrei Sabelfeld, and Andrey Chudnov. Tracking information flow in dynamic tree structures. In Michael Backes and Peng

Ning, editors, *Computer Security - ESORICS 2009, 14th European Symposium on Research in Computer Security*, volume 5789 of *Lecture Notes in Computer Science*, pages 86–103. Springer, 2009.

[65] A. Sabelfeld and A.C. Myers. Language-based information-flow security. *IEEE Journal on Selected Areas in Communications*, 21(1):5–19, January 14 2003.

[66] Andrei Sabelfeld and Alejandro Russo. From dynamic to static and back: Riding the roller coaster of information-flow control research. In Amir Pnueli, Irina Virbitskaite, and Andrei Voronkov, editors, *Perspectives of Systems Informatics, 7th International Andrei Ershov Memorial Conference, PSI 2009*, volume 5947 of *Lecture Notes in Computer Science*, pages 352–365. Springer, 2009.

[67] Andrei Sabelfeld and David Sands. Dimensions and principles of declassification. In *18th IEEE Computer Security Foundations Workshop, (CSFW-18 2005)*, pages 255–269. IEEE Computer Society, 2005.

[68] Helmut Seidl, Reinhard Wilhelm, and Sebastian Hack. *Compiler Design: Analysis and Transformation*. Springer, September, 2011.

[69] Kuo-Chung Tai. The tree-to-tree correction problem. *Journal of the ACM*, 26(3):422–433, 1979.

[70] Motion-Twin Technologies. XML-Light Version 2.2. Available on: http://tech.motion-twin.com/xmllight.html.

[71] Tachio Terauchi and Alexander Aiken. Secure information flow as a safety problem. In Chris Hankin and Igor Siveroni, editors, *Static Analysis, 12th International Symposium, SAS 2005*, volume 3672 of *Lecture Notes in Computer Science*, pages 352–367. Springer, 2005.

[72] Ming-Hsien Tsai, Yih-Kuen Tsay, and Yu-Shiang Hwang. GOAL for games, omega-automata, and logics. In Natasha Sharygina and Helmut Veith, editors, *CAV*, volume 8044 of *Lecture Notes in Computer Science*, pages 883–889. Springer, 2013.

[73] W. M. P. van der Aalst and A. H. M. ter Hofstede. YAWL: yet another workflow language. *Information Systems*, 30(4):245 – 275, 2005.

[74] Wil M. P. van der Aalst and Kees M. van Hee. *Workflow Management: Models, Methods, and Systems*. MIT Press, 2002.

[75] Moshe Y. Vardi. An automata-theoretic approach to linear temporal logic. In Faron Moller and Graham M. Birtwistle, editors, *Logics for Concurrency - Structure versus Automata (8th Banff Higher Order Workshop)*, volume 1043 of *Lecture Notes in Computer Science*, pages 238–266. Springer, 1995.

[76] Moshe Y. Vardi and Pierre Wolper. Reasoning about infinite computations. *Inf. Comput.*, 115(1):1–37, 1994.

[77] V. N. Venkatakrishnan, Wei Xu, Daniel C. DuVarney, and R. Sekar. Provably correct runtime enforcement of non-interference properties. In Peng Ning, Sihan Qing, and Ninghui Li, editors, *Information and Communications Security, 8th International Conference, ICICS 2006*, volume 4307 of *Lecture Notes in Computer Science*, pages 332–351. Springer, 2006.

[78] Dennis M. Volpano, Cynthia E. Irvine, and Geoffrey Smith. A sound type system for secure flow analysis. *Journal of Computer Security*, 4(2/3):167–188, 1996.

[79] Christoph Weidenbach. Towards an automatic analysis of security protocols in first-order logic. In Harald Ganzinger, editor, *Automated Deduction - CADE-16, 16th International Conference on Automated Deduction*, volume 1632 of *Lecture Notes in Computer Science*, pages 314–328. Springer, 1999.

[80] Christoph Weidenbach, Dilyana Dimova, Arnaud Fietzke, Rohit Kumar, Martin Suda, and Patrick Wischnewski. SPASS Version 3.5. In Renate A. Schmidt, editor, *Automated Deduction - CADE-22, 22nd International Conference on Automated Deduction*, volume 5663 of *Lecture Notes in Computer Science*, pages 140–145. Springer, 2009.

[81] Martin Wirsing, Allan Clark, Stephen Gilmore, Matthias Hölzl, Alexander Knapp, Nora Koch, and Andreas Schroeder. Semantic-based development of service-oriented systems. In Elie Najm, Jean-François Pradat-Peyre, and Véronique Donzeau-Gouge, editors, *Formal Techniques for Networked and Distributed Systems - FORTE 2006*, volume 4229 of *Lecture Notes in Computer Science*, pages 24–45. Springer, 2006.

[82] Christian Wolter, Philip Miseldine, and Christoph Meinel. Verification of business process entailment constraints using SPIN. In Fabio Massacci, Samuel T. Redwine Jr., and Nicola Zannone, editors, *Engineering Secure Software and Systems, First International Symposium ESSoS 2009*, volume 5429 of *Lecture Notes in Computer Science*, pages 1–15. Springer, 2009.

[83] Mirko Zanotti. Security typings by abstract interpretation. In Manuel V. Hermenegildo and Germán Puebla, editors, *Static Analysis, 9th International Symposium, SAS 2002*, volume 2477 of *Lecture Notes in Computer Science*, pages 360–375. Springer, 2002.

i want morebooks!

Buy your books fast and straightforward online - at one of world's fastest growing online book stores! Environmentally sound due to Print-on-Demand technologies.

Buy your books online at

www.get-morebooks.com

Kaufen Sie Ihre Bücher schnell und unkompliziert online – auf einer der am schnellsten wachsenden Buchhandelsplattformen weltweit! Dank Print-On-Demand umwelt- und ressourcenschonend produziert.

Bücher schneller online kaufen

www.morebooks.de

 VDM Verlagsservicegesellschaft mbH
Heinrich-Böcking-Str. 6-8　　Telefon: +49 681 3720 174　　info@vdm-vsg.de
D - 66121 Saarbrücken　　　Telefax: +49 681 3720 1749　　www.vdm-vsg.de

Printed by Books on Demand GmbH, Norderstedt / Germany